Trinity Tales

Trinity College Dublin in the Sixties

'A wonderful book … of amazing charm and real candour … a valuable map of the cultures and conversations which then animated Trinity … the editors and their contributors have produced a book of immense value. It manages to be a portrait of an institution that is not institutional. It provides access to a moment that is more human than historic. Best of all, you don't need to have been a Trinity student to enjoy reading it. Just young.'

Eavan Boland, *The Irish Times*

'This is a terrific read, a portrait not only of a unique institution at a uniquely interesting time, but also of the very different Dublin which then surrounded it.'

John Spain, *Irish Independent*

'Fascinating … what we find here is love, youth and charm – that note sounded in *Brideshead Revisited* and adored by generations of readers.'

Bridget Hourican, *The Dubliner*

IN MEMORIAM
MICHAEL DE LARRABEITI
1934–2008

Trinity Tales

Trinity College Dublin in the Sixties

Edited by SEBASTIAN BALFOUR, LAURIE HOWES,
MICHAEL DE LARRABEITI *and* ANTHONY WEALE

THE LILLIPUT PRESS
in association with Trinity Foundation
DUBLIN

First published 2009 by
THE LILLIPUT PRESS
62–63 Sitric Road, Arbour Hill
Dublin 7, Ireland
www.lilliputpress.ie

ISBN 978 1 84351 154 0

3 5 7 9 10 8 6 4 2

A CIP record for this title is available
from The British Library.

Set in 11 on 16pt Minion by Marsha Swan
Printed in Dublin by ColourBooks

CONTENTS

Preface • Sebastian Balfour, Laurie Howes, Anthony Weale • **vii**

Introduction • Brendan Kennelly • **xi**

The Greenhorn • Bernard Adams • **3**

The Quays • Terence Brady • **9**

In the Steps of the Ginger Man • Peter Hinchcliffe • **14**

Tarnished Buttons • Michael Longley • **23**

To TCD via the Gala, Ballyfermot • Mike Dibb • **30**

Beyond the Dalkey Bus • Edna Broderick • **36**

Ireland's Tangier • Damian Duggan-Ryan • **44**

No. 10 • Sebastian Balfour • **50**

The Absence of Whales • Mary Carr • **60**

All the Golden Oldies • Ian Blake • **66**

Castaway • Laurie Howes • **73**

Forty Years On • Harriet Turton • **89**

Ghostly Rumble among the Drums • Derek Mahon • **94**

Craic and Carpe Diem • A tribute to Rosemary Gibson (1942–1997)
by Andy Gibb • **99**

First Impressions • Jeremy Lewis • **106**

Turning Cartwheels • Deborah de Vere White • **117**

Remembrance of Things Pissed • Tom Haran • **123**

French Leave • Jacques Chuto • **131**

Just Fumblings • John Wilkinson • **139**

Moving On • Anthony Weale • **146**

The Corrugated Cottage • Michael de Larrabeiti • **155**

Banana Sandwiches • Heather Lukes • **165**

Cooking for Kennelly • Mirabel Walker • **173**

Look Back in Awe • Andy Gibb • **177**

Rats, Mice, Coffee and Buns • Ann Heyno • **185**

An Age of Innocence • Gill Hanna • **191**

The Trinity Idyll • Douglas Henderson • **198**

In Search of an Author • Rock Brynner • **205**

Finding a Voice • Fawzia Salama • **209**

Sleepwalking through the Sixties • Nicholas Grene • **218**

A Trinity Tale 1965–1969 • Turlough Johnston • **227**

Tribalism, 1967 • Roy Foster • **234**

Angela of the Buttery • Ray Lynott • **240**

Maiden Speaker • Donnell Deeny • **246**

Certain Good • Christopher Jane Corkery • **255**

The Students are Revolting • John Stephenson • **261**

PREFACE

A BOOK on Trinity College Dublin in the Sixties was our friend Michael de Larrabeiti's idea. It surfaced during one of our frequent reunions with him when we used to get together to enjoy good food and wine and share memories. Four TCD graduates from 'across the water', we went our different ways but kept in touch for over forty years. Our growing perception over the intervening years was that Trinity in the Sixties had been a rather unusual place. Of course, many graduates tend to claim something similar for the universities of their youth. The implicit concept behind this book is that the TCD of the 1960s was a truly idiosyncratic place.

Trinity brought together a post-war generation of Irish, British and international students at a particularly innovative time. And it brought them together in an institution, a city and a country that, at the beginning of the decade, were eccentric and beautiful as well as old-fashioned, still rooted in a culture of ritual, religious bigotry and male privilege. Contraceptives were forbidden, many books were banned, and women students in Trinity were obliged to leave the premises by early evening. In order to study at TCD, Catholics had to obtain a special dispensation from John Charles McQuaid, Archbishop of Dublin; otherwise they were committing a mortal sin. It was only at the end of the Sixties that the requirement of the dispensation was lifted, bringing to a close decades of theological intolerance. Part of the excitement of being a student in TCD at the time was evading or challenging the archaic rules of the institution and the Church. The seditious nature of the TCD students of the Sixties derived also from the confidence born of the post-war boom in Europe.

But what also made Trinity in the Sixties a special place was the multicultural nature of its student intake. Students from the Republic rubbed shoulders with students from Northern Ireland, Wales, Scotland, England, the United States and many other countries across the world. While other universities in Ireland and Britain still had a largely culturally homogenous body of students (although students from working-class families were beginning to penetrate academia), Trinity provided an extraordinarily creative environment for students of very different backgrounds. The evidence for this lies in the talent that TCD of the Sixties spawned in the arts and academia in both Ireland and Britain.

So what was this so-called 'golden generation' like? Were they really, in the words of Dr McDowell, 'remarkable people'? Or were they, as others claim, 'intolerably arrogant', 'self-indulgent', 'unaware' and 'self-obsessed' – or was that simply the English? The 'wonderful absence of gravitas', which Derek Mahon (1961–5) says characterized students in the early Sixties, was not simply due to these 'Sloane Rangers' (as they were later called), the 'chasps and chaspettes' with loud voices from across the water. Students nearer home, like Damian Duggan-Ryan (1960–4), confess to being attracted by the 'liberatingly foreign' quality of the 'Irish Tangier' they found on their doorstep, especially in a student community where 'conspicuous sobriety was frowned upon'. Throughout the Sixties 'invaders' from the North, England, the US and beyond, Edna Broderick (1958–62) suggests, 'hybridized the inbred Irish Protestant ethos … forging a milieu that glamorized various permutations of sex, alcohol, creativity and mortal sin'. No wonder the Archbishop of Dublin was worried. For one 'invader', Jeremy Lewis (1961–5), Trinity in the mid-Sixties was 'benign, tolerant, indolent and indifferent … a place in which the idle and the industrious … were left to sink or swim'.

ONE DELIGHT of the collection is that the thirty-seven contributors had different experiences, have different memories and, unsurprisingly, disagree on the meaning of the decade. Their accounts combine social anthropology with the confessional – or so Bernard Adams (1957–61) claims. What becomes clear from these memoirs is that Trinity, and indeed Dublin itself, were very different places at the beginning and the end of the decade. But this was only to become apparent in the Seventies, reminding us that while history is written backwards, life is lived forwards.

Life in the 'charming eighteenth-century pleasure dome' that was Trinity in 1960 continued well into the second half of the decade. For many female students the greatest political struggle was the battle to secure a flat, far from the prying eyes of the accommodation officer. Accommodation issues link the student generations throughout the Sixties, as these confessions demonstrate. It is either illegal flats or corrugated cottages (in the case of Michael de Larrabeiti, 1961–5), or the problems of living in College (if you were male of course), which thread their way through these stories. Roy Foster (1967–71) remembers in his time that 'it was 'five shillings for a boy; ten shillings for a girl'. Thankfully this was not the purchase price, but the consideration to your 'skip' to turn a blind eye to an unlawful overnight guest.

Five years earlier students were being 'rusticated' (sent down) for entertaining the fair sex to hot chocolate in their rooms after the witching hour.

What many agree, and some are now embarrassed by, is that it was such a privileged life. Students had time and space. Gill Hanna (1964–8), amongst several, records the innocence and optimism of her generation – the last before 1968 – but also the fact that, on reflection, they appeared to be 'unaware … careless and blinkered'. And then came 1968, when the outbreak of student political activism and soon after that the collapse of resistance to women, and Catholics becoming fully legitimate members of the University, created shock waves. By the end of the Sixties, Donnell Deeny (1969–73) writes, 'Trinity was on the cusp.'

As the Sixties unravelled, Christopher Jane Corkery (1970–2) suggests, Trinity was no longer 'caught in amber suspension'. 'The North had not fully imploded yet, but that was coming … The male control of all at Trinity would start to crack, the social classes were already blending and blurring, creating wholly new identifications and divisions.' The Trinity that had largely ignored Sharpeville in 1960 turned out in thousands to protest against the Springboks rugby tour in 1970. The social rebels of the mid-1960s had been predominantly Protestant and British, John Stephenson (1969–76) claims, but their 'collaborative rebelliousness' was mainly 'anachronistic and harmless'. By contrast the steady and growing stream of Southern Irish Catholics now flooding into Trinity was part of a more serious enterprise. Women could now speak in The Historical Society and were finally full members of the University. The new decade, Stephenson suggests, marked a transition from the fun, tolerance and indulgence of the Sixties to the more serious concerns of the Seventies. Not all the contributors would agree unreservedly. It is good to record that those sitting in overnight in the New Library protest in 1970 entertained themselves watching Polanski's *Cul-de-Sac.* Earlier generations would have been proud.

This book, then, is an effort to bring together essays exploring that decade at Trinity and in Dublin through different autobiographical lenses. The approach ranges from the lyrical through the anecdotal to the lite-sociological. They are organized in chronological order according to the period spent at TCD by the contributors through the Sixties. Female contributors fly under their maiden names as they did at Trinity to aid recognition. We have deliberately interpreted the decade of the Sixties generously. So the collection spans contributions from those whose final year was spent at the beginning of the decade to those who began their studies at Trinity at the end of it. We make no pretence that the views represent a cross-section of life in TCD of the time. Inevitably, many of the contributions arise from our networks of friends or acquaintances, though we have tried to reach beyond them to reflect other experiences of Trinity and Dublin. We hope the book will stimulate nostalgia or cast light on the past for those who studied there during that decade as well as arouse curiosity among those who came after and among others interested in the bizarre and strangely innocent world of the Sixties in Dublin.

Both the editors and the contributors have agreed that all royalties from the sale of the book should go to the Long Room fund of Trinity College; this was the plan from the beginning. We would like to thank the administration of the College, in particular Simon Williams, for encouraging the production of the book in its final stages. We would also like to thank all the contributors for their memories and their patience. We hope that this volume might encourage Trinity graduates from other decades to record their experiences. Finally, we are grateful to Rose de Larrabeiti and James Benstead for their help with documents and photos left behind by Michael de Larrabeiti, to whom we dedicate this book.

Sebastian Balfour, Laurie Howes, Anthony Weale
January 2009

INTRODUCTION

brendan kennelly

IN THE SIXTIES, Dublin was beginning to emerge from the poverty that had produced writers like Sean O'Casey and Brendan Behan. Louis MacNeice, the great Ulster poet, had commended Dublin for 'the glamour of her squalor' and 'the bravado of her talk'. This atmosphere of social deprivation and verbal dynamism was still prevalent in Dublin in the Fifties and Sixties. James Joyce had described Trinity as 'a dull grey stone set in the ring of the city's ignorance'. In the Sixties, however, Trinity was anything but dull. It was a lively place, full of characters from different parts of the world who added colour, charm, difference and mischief not only to the College but to the city itself. Today there are five times as many students in Trinity as there were then, but I doubt if the place has quite the same vibrant air of creativity that it enjoyed when the Celtic Tiger was unheard of. I am not being nostalgic when I say that Trinity in the Sixties was both poorer and richer than it is today.

For me, the deepest source of joy was knowing poets like Michael Longley (the 'Homer of Botany Bay'), Derek Mahon, Eavan Boland, Tim Webb, Terry Brady, Timothy Brownlow, Deborah de Vere White, Ron Ewart, Ronnie Wathen, Rudi Holzapfel, Michael Leahy, Donald Carroll, Richard Stack, Kate Lucy and Bruce Arnold (who went on to become an accomplished novelist and essayist as well as an incisive political analyst). There were other productive prose writers such as George Hodnett, John Jay, Eliza Collins, Tony Hickey, Max Stafford-Clark, Brian Osman and Michael de Larrabeiti. I am currently reading, and very much enjoying the latter's *Foxes' Oven*, published in 2003.

Other writers from that period include Jeremy Lewis whose excellent memoir, *Playing for Time*, contains a witty, vivid evocation of 'Unholy Trinity' and Dublin in the Sixties. A book I delight in is Charles Sprawson's *Haunts of the Black Masseur: The Swimmer as Hero*, which explores mythology, literature, history and the culture of different countries, tracing the swimmer as heroic figure. It is beautifully written. And so are *Radon Daughters* and *White Chappel, Scarlet Tracings* by Iain Sinclair, who has also published several volumes of poetry.

Ian Blake, a Sixties man who wrote poems and short stories, published an epic novel, *School Story*, in 2005. It is a piercing scrutiny of the complex, sometimes dark and corrupt world of education. As the decade pushed on, worked on, talked on, sang on, I was privileged to meet people like John Kelly, now a distinguished Oxford don who has done excellent work on Yeats and other Irish writers.

Then in the latter part of the decade there are two students I remember in a special way because they became teaching colleagues of mine and went on to become distinguished professors, writers, scholars and critics. They are Terence Brown and Nicholas (Nicky) Grene, who are still working hard in the School of English.

Declan Kiberd, Professor of English in UCD, was in Trinity from 1969 to 1973. He has produced some epic works, such as *Inventing Ireland*, and is, as so many of his students have told me, an inspiring teacher.

IT WAS BEATLES TIME and that meant music, wine, dancing, singing, parties in College rooms, in different flats and houses throughout Dublin, and outings to warm, welcoming places in Wicklow, Kildare and Meath. And the young women of Trinity were bright, articulate and beautiful. I recall conversations, both serious and giggling, with Hilary Mitchell, Suzanne Lowry, Dorna Farzaad, Sara Abernethy, Anne Mullen, Marian Lurring and Jean Scott – a sparkling young lady known as 'Scottie'. And there was Edna Broderick, who married Michael Longley and went on to become an eminent professor in Queen's University

Belfast, and a vigorous, fearless critic with an international reputation.

The most famous student of the Sixties is Mary Robinson, of course, who became president of Ireland and United Nations High Commissioner for Human Rights. She was, and is, a truly brilliant, deeply humane person with a passionate love of justice. Her husband, Nick Robinson, was a student at the same time as Mary. So too was David Norris, a distinguished senator for many years, a witty, erudite Joycean and an eloquent, energetic politician.

A crucial aspect of that spirited Sixties atmosphere was the love of sport. Trevor West, editor of *150 Years of Trinity Rugby*, was a tireless worker for several decades promoting interest in sport among the ever increasing flood of students into the College. In Gaelic football, Dublin stars such as Kevin Heffernan and Tony Hanahoe worked hard for the advancement of the national game. And cricket, a game beloved and well played by Samuel Beckett when he was a lecturer in the French Department, thrived during that time. It still does. Games played in those beautiful green fields in the heart of Dublin continue to attract and delight spectators every year.

I am writing about people and events of almost fifty years ago and I realize there are those I have forgotten.

Over the decades, the numbers of students increased each year so that for me to recall the Sixties is to see a picture that is both blurred and clear, vague and precise, muttering, candidly articulate. And yet, of the five decades I've been privileged to work in Trinity, the Sixties are somehow the most varied and vibrant. Perhaps this is so because I was almost the same age as many of the students, and we talked and partied and argued together. In this respect I think of Geoffrey Thurley, for example, a brilliant young Englishman, a fellow lecturer and friend of mine, who would spend whole nights passionately discussing the poetry of Pound, Eliot and Yeats with anyone who chose to engage with him. Fresh from Cambridge, he loved Dublin and 'the bravado of her talk'. He made many memorable contributions to that same bravado, whether lecturing to students in College or chatting with them in cafés or pubs. At once passionate and relaxed, modest and eloquently assertive, he shared his ideas with those who were interested, and he listened intently to all responses.

Looking back now, I see that all the genuine fun and frolics co-existed with forms of strict, rigid Victorianism. For example all females had to be out of College by six o'clock every evening, and were fined heavily if they failed to comply. On the whole this rule was observed, though there were some delightfully sly, effective ways of breaking it. Rule-breaking added to the delights of love-making. Every year on Ash Wednesday priests announced from pulpits that it was a sin to go to Trinity College without permission from Archbishop John Charles McQuaid. Gay Byrne, the leading television personality in Ireland at the time, had a discussion about this Trinity–McQuaid matter on his famous *Late Late Show*, and following this the Archbishop's grip seemed to loosen, so that Catholics began to stroll and study in Trinity just like the visiting English, Swedes, French, Belgians, Italians, Germans and Americans, as well as all the friendly Protestants from different parts of the island of Ireland. On that *Late Late Show*, Trinity academics such as David Thornley and Jim Lydon put 'the Trinity case' with eloquence and controlled passion. They showed that a university where everyone qualified to enter has the right to enter. I believe that Trinity today is inspired by that spirit. I still remember the sheer joy I felt in the late Fifties and early Sixties when I, a rather shy young country Catholic, met and enjoyed these marvellous, challenging, endlessly surprising students from all around the world. I realized then that the day we cease to be surprised is the day we cease to be educated. And a crucial part of education is how students educate each other in moments serious and daft, solemn and loopy, stylish and scruffy.

Trinity College is situated in the very heart of Dublin. It is surrounded by a wall that gives it a certain distance, a kind of detachment from the city that pulses and roars all around it. This strange mixture of distance and intimacy, walled privacy and intense involvement, green parks and loud, stinking, endless traffic, is part of Trinity's special character. It is insider and outsider at once. And it must be said that Trinity in the Sixties was a crucial, colourful part of the fascinating development. Today there are more than fifteen thousand students in the College, up from three thousand in the Sixties. But these men and women from forty years ago, and more, brought fun and creativity, laughter and inspiration into Trinity, and Dublin, for which I and many others are and always will be grateful.

Brendan Kennelly (TCD 1957–61; English) is Emeritus Professor of Modern Literature at Trinity College Dublin. He has been there for much of his life, first as a student and then as a lecturer and professor. He is one of Ireland's most distinguished poets and has published over twenty books of poetry, including **Cromwell** (1983), **The Book of Judas** (1991), **Poetry My Arse** (1995), **The Man Made of Rain** (1998), **Glimpses** (2001), **Martial Art** (2003) and **Familiar Strangers: New & Selected Poems 1960–2004** (2004).

Statue of Oliver Goldsmith by John Henry Foley.

Trinity Tales

Trinity College Dublin in the Sixties

TRINITY COLLEGE DUBLIN FROM THE NORTH WEST

THE GREENHORN

bernard adams

I LIKE THIS WORD because it so exactly describes the person who arrived to study modern languages at Trinity in September 1957. I was remarkably green and certainly horny. I was Green in the Irish political sense, a little proud of being a Dubliner and rather less proud of the odd, repressive Free State that was my native land. I was a United Ireland man, I suppose, but also strongly aware – having spent six years at school in Northern Ireland – of just how hard and immovable the Orange stumbling block remained.

No, it was socially, interpersonally, that I was really green – timid, uncertain, blushing inexplicably, unreasonably in awe of the boundlessly confident young men and women who came from across the water to study at a university that had a remarkably persistent social and intellectual cachet. This greenness was not really supposed to be part of the plot – send boy to public school, tough regime, bleak buildings but inspirational shades of Oscar (Wilde) and Sam (Beckett). A polished, sporty, intellectually curious young man was supposed to emerge – ready to leap from his schoolboy diving board into the cerebral swimming pool of university life.

But it was a very young, very unpolished eighteen-year-old who actually emerged from this educational process in 1957 to study 'Mod. Lang.' – Spanish and English. It's perhaps better to dispose of the horny teenager here; he remained soppily romantic and unrequitedly lustful (Larkin was almost right in my case) for the whole of his university career. It would be ungallant and unwise to name or count those who were the recipients of his bungling attentions.

There was to be no swimming-pool dive – more a cautious toe-in-the-water approach followed by slow acclimatization. Disgracefully, I chose to live for at least half of the time at home – delighted with the comforts after the damp rigours of the Enniskillen monastery, Portora. This homeiness hobbled for a start my participation in what was potentially a lively environment – and one that benefited enormously from the benign invasion of more worldly-wise English students. I was not adept at sherry – yes, sherry – party conversation. I did not have the skills for a Brideshead-over-the-water existence. I was a far too occasional visitor to the debating societies that relieved the splendid cultural isolation of a student body, parts of which tended towards a vague Home Counties conservatism. We needed reminding that Ireland and The World lay outside the gates of our charming eighteenth-century pleasure dome where many – including me – lived in Keats' 'Chamber of Maiden Thought' and the pleasure principle ruled.

I did a bit more of a plunge with *Trinity News*, the rather more tabloid of the two College newspapers. I jumped in largely because I was pushed by one Frances-Jane ffrench, an older female person with an elevated pedigree and a lot of patience. She printed my articles and helped me eventually to become editor for a term. During that spell I had the good fortune that a natural-born columnist, William Oddie, the tall, pleasantly padded son of a Yorkshire woollen mill, began to write his delightfully witty Martin Marprelate letters. (Prelates and priests played a sizeable role in his later career: he ended up as editor of *The Catholic Herald*.)

The English Department was a polite shambles for most of my time at Trinity. There was a huge syllabus, patchy lectures and exams at the end of the summer vacation – now hard to believe, but a huge incentive to term-time social excess. Course work, essays and tutorials were almost unknown. H.O. White had been in charge since, I believe, the late 1930s when legend has it he was chosen ahead of Louis McNeice for the Chair of English. White seemed incredibly antique to me, a man with a shiny pink face often scarred by a rashly wielded razor. I cannot remember a single word of any of his lectures and, looking back today, it seems to me that he presided over a huge missed opportunity – to specialize in the study of the Anglo-Irish cultural heritage – much of it provided by former TCD alumni, Swift, Burke, Goldsmith, Synge and Beckett, to name but a few. (Thankfully, that opportunity was grasped soon after I left.)

There must have been fifty students in my English year – worryingly, only two stand out. Brendan Kennelly was a little older than me. He was a lot wiser – having already spent time working in London. He looked a little like a young priest who already knew that the seminary was not for him; he had begun to write his poems and to help others, like me, struggling to express raw feelings in memorable words. Harden Rogers, brilliant and mysterious and Northern, I sadly never got to know. My memory of her is that she smoked with dedication and seemed to be always surrounded by a male phalanx of formidable Ulster bodyguards. This must be a fantasy. Why didn't I just go up and talk to her?

I remember enjoying the lectures of A.J. Leventhal, who, I later discovered, was the lover of the marvellous Trinity star of the 1920s, Ethna MacCarthy, whom Beckett admired to distraction. Also I have a vivid image of Alec Reid – with his shock of white hair; his poor sight, his physical helplessness contrasted with great intellectual energy. In my last year, 1960/61, the English Department was taken over by Professor Philip Edwards. He brought order and focus, and a new lecturer – a Dr Walton, who introduced us to the revolutionary idea that there was a huge critical literature out there and that reading our set texts and simply giving our own views on them was insufficient. The shock of the new was considerable but healthy. Nevertheless I found that in my finals I had to face the formidable but kindly Dr Pyle for a Chaucer viva – which involved reading some of the text out loud. Now I don't think there were any Chaucer lectures, nor any tutorials – or maybe I was just such a head-in-air that I missed some academic trick. My performance was a disaster – and I do believe, an unnecessary one.

The Spanish Department was a different matter. Lean, streamlined, focused, properly managed by an ex-naval officer and immensely distinguished Cervantes scholar, E.C. Riley. 'Ted', as I got to call him much later, did not do inspirational, flamboyant lectures. All that was required was for him to tell us in his incisive way about Federico García Lorca, read a poem or two, analyse *The House of*

Bernarda Alba and I was hooked, enchanted – for life, as it turned out: in 2001 I wrote a play about Federico and his relationship with Dalí and Buñuel.

Like many fellow students I had taken up Spanish at the age of eighteen and my grasp of the written language has always been shaky, so doing English-into-Spanish prose for Ted was an ordeal. How I longed for them to come back with minimal red ink marks, but how rarely they did. Daniel de W. Rogers and Keith Whinnom were the other lecturers in the Spanish Department. Señora Doporto, if I'm not wrong a Civil War refugee from Soria, charmingly taught us to speak. I remember a delightful remark from a fellow student after one of these classes, a very clever girl from the Isle of Man called Judith Cowley. I had been deploying a small talent for mimicry and speaking fairly confidently if not very correctly in Spanish. 'It's funny,' she said, 'you know … you sound so much more in command of the situation in Spanish than you do in English.'

Dan Rogers was a young, friendly lecturer with an infectious laugh and a love of cricket – which he was able to exercise to the full when he moved to Durham where he haunted the county ground. Later, I believe he grew a little sad, but in the late 1950s he encouraged me, perhaps more than anyone, in my uphill battle to write Spanish decently and inspired us all with his gloriously full-blooded account of the amorous Nicaraguan poet Ruben Dario. Keith Whinnom, sandy hair, dry, accentless voice and with a wit to match, had the difficult task of turning us on to linguistics. This he tried manfully to do, but the hormones turned us – or perhaps just me – towards the Golden Age drama, the swashbuckling Lope de Vega and Tirso's *Don Juan*.

This Spanish Department had youth, scholarly distinction and personality. It's not surprising that, despite its small size – perhaps just a dozen in my year – a remarkable proportion of its students went on to make their mark. The hard-hitting historian of modern Spain, Sebastian Balfour, is one; the distinguished BBC film-maker Mike Dibb, is another … and the list goes on. Perhaps the most extraordinary of all E.C. Riley's intellectual scions is Ian Gibson. Writing in Spanish, he has, more or less single-handed, invented literary biography in modern Spain, and in a long writing life has mapped a huge swathe of his adopted country's twentieth-century cultural and political history. Oddly enough, my first connections with him were sporting – he was an outstanding natural athlete. I first met him playing in the final of a badminton tournament, saw him score a fine try in a club rugby match at Lansdowne Road and, later, take an astonishing running, diving outfield catch for my cricket team on our local London suburban ground. He was a year ahead of me at Trinity and I remember making fun of his meticulous organization of his lecture notes and reading lists. Imitation might have been a better reaction. He worked hard and played hard. I seem to remember him hanging rather precariously from one of the higher balconies at some rowing event at Islandbridge. What a loss to Spanish studies might have been incurred if that alcohol-emboldened grip had slipped or the timbers given way! But the strength, determination and sheer cussedness that have taken him through more than thirty years of mighty literary endeavour allowed him to scare his companions to death but remain unscathed.

A brief section on parties is indicated here. James Joyce's Martello Tower at Sandycove seemed like a good venue. Young Michael Scott – whose father, the architect, I think owned the Joycean shrine at that point – took the risk of inviting us there. It was windy out on the roof, where soldiers used to scan the horizon for invading Frenchmen; it was dark and cold inside – and easy to understand why James Joyce left fairly smartly, quite apart from the unpleasant attentions of Oliver St John Gogarty. I remember other parties on the south Dublin 'gold coast' – several at a wonderful house high on Killiney Hill. One was given by Tony Hickey and his partner Alan, and it gave me a model for what a good party might be like – fine food and wine, a beautiful setting and some indefinable excitement – as though something or someone new was just round the corner.

If my mother were to read all the above – which, sadly though alive, she can't – she'd probably say: 'It's quite interesting about you, dear, but you really haven't said very much about the College.' Likewise, the editor may well be thinking: 'This is supposed to be social anthropology, not the confessional.' So let's attempt the analytical for a moment. It's hard without having a suitable history of TCD at my fingertips. But, impressionistically, my guess is that my time there was the beginning of the end for an expat university, which benefited from the generosity of British local authorities that in the Fifties and Sixties paid for students from a wide variety of backgrounds to go to our slightly exotic but prestigious seat of learning. Students from the rest of Europe were rare, so the place sometimes felt as if the vice-chancellor might be Harold Macmillan.

This hybrid did not last very long. As the Celtic Tiger began to make a few exploratory growls in the Sixties, Dublin and Ireland began to re-colonize TCD. Now it is a huge, laudably international, utterly different, Irish university. But when I go back I find that although so much has changed, a great deal of Trinity remains the same. It still has that look of Georgian confidence, its green spaciousness and, above all, its unique situation at the heart of one of the world's great small cities.

Recently when I've been toiling away at literary projects in the Manuscript Room of the world's most atmospheric library, high above the squares and milling students, I've thought that perhaps now I could join them down below, go through the gate and take my place with the first-years. I've had my gap years. Now I'm really ready.

Bernard Adams (TCD 1957–61; Modern Languages: Spanish and English) was a freelance journalist on the **Belfast Telegraph** and **Radio Times,** and subsequently a television producer and director for BBC Education. Now a journalist again (**The Irish Times, The Independent, Times Educational Supplement**), he is also the author of **Denis Johnston: A Life** (2002) and is currently working on a biography of Christabel Bielenberg. In 1966, he married Mona, a rock from the Hard Place (Belfast). They have two fantastic daughters, and three grandchildren. Things are looking up.

THE QUAYS

terence brady

HALF A CENTURY ON yet so clear the mind it seems only yesterday so perfectly recalled booted and boated I disembark at North Wall do not take cab the Da cajoled me do not be had by them jarveys offering you a cab when what you must have is a taxi but then he hadn't bothered to tell me had he that I had a first-class ticket for the packet so when I present myself plus ticket at steerage at the Holy Head port the officious tears the billet in two and never redirects me so all night is spent roughing it above and below deck but now I am here on the quays along alone at last where a man in a vast black coat down to his shoes gangplanks aboard and asks me do I want a taxi I say yes I do want a taxi remembering the words of the Da not to be had only to see the man in the vast black coat down to his shoes now loading my stuff my life on top of a whacked out horse drawn stop that I cry but the cases and trunks are up atop the shaking hansom this isn't a taxi I protest sure it is he retorts showing no teeth at all this is what you lads call a taxi now but what we calls a cab here so hop in and I'll have you at Side Gate in no time so I have no alternative but to jump in as the cab is now moving I do as bidden while two urchins jump on the runners pressing candlestick noses to the dirty glass begging so I give them two pennies and the jarvey shouts don't they'll be in the cab if you gives them money and the childer hang on to the quickening carriage banging on the glass and shouting hey mister give us a penny for some woodies will ye they can't be older than six or seven they finally fall off as the cab wheels round a cobbled stone corner to swing up a hill and the no time at all takes a near hour as we pass St Patrick's on wet stoned streets near empty except for huddled shawlies beetled up in doorways while shabby dressed men search bins for survival Dublin glistens grey from the rain of years and the tears of centuries great Georgian buildings dying from neglect their fanlights cracked over fine doorways and half starved dogs raising weary legs to sprinkle yet more water on lamp posts and green pillar boxes there are policeman in long dark blue coats and officers' hats patrolling the streets one of their number long armed on point wearing white gloves to wave through recklessly speeding buses shaky cyclists and pre-war American cars old Oldsmobiles packed up Packards crippled Cadillacs now serving as taxis the transport I should have selected instead of this flea wheeling jalopy now pulling up at Side Gate my luggage is dumped on the rain washed pavements my pockets are emptied by the toothless jarvey who has given me the student run round now I am four floors up at the top of Botany Bay my home for the next two years at least there is only the one lavatory at the foot of eight flights of wooden stairs one fire bucket one escape appliance welded solid by non use not that anything could catch fire it's far too damp the walls are running with it and so finally here are my rooms They make school look like the Ritz bare boards two wooden chairs a small wooden table three ancient iron beds own mattresses to be supplied no hot water one gas ring no sink one chipped enamel bowl one half functional gas fire with meter four naked electric light bulbs no curtains it's a prison no prison must be better furnished than this place where are we going to sit how are we going to live we have to buy at auction down the quays a small Ulsterman eating cornflakes at the three legged table tells me we have to furnish rooms ourselves he's called Brian and he is very dour I was given him like he was given me random selection put them together any old how did you hear the one about the Ulsterman the Dubliner and the Anglo rooming together it's not very funny and something will have to be done we're all thinking of that as we regard each other with deep suspicion and now there's another one the third room mate James who's wandered in from the single bedroom reading the Bible on the move are you studying Divinity I wonder but he's not he's reading Economics then I see the lapels on his thornproof are decked out with Scripture Union badges and other symbols of piety and godliness and I wish I wish I had gone to Oxford this is a barbaric place altogether and things don't improve when a man with a bad gimp and cunning eyes shuffles in he's our skip our manservant would you believe he can never have been out of his clothes he goes into what I am told is the kitchen to throw days old dirty crockery from a great distance into the chipped enamel washing up bowl and brew the filthiest cup of tea for the new arrival in a matching chipped enamel mug it's only early in the morning and I see four years stretching ahead of me like a life sentence now I think perhaps I should have gone into the army after all because this is worse than any army could be I find a coffee bar along O'Connell Street share a table with three large Teddy boys who push and punch each other constantly talking a nasal tongue I do not know while the juke box blares Presley hey yous I'm enquired after do yous loike Elvis you bet I affirm teeth a clatter good man yerself I'm told good on ya they buy me coffee in a clear cup and matching saucer and offer me Sweet Afton and by the third cup o' cappo I wish they were my room mates I wander the streets with nothing else to do have my photograph taken by a sharpic on the Bridge who says half a dollar young sir for colour I still have the print it's brown altogether brown and always was from the moment of delivery I complain of course who wouldn't I said give me my money back it's not in colour oh yes it is young sir brown's a colour is it not Later gown on and into Commons for the first time the noise is terrible everyone seems to know everyone else no one talks to me and I don't know what to say to anyone because they all seem to know each other the beer is indescribable as is the food I look for someone my own age and stamp but everyone at my table are older than me and then I twig that them who are like me are not like me because they have done National Service these are the elite the ones I later see in faded military camel coats drinking large Cork gins in Jammets front bar eating oysters their cavalry twills tapered thin their sports coats patched leather at elbows and cuffs they have double-barrelled surnames and first names like Graham and Larry and Mike and Rod Andrew Fergus Jerry and Teddy Simon George and Ian chaps' names names of chaps who'd been in Cyprus Malta Borneo driven tanks macheted their way through jungle seen life learned how to drink owned their own MGs and are on permanent prank standby the sort who are ready at the drop of a bottle to climb the Campanile and stick a chamber pot on the top of it they are the Boat Club the Rugger Club mountaineers motor bike men one of them has already climbed a lot of Everest if not most of it another is a certainty for an Irish rugby cap and they all have drop dead gorgeous women on their tweed arms my first evening I drink in Davy Byrnes where else have my first draught Guinness and wonder seriously about a nation whose national brew could possibly taste like this did there are no grown up students in Davy's just a handful of Freshers putting a toe in the water boys who thought they were men leaving public school only to arrive at Trinity and find themselves back being boys again boys in pink plastic spectacles called Glyn and Brian Derek and Jeremy Ronald and Basil all in waistcoats red green or ochre ones we all wear waistcoats then I have a dark green one with brass buttons and a check Burtons suit and everyone has ties generally with red or yellow backgrounds with fox head or horse shoe motifs sport bow ties bow ties are always sported never worn some already wear the Trinity tie born to be club men to live as club men and to die as such wearing the Now Dead Club tie to the grave young old men trembling on the brink telling tales of aged Egyptian students rumoured to be thirty-eight years old and rich as only Egyptians might be rich certainly rich enough to fail Little-Go twenty times yet still remain at Trinity stuck forever in his Second Year and of similarly wealthy African students cleaned out every term at the poker tables and paying their debts off in carpets and jewellery bracket on gold bracket off and silk suits and fine wines and tales of girls with exotic names who could drink the Irish front row under the table of an eccentric and brilliant lecturer with Albino hair and pink eyes whose best friend was Samuel Beckett and of an equally eccentric Junior Dean who took his occasional bath standing naked in his ground floor rooms on sheets of *The Irish Times* while pouring a kettle of water over himself my appetite begins to get whetted I begin to sense an altogether different place to the College at which I have just arrived and sure enough in no time at all Brian has been swapped for Ronnie and James for John and by the end of my first week in Trinity I have got the point of the place and had my Burtons suit trousers tapered and so begins four tumultuous unforgettable incredible riotous enlightening edifying astounding and wonderful years spent in one of the greatest and most distinctive universities in the world thanks be

Terence Brady (TCD 1957–61; History and Political Science) is a playwright, actor, novelist and horse breeder. He has over three hundred roles on stage, film and television to his name, and has written **The Fight against Slavery** (1976) and **A History of Point to Pointing** (1990), plus two novels, **Rehearsal** (1972) and **Yes Honestly** (1977).

TCD Magazine, *25 May 1966.*

IN THE STEPS OF THE GINGER MAN

peter hinchcliffe

I CAME TO DUBLIN in October 1957 hotfoot from two years in the British army to start a four-year honours degree course: Modern History and Political Science – an easy option, so I was assured, for a stress-free existence within the high walls of Trinity.

I had much in common with many others of the Junior Freshman class of 1957, including my English public-school background with its uniform of tweed sports jacket and cavalry twill trousers, loud voice, braying vowels and regulation thick skin. Many of us seemingly brashly insensitive to our novel existence in a foreign land. And like so many of this new generation of students from across the water I had failed to find an Oxbridge college that felt it would benefit from my attendance. At least (unlike so many others in my intake or who would arrive over the next four years), I had not been sent down from another institution of higher education. And together with others from a similar back-ground I had been matured, to a certain extent, by two years' service in HM forces – in my case as a volunteer from the 'North' as those 'domiciled' in the Six Counties were not subject to compulsory call-up for obvious reasons. I had been commissioned, and had seen active service in the Suez fiasco of 1956. I felt strongly that farce or no, this gave me an edge over my service contemporaries who had failed to pass the War Office Selection Board, thus remaining in the ranks 'for the duration'. And I felt sorry for those timid souls, commissioned or not, who had never left England, had not heard a shot fired in anger and had not faced down the Queen's foes in foreign lands.

But in contrast to most of my fellow newcomers I had some claim to Irishness. On my mother's Six Counties side we went back to Plantation times. When interviewed by the Junior Dean, Dr R.B. McDowell, he warned that the minimum qualification for overseas entry was an Irish grandparent and one O level. I could assure him, more or less straight-faced, that I was doubly qualified on both counts. (In idle moments I used to ponder how many Irish grandparents the seventy-strong Nigerian contingent could muster between them.) But truth to say, it was the twenty-five or so golf courses within seven miles of Trinity, which was the clincher for my seeking admission.

I got to know the famous Junior Dean well. An unrepentant snob, he 'collected' English public schoolboys in whose company he could recall the happiest days of his life as a junior master at Radley College on the English south coast, evacuated during the Second World War for fear of invasion, to another school, Radley College, Berkshire. My old Alma Mater. He had a particular high regard for Radleians – so anyone from Radley who arrived at TCD was sure of attracting the attention of R.B. McDowell.

He asked me towards the end of the first term to give a party in my rooms for as many former Radley boys as I could muster. I found twelve or so supplemented by a few other chaps of the right background. McDowell kindly paid for the booze – good dry sherry and poor plonk – and we all had a lively evening. Except, I fear, for the Junior Dean who on arrival had been seized by two hulking brutes from the former Radley XV front row and immobilized by being hung by the back lapel of his tightly buttoned filthy blue overcoat from the hook at the back of my sitting-room door. He remained marooned there all evening jabbering away at the nearest group of partygoers but was mostly ignored by (my/his) guests. He seemed to take it all in good part but I heard subsequently that he was very irritated at being unable to get to know the freshest faces of the public-school set and thus denied the chance of making a new special friend or two for an intimate glass of sherry in his rooms.

I was grateful for one of Dr McDowell's acts of social engineering. He prided himself when allocating rooms in Trinity for Junior Freshmen in putting like-minded people together – public schoolboys with others for instance. In my case the 'wife' he selected remains a good friend to this day though, on the face of it, apart from our public-school background we had little in the way of common interests, he being of an aesthetic tendency whilst I was an out and out Philistine. I inevitably got on his nerves after a bit and he moved out after two years leaving the Junior Dean to fill the vacancy with my second wife, curiously not a public-school man but the son of a Strabane solicitor, much given to plastic flowers, air fresheners and ringing up his mother when either I or one of my crassly insensitive friends had upset him. He also was a nephew of George Otto Simms, the Church-of-Ireland Archbishop of Dublin who occasionally dropped by in search of Patrick. One Saturday morning he knocked on our door at the ungodly (no offence intended, Your Grace) hour of 10.30 am. Patrick had gone north to deliver his laundry to his mum for a second opinion; I had retired to my pit only a couple of hours earlier and was not pleased to be disturbed by the gentle but persistent knocking. In the end I went to the door and shouted, 'Whoever you are just **** off!' He didn't and I eventually opened the door to be greeted by this vision in purple, apologizing for the intrusion but anxious to hear about his nephew's progress at TCD.

I subsequently saw quite a lot of him and got greatly to admire this gentle scholar who once amazed an audience of Irish speakers at a Sinn Féin rally in Cork with his fluent and erudite Gaelic, lauding the contribution made by the rebels of the 1916 Easter Rising to the cause of Irish independence, thus destroying, in a few sentences, many of their long-cherished preconceptions of a remote, stuffed shirted, 'heretical' churchman irredeemably wedded to the 'British connection'.

Although the student body in the late 1950s was much smaller in number than now, it was impossible to get to know even just your fellow Freshmen. The Ginger Man was no longer with us but there were larger-than-life characters that would have stood out in their own right in the pages of J.P. Donleavy. Nikolai Tolstoy was one, the grandson of the novelist – a dashing tall figure who often featured in the *Trinity News* gossip column, 'Four & Six', usually in the company of one of a variety of attractive young ladies who seemed to be on some kind of permanent roster system for escorting this enigmatic and romantic aristocrat. In the edition for 25 February 1960 he is referred to as the 'tall, piratical Count Nikolai Tolstoy-Miloslavsky', 'a Russian who spoke no Russian'.

Then there was the Hon. Andrew Bonar Law, another grandson of a well-known public figure – Britain's shortest-serving prime minister, also Andrew. He had a penchant for outrageous practical jokes including engineering the ancient organ in the Examination Hall – salvaged from a sunken galleon of the Spanish Armada – to burst into martial music during a finals exam. Less flamboyant but well known to all inmates was Frances-Jane ffrench, an imposing lady of uncertain age who was supposed to have done over twenty years as an undergraduate without reaching the third year in any course. The myth had it that she was the inspiration for a character in a Richard Gordon novel about a young man who received a generous allowance from a family trust only as long as he was a student. She was there when I arrived and started on a new course the year I graduated.

TCD was no academic hothouse. There were many of my fellow students who seemed to be under little pressure to complete their degree or even pass an exam. None could quite emulate the institutional longevity of Miss ffrench but many went into fifth or sixth years having changed degree courses a couple of times. The official attitude seemed relaxed – as long as you could pay your fees you could stay on. I never really did any work until just before Part One of my finals towards the end of my third year. But I really wanted to get a decent degree, a Second, so I tried. Lots of my friends didn't and one or two never graduated at all. Nor was I, looking back, much impressed by the quality of the teaching in the Modern History Department. Professor Moody and the 'Lecky' Professor Jocelyn Otway Ruthven were eminent historians. Both were severely tweedy and seemed ill at ease with the younger generation. Moody was said to be a Beethoven aficionado, and looked the part with his huge hirsute head; it was said that he believed that he was a reincarnation of the great composer. Otway Ruthven's lectures, erudite no doubt, were delivered in a low monotone, head down, obviously anxious to do the business and get back to the safety of her rooms.

David Large, lecturer in economic history, spoke almost entirely in clichés; so much so that I, aided by some fellow conspirators, noted them all down as they came burbling forth, catalogued them by topic and later turned them into an updated *1066 and All That*, which we called *History By and Large*, and sold over 200 copies. And we had two Irish historians. The first, Dr Gerald Simms, was George Otto's younger brother. He was regarded as weedy, tentative and boring. This did not apply to the other, R.B. McDowell himself, who knew his stuff but rarely got around to telling us about it. Within the first two minutes of starting his lecture he was usually diverted and distracted by some rarely innocent question that would send him off on flights of fancy, totally absorbing, and far, far removed from Ireland and its sombre history. Now that I am a part-time university teacher I often wonder what my students think of me. Outwardly their courtesy and apparent attentiveness is in marked contrast to how we cocky young people behaved in the presence of our lecturers – uninspiring teachers maybe but eminent scholars in their chosen fields. I had much more respect for my tutor, Dr F.S.L. Lyons, a world authority on Charles Stewart Parnell, who inspired me to take a real interest in the nineteenth-century Home Rule issue. But sadly he never lectured to us.

Our group, predominantly male with a few peripheral and occasional distaff attachments, was spread over a number of academic disciplines and University institutions. We included a number of engineers and scientists – the former being the backbone 'hearties' of the Rowing Club and a significant source of income to Davy Byrnes and other Dublin hostelries. The latter tended to support the more arty societies such as the new College gallery established by a TCD lecturer, Dr George Dawson. My immediate circle was heavily into 'The Hist' – The Historical Society, whose all-male debates were generally of a high standard and whose 'Private Business' sessions with their archaic rituals and pompous white-tie formality must have been an inspiration to successive generations of ardent Freemasons.

We successfully fought to keep women from our gates. I really can't remember why, except that females had been banned since 1747, Edmund Burke having been our founder. So why spoil it all now?

It is a cliché to say that in our time Trinity was not regarded as an Irish university so much as a West British establishment in Ireland. The student body was cosmopolitan and, so we were told, made up of over seventy different nationalities. Southern Irish Catholics, in the leading institution of higher learning in their capital city, were almost an endangered species. The Catholic

Archbishop of Dublin, John Charles McQuaid, had seen to that by forbidding his parishioners, taken to include all Ireland, to darken the doors of a sinful Protestant establishment. Some, mainly offspring of prosperous, mostly middle-class professionals, many of them educated at Clongowes in Ireland or at English Catholic public schools, ignored the ban. The North of Ireland was represented by those who did not fancy Queen's and some of them were also from Catholic families looking for a university in Ireland away from the stifling sectarianism of the Six Counties.

TCD seemed to reciprocate any local suspicions about attitude and ethos by being fairly isolationist, isolated within its walls from the pressures of 'real' Ireland. Most of my friends took little interest in domestic politics – the Troubles in the North were at a very immature stage and political parties in the Republic, whether Fianna Fáil or Fine Gael, seemed quaintly foreign. The debates in The Hist were usually more international than national in theme; the University Philosophical Society ('The Phil'), dismissively referred to by Hist people as 'The Other Society', had a greener tinge to its membership. It was accordingly more parochial than we were with our mainly English 'Anglican' students leavened with across-the-water Catholics and other folk from Nigeria, south Asia and the Arab world. The image of gown in town was not helped by a group of young gentlemen known collectively as the 'Nags'. Double-barrelled names, tweed-jacketed and -capped, they had attended rather than been educated at Harrow, or somewhere equally 'upmarket'. Many having been rusticated from their institutions of first choice, they had eventually come to Ireland because they liked horses. At least they mixed with the natives, no doubt getting very drunk in the process; but the Ireland that they knew was limited to Leopardstown and the other race courses, where they lived, drank and had their being. One wit when asked about a Nag's previous educational background responded, 'Eton and Christ knows.'

I often wondered how the really foreign students felt about the institution. The group of aristocratic Egyptians in exile since the revolution that had overthrown King Farouq? One of them, a Greek Egyptian from Alexandria, Boutros had been at TCD for ten years and had no intention of returning to the Egypt of Jamal Abdul Nasser. Or the band of small quiet Yemenis who had been awarded government scholarships, perhaps to get them out of the way as presenting a political threat to the medieval Imamate. That may have been good thinking, if short on foresight, as after the Imam was overthrown by a revolution in 1962 TCD graduates formed about 70 per cent of Abdullah Sallal's first cabinet. But these nice gentle Trinity men were not apparently tough enough to survive subsequent counter-revolutions. One very distinguished Nigerian student, a chief no less, always immaculately dressed in a three-piece Saville Row suit, with an Oxford drawl reminiscent of the 'Nags', would not have enjoyed being chased through the streets of Dublin by an angry mob protesting at the massacre of an Irish UN patrol by Baluba tribesmen during the UN intervention in the Congo. I met him dishevelled and exhausted just inside Front Gate, having been rescued in the nick of time by the gardaí. 'They called me a bloody Baluba! I tried to explain that I was not a bloody Baluba but a ******* Ibo. But they didn't want to know. And they call us savages!'

I suppose our group was not much better than the 'Nags' in taking advantage of our new environment and we went around in a little bubble of English-ness. Most of us would know the name of the current taoiseach but few of his ministers. We read *The Irish Times* and cursed the sports page for its obsession with racing and disregard for what really mattered like county cricket in England. RTÉ seemed so parochial, and we were the generation before *The Late Late Show* with Gay Byrne, which became required viewing for undergraduates from 1962 on. Most of us were in receipt of generous allowances so could afford to eat out at the better restaurants now and again. To a man we avoided 'Commons' (despite having paid for it upfront) and preferred a local greasy spoon, the Royalette or the Log Cabin, not far from Pearse Street Gate.

Part of my military service had been in the North – the army of occupation, as the IRA described us, and I tended to be very critical of the Irish government's apparently ambivalent attitude towards Sinn Féin and its unsubtle encouragement of northern nationalists. Many of my English chums made no secret of their distaste for Irish neutrality not only in the Second World War but in post-war Europe, refusing to have anything to do with NATO. We all made a point of importing Earl Haig Fund poppies and attending, poppied to the gills, the Remembrance Day service in St Patrick's Protestant Cathedral, studiously ignored by the Catholic establishment despite the huge numbers of Irishmen who fought (and died) with the Allies against the Axis powers. And perhaps fortunately there was no official government representation as my diary for 8 November 1959 records that a 'packed congregation' sang the British national anthem! I took particular pleasure in wearing my highly polished Suez campain medal to the service, flaunting my military past on the top of the bus as a message to the natives that some of us had to stand up and be counted. The effect was slightly spoilt on one occasion when a very inebriated Dubliner, peering closely at my gleaming gong asked, 'Is that one of them newfangled Pioneer badge yokes?' I said nothing but felt that if anyone needed to take the pledge it was he who should be first in the queue!

One of our group, Angus Bainbrigge, a very loud and professionally eccentric person, widely regarded (and never denied by him) to be fabulously rich, believed in occasionally letting the town know about how badly the craven Irish government had behaved in the fight against Fascism. In January 1959, on Winston Churchill's eighty-fifth birthday, he borrowed equipment from the Gramophone Society and using its most powerful amplifier broadcast selections from the great man's wartime speeches from a set of rooms in Botany Bay. This performance ended with a rousing rendition of 'God Save the Queen'. We never had any public reaction despite the volume. Sir Winston was clearly audible in Bewley's Coffee Shop halfway up Grafton Street and the only complaints were from fellow Botany Bay inmates wrestling with hangovers or overdue essays. I suspect long-suffering Dublin people just took it as yet another indication of inappropriate behaviour from an alien institution in their midst.

Like the Hon. Andrew Bonar Law, Angus Bainbrigge and I were into practical jokes. But subtler, we felt, than Bonar Law's boorish exhibitionism. Our most spectacular wheeze misfired spectacularly. We put a notice in *The Irish Times*, the *Irish Independent* and the evening papers appealing for old toys and dolls for a 'Christmas Presents for Refugee Children Campaign'. The idea, it was explained, was to have the toys renovated and sent to Germany for refugees as part of World Refugee Year. The address for donations was a set of rooms in No. 3 New Square – namely those of a certain Guy Milner mentioned by name in the public notice. Angus and I had a great distaste for this young man as a well known activist for 'good' causes, of an ostentatiously Christian tendency and too smug by half. We hoped that his rooms would be embarrassed by floods of broken-down dolls and useless toys. They were, but he cleverly capitalized on this windfall by adopting the cause as his own and enthusiastically pursuing it. Worse, we were blackmailed by Guy: someone had leaked our role (or more likely Angus had publicly bragged about it) and under threat of public exposure we undertook to organize a 'bring a toy' reception at the Gresham Hotel. We did our best at some considerable expense and even had the Lord Mayor of Dublin and the Protestant Archbishop amongst the guests, but too few others to make a success of the venture. This was further egg on our faces but at least we were saved total public humiliation. An additional irritation was that Milner and Co. (including Bill Jackson who was later to be a prominent figure in Irish charity circles) did very well. 'A boorish practical joke developed into a worthwhile Movement' (*Trinity News*, 19 November 1959). By early December 1000 gift parcels were on their way to Germany and Guy Milner had attracted widespread public recognition for one of the most successful operations in a city that was inherently punch-drunk from innumerable 'Flag Days' for this deserving cause or that. Bah. Humbug.

Perhaps we should have put much more into TCD and got more out of our Dublin experience than we did. I, for one, remember it as certainly high amongst 'the best years of my life'. Especially my last year when four of us shared a house in Sandymount; we appreciated living more like ordinary Dubliners than was possible in the isolation of College rooms. My debating skills (I was in a team representing Irish universities in the Observer Mace competition), my contact with people from so many different countries, and the necessity, belatedly, of having to work very hard under extreme pressure (an own goal, that one) was an excellent preparation for two overseas careers – in the former Colonial Service and in the Foreign Office. And oh yes: two other plusses: my golf handicap into single figures and meeting my future wife, a physio student at the Adelaide. I once asked a former close friend what he had got out of TCD. After a bit of thought he said, 'Well at least it didn't do me any harm.'

Peter Hinchcliffe (TCD 1957–61; Modern History and Political Science) later joined HM Overseas Civil Service in Aden, then the Foreign and Commonwealth Office. He was Ambassador to Kuwait and to Jordan, and High Commissioner in Zambia. He is currently an Honorary Fellow at the University of Edinburgh.

TARNISHED BUTTONS

michael longley

> tar nished buttons
> all have lil anchors
> Rudi Holzapfel

MY UNDERGRADUATE DAYS began under a cloud. At my Belfast school I had been singled out as a likely star in classical studies, and had been drilled thoroughly in anticipation of an entrance scholarship to an Oxbridge college or to Trinity. But love broke in and destroyed my concentration. At sixteen I became obsessed with a girl from Methodist College and craved her company. We spent weekends together and met in each other's homes on Tuesdays and Thursdays to do our homework at the same table. Sexual fervour and jealousy had me teetering on the verge of craziness. After eighteen passionate months the lovely girl made her sensible getaway, and I embarked on a sequence of compensatory relationships, all of them heated and doomed. My Latin and Greek studies went up in the blaze. I didn't score in the exams for Entrance Scholarship, and arrived in College in October 1958 feeling a bit of a failure and emotionally burnt out.

At first I lodged with an elderly couple, Mr and Mrs Leeson, in Wellington Road. Their son Victor, with whom I breakfasted, worked for Arthur Guinness and devoted all his free time to the St James's Gate Choral Society, which he had founded in 1951. Intense and introverted, he lived for music, and showed no inclination to chat with me over the fried eggs. I cycled to College, and attended lectures for a brief period – before the bad habits set in – and did some work in the Reading Room. Then back to Wellington Road and my bedroom at the front of the house. I lay in bed and listened to the traffic and to Victor playing the piano a floor below me. Melancholy months.

John Murray, another classicist and a fellow Ulsterman, was my first 'wife'. His chief enthusiasm was Esperanto. I still have a couple of his paperbacks with inscriptions written in Esperanto. Our spacious rooms were in No. 27 above the coffee shop. Was I shy or depressed or both? For a long time I wasn't plucky enough to go into the coffee shop where all the bright young things congregated. I would glance in at them on my way up to rooms, and I could hear their starling-chatter through the floorboards. Although I didn't open a book for months on end, I was able for a while to bluff my way, thanks to the schoolteachers who had hammered the basics into me. Then, in a viva with the Professor of Ancient History, Herbert Parke, I could barely translate a straightforward passage from Livy. He asked me if I really wanted to continue with Classics.

I could hardly breathe with the shock. Dejection stifled me. Round about that time I started to spew into a notebook my perplexities. A few years earlier I had tried to write poems to impress my sweetheart and her friends. This time I needed to impress myself. I wrote a crazy prose poem, a wild dog's howl, which John Murray encouraged me to submit to *Icarus*. When I dropped my first-born into the magazine's postbox, I wasn't expecting it to disappear forever. But it did – mercifully. At school I had immersed myself in classical music, and explored in a daze of pleasure all the beautiful big art books in the library. Now it was poetry, or the idea of poetry, that took me over completely. I filled notebooks with formless outpourings, writing several bad poems a day. I showed them to a beautiful girl called Averne and to a scholarly friend, who said they liked them. But there was one person whose opinion I was particularly keen to hear.

EDNA BRODERICK was a brilliant student. I was attracted to her but feared rejection and postponed making a move. Giddy with nerves I brought my maroon-covered notebook to her in the Reading Room and asked her if she would mind looking over my poems. She turned out to be a kind-hearted critic. Warily I started inviting her and her friends to my rooms in Botany Bay for cups of milky Nescafé and the occasional fry-up (a virtuoso performance on a single gas ring). Bruce Arnold included two of my poems in the March 1960 *Icarus*. The thrill of that reverberates to this day. When I was home for Easter my father read one of them, 'Marigolds', and told me it wasn't worth the paper it was printed on. Brendan Kennelly encouraged Tony Hickey, the editor of the next issue, to publish six more of my poems. (In my latest collection *Snow Water* I have rescued from oblivion the best of these, 'Tra-na-rossan', by encorprating all of it into a new poem.) Edna gave me my first favourable review in *Trinity News*. In June of that year I held her hand in the Astor cinema: *Les Enfants du Paradis*. We parted as soon as we had come together, she to a study course in Italy, I to a holiday job in a pea-canning factory in England. My father died in July of a terrible cancer. Edna didn't come back to Ireland until the beginning of October, not many days before my Senior Freshman examinations. Mourning my father and terrified of losing my new love I had driven myself demented, and went on to fail my exams. I was allowed to resit in the New Year. Edna and I picked up the pieces and embarked without knowing it on our lifetime together.

Brendan Kennelly and Rudi Holzapfel were the best-known 'College poets' ('Sounds like "village idiot"', my friend Victor Blease said). I was jostling to lay claim to the title when Derek Mahon breezed in from Belfast, fully fledged, brilliant, self-confident. I was flummoxed: one of the best things ever to happen to me. We became (and remain) close friends. As I've said elsewhere, we inhaled poetry with our untipped Sweet Afton cigarettes. We smoked and drank like troopers. We read our poems in public for the first time towards the end of a performance by Kennelly and Holzapfel at the Laurentian Society (a Catholic outfit). They generously invited us to join them on the platform. So intense was my involvement with Mahon that I missed out on getting to know Kennelly better. I now regret this. He seemed to encompass everything I had been missing. He was culturally astonishing. In my poem 'The Factory' I pay tribute to his genius: 'Already the tubby, rollicking, broken Christ / Talking too much, drowning me in his hurlygush.'

Joining the editorial board of *Icarus* felt like promotion to the officer ranks. I remember a board meeting where the American poet Cheli Duran criticized obscurities in a poem by Michael Leahy ('balloons have habits of points'). He was a dapper philosophy student and the most self-assured of us. I can still recite the opening lines of his 'This Particular Cat'. He was really smart and paid his way through College with poker winnings. We took ourselves very seriously, with Rudi Holzapfel the only poet who was any fun. His lower-case whimsy could occasionally be beautiful: 'tar nished buttons / all have lil anchors.' When I became editor I included 'lullablues', along with four startling poems by Mahon, and a precocious essay by Edna about e.e. cummings. In 'Interpreter of Roses' she wrote: 'Renew the lost connection between man and the poetry of earth, and a moral universe seems possible.' I loved the whole editorial process, corresponding with Turner's Printing Company in Longford, the folds of galley proofs, red ink and blue pencil, hustling for advertisements, flogging the magazine at Front Gate. Alec Reid gave my issue the thumbs-up, but criticized the blank pages at the very end ('If you can't get ads, then fill them with info about past issues') and for over-punctuating quotations in the review section.

I hung on his every word. We all did. An inspirational lecturer in the English Department, Alec Reid was fat and untidy, albino and nearly blind. As he walked he swayed and rolled his head and boomed and laughed. Like adoring little Boswells we shadowed him to O'Neills or Flynn's where he would squat on a stool with his legs apart, his pudgy fingers round a pint, and quote poetry by heart or monologue about Beckett and cricket. He had been one of the founding editors of *Icarus*. We craved his approval. Some of us felt anxious when we learned that he was going to review the magazine in *Trinity News*. Mahon told me ahead of publication that Alec had singled out for praise my poem 'Konzentrationslager'. For us such news was worth leaking and, now, forty-five years later, worth remembering. Trinity treated Alec ungenerously. We suffered the slights on his behalf. We were devastated when his young son Michael died in America after undergoing open-heart surgery. Alec and Beatrice had scrimped and saved to take Michael across the Atlantic where the odds were supposed to be better. We all grew up a bit. Alec's passions included Edward Thomas and Louis MacNeice. Edna's and my subsequent work on these poets owes so much to him. In the tenth-anniversary issue of *Icarus* (March 1960) Alec wrote: 'It could well be that it owes its survival in part to the fact that it has so little to offer the ambitious. Claiming little it has achieved much. In its modesty, its empirical approach and its balance, it is very typical of Trinity.'

W.B. Stanford was a world figure, a great Homeric scholar, a startlingly handsome man, reserved and grave. His Macmillan edition of *The Odyssey* had been part of my mental furniture since schooldays. I was selling *Icarus* at Front Gate when he approached the table and bought a copy.

'You weren't at my lecture this morning.'

'I slept in, sir.'

'My lecture was at eleven. Don't you live in College? Come and see me first thing Monday morning.' Lectures were compulsory and I had missed so many he could with justification have failed me my year. A nail-biting weekend. He scolded me, then smiled: 'I suppose you think that because you're a poet I'm going to let you off?'

'Of course not, sir.'

'Well, I am. I very much liked those new poems in the magazine.' Many years later at his retirement dinner he came and sat beside me after the speeches. 'If I had my life over again, I would choose to be a poet rather than a scholar,' he said. I now wish that I had been a bit more of a scholar. I enjoyed those lectures of his that I did attend. Occasionally he would take flight. 'The Golden Mean, Ladies and Gentlemen, is a tension and not a dead level.' He believed that Homer's poetry had been sung and bravely showed us how he thought it might have sounded. He gave me my one and only distinguished academic moment. In a class on Aristotle's *Poetics* he asked us to compose for the following week our own definitions of poetry. Mine was: 'If prose is a river, then poetry's a fountain.'

I quote this in the section about Stanford in 'River & Fountain', the poem commissioned by Trinity in 1992 as part of their quartercentenary commemorations. Its structure of twelve self-contained six-line stanzas had a life of its own, with the result that Alec Reid may be a presence between the lines, but is not, alas, a subject – nor is Donald Wormell, the Professor of Latin. He read aloud from Propertius and Tibullus as though they were living poets. He recommended, with reservations, Pound's 'Homage to Sextus Propertius', and began his lecture on Catullus by quoting Yeats' 'The Scholars' ('Lord what would they say / Did their Catullus walk that way?') When my father died and I failed my exams, I went to Wormell with my confusions. Gentle and sympathetic, he helped me to save my year. Later, I showed him my first translations from Propertius, and he was wonderfully encouraging. Inspired by Wormell I chose the Latin love elegy as my Special Subject for moderatorship. I even gave a paper on Propertius to the Classical Society – with some assistance from Edna. I remember expatiating at length on the poet's use of 'et'. Since 1990 my poetry has been energized by a belated (and still woefully inexpert) involvement with the Classics, especially Homer, and Ovid's glorious ragbag, *Metamorphoses*. The seeds sown by Stanford and Wormell did eventually germinate.

Among the small student population there was a goodly proportion of folk who would have been bracingly new to a youth from Northern Ireland – English public-school toffs, an ex-GI or two, students from France, Sweden, colonial Africa, post-Farouk Egypt. The toffs turned out to be human, the Swedish girls heartbreakingly beautiful. One of the GIs, Paul O'Grady, became a good friend. But I depended most deeply on the companionship of fellow Ulstermen – Bill Jackson, Alan Elliott, Tony Taylor, Robin Harte, Harry Gilmore – but not in a parochial way. We took Dublin to our hearts and were in no hurry to get back across the Border. Bill and Alan went on to hold top jobs in Oxfam and the Northern Irish Civil Service. Robin still pursues mathematical will-o'-the-wisps. Harry, a self-employed horologist, lives just around the corner from me in south Belfast. I lament Tony in a section of 'River & Fountain': 'Oh, to have turned away from everything to one face, / Eros and Thanatos your gods, icicle and dew.' All the while poetry was pulling me off balance. I was stretching my creative abilities to breaking point and at the same time neglecting my Classical studies. In October 1962 I suffered a brainstorm and walked out of my finals or, as they put it, 'surrendered my papers'. Brendan Kennelly, I recall, was invigilating the examinations in the Old Museum Building at the time. Derek Mahon, who was more usually the lawless one, tracked me down to the station and tried unsuccessfully to persuade me to return to the ordeal. A year later I resat my finals and struggled through. 'We're delighted you came back,' Stanford told me at the results notice board.

A few years ago I was asked by Peter Rowan, a Belfast book dealer, to look over and write a catalogue note for the late Victor Leeson's comprehensive collection of contemporary poetry. It was a big surprise to learn that Victor had been a poetry lover, a collector on such a scale, and then a relief to find my own books and pamphlets in their alphabetical nook. I was brought back full circle to Wellington Road and gawky conversation over breakfast. It is 1958 and I am about to cycle in October sunshine to my first day in Trinity.

Michael Longley (TCD 1958–62; Classics) joined the Arts Council of Northern Ireland after several years' teaching, where he initiated programmes for literature, the traditional arts (mainly Irish music) and arts-in-education. A freelance writer since 1991, he has published eight collections of poetry including **Gorse Fires** (1991), which won the Whitbread Prize, and **The Weather in Japan** (2000), which won the T.S. Eliot Prize, the Hawthornden Prize and the Irish Times Prize for Poetry. His most recent collection **Snow Water** (2004) was awarded the Librex Montale Prize (Milan). **Selected Poems** was published in 1998 and **Collected Poems** in 2006. He is the editor of **20th Century Irish Poems** 2004), and selections of the poetry of Louis MacNeice and W.R. Rodgers. In 1996 he received the American Ireland Fund Literary Award, in 2001 the Queen's Gold Medal for Poetry, and in 2003 the Wilfred Owen Award. He was the recipient of an honorary degree from Trinity in 1999, and is a Fellow of the Royal Society of Literature and a member of Aosdána.

TO TCD VIA THE GALA, BALLYFERMOT

mike dibb

PERHAPS, LIKE OTHERS, I arrived at TCD more by accident than design. I studied science at school and had already been accepted to read Chemistry at King's College, Cambridge. But I then realized that at heart I wasn't a scientist but was much more interested in painting and literature. So I asked the Cambridge authorities whether I could switch my degree course from Chemistry to English. In my naivety I thought that all you needed to study English was the ability to read, an interest in books and a curiosity about the relationship of literature to life. It also seemed to me that, after the C.P. Snow-inspired debates of the 1950s on the regrettable divisions between the 'two cultures', a scientifically educated student would be welcomed by the English Department. Such an idea was unthinkable to the Leavisite moral guardians of literature. They firmly rejected me as a scientific trespasser, and I found myself looking around for somewhere else to go.

An old schoolfriend, Nick Carey, who was already halfway through his first year at Trinity (ironically studying Chemistry) suggested that, although it was a bit late in the day, I should apply to join him. He told me Dublin was a great place to be, the cost of living was cheaper than England, the courses lasted four years and, best of all, the qualification threshold was just five O levels (including Latin), on the basis of which you could apply to read anything you liked. And so it was that in the summer of 1958, five months after the official closing date for entries, I sent off an application form. A short welcoming note from my prospective tutor, Professor E.C. Riley, came back by return post. The only hitch, he wrote, was that, Ireland being Éire, English was just another continental Western Romance Language and could only be studied in tandem with another language for a full honours degree. In the end I chose Spanish (it took beginners). It was a good choice. Professor Riley, known internationally as an authority on Cervantes, was in charge of the Spanish Department. I'm sure he was never happy with my stumbling Spanish and certainly neither of us could have then imagined that much later in our lives – by which time he was no longer 'Professor Riley' but plain 'Ted' – we would collaborate on a TV documentary about the cultural afterlife of Don Quixote. Of course, while at TCD I could not imagine myself as a documentary film-maker: the term meant almost nothing to me. The word 'film' meant going to The Cinema and in Dublin this became the passion of my life, as well as being a wonderful way of exploring every corner of the city and taking me beyond the restricting, if beautiful, spaces of the University.

My interest in movies was first kindled by my father. A GP on the east coast of Yorkshire, he was the most organized man I've ever known. Despite a gruelling town and country round each day of many miles and visits, he was always back home for lunch or tea exactly when he said he would be, to the minute. He was a passionate musician and kept his large collection of classical records meticulously numbered and catalogued in a book, which I still use. He was also a keen cinema-goer. He went at least once and often twice a week and kept a little book about that too. Every Sunday he would enter the titles of the new films and would place one, two or three stars against each based on the opinions of *The Observer*'s film critic, C.A. Lejeune. There was a column for his own starred estimate and space for a very brief comment. I would love to refer to it now but, being my father, he threw it away without sentimentality when he no longer thought it useful. One thing I do remember is his response to *The African Queen*. He was a great fan of Katherine Hepburn but after Lejeune's three-star recommendation he merely entered his own blob of disappointment, adding the two words, 'Oh Dear!' (Personally I've always thought John Huston an overrated director and perhaps the seed of that judgment was sown in my father's book.)

As is often the way, I resisted much of my father's neatness, punctuality and sense of order, but in discovering my own love for the cinema I found myself following his example. The year was 1960, and I was halfway through my degree course in Dublin. By chance I met that very rare thing in those days, a postgraduate film student – Charles Barr – over on a visit from the Slade School of Fine Art in London. Later Charles was to publish exemplary studies of Laurel and Hardy and of Ealing Studios, but at the time he was writing a thesis on cinemascope. He was the first person I had ever met who had actually seen a film ten times. I couldn't believe it. And the film in question was not a 'serious' European art house movie but *The James Brothers*, a Western directed by Nicholas Ray. This was a revelation, both for me and my close friend and fellow student, Peter Bell. Soon Peter and I were taking in two more extraordinary Westerns – *Ride Lonesome* and *Commanche Station*, both directed by Budd Boetticher, someone I'd never heard of then, but whom much later in 1993 I had the pleasure of meeting at his ranch near San Diego. I filmed an interview with him about the Alabama Hills in Lone Pine, California, where he'd directed so many of his Westerns.

Back in 1960, Peter and I realized, to our amazement, that we were not in a cinematic backwater but in a city that was a cornucopia of undiscovered American masterpieces. Indeed, Dublin was the perfect place for us to be. Telefís Éireann hadn't yet started and Ireland had the highest per-capita cinema-going public of any country in Western Europe. Dublin and its suburbs were awash with thirty or more small cinemas, each with a double bill that changed three times a week, Monday to Wednesday, Thursday to Friday, and with a complete change of programme on Sunday when you often had to book in advance.

Next, we had to find a more efficient way of accessing the gems in this ever-changing public library of British and American films. Peter took out a subscription to *Cahiers du Cinéma*, then in its heyday of Truffautesque and Godardian hyperbole for all things US. But it was another French publication that became our bible. *Vingt Ans de Cinéma Américain* had just been published in Paris. It was edited by Jean-Pierre Coursodon, and among its contributors was the French director Bertrand Tavernier. Along with a year-by-year summary of the evolution of Hollywood from 1940 to 1960, it offered opinionated biographies of all the major and minor directors, stars and supporting actors. What it didn't contain, however, was a list of the films referred to. This became our next task. In the spirit of my orderly father, Peter and I went painstakingly through the whole book, extracting all the film titles, often translating them from the French, and recompiling them into an alphabetical dictionary, of which we each still have a copy. We invented our own star system of directorial evaluation and, needless to say, bought the whole 'auteur' theory lock, stock and barrel.

Every day the Dublin evening papers devoted several columns to complete listings and times for all the films being shown across the city. After a quick glance at our dictionary, we would rush off to catch *The Stranger* (Orson Welles, 1946), given only supporting picture status at The Rialto, Dundrum; next day it was off to The Gala, Ballyfermot, to catch Burt Lancaster swinging his way through *The Crimson Pirate* ('bondissant et savoureux', Robert Siodmak, 1952), followed by an Anthony Mann Western or Don Siegel's *Invasion of the Body Snatchers* ('le meilleur film de science fiction que nous ayons jamais vu') or another particular favourite, Budd Boetticher's gangster movie, *The Rise and Fall of Legs Diamond*, a new release in 1960. Indeed, if I had to think of a single group of films that encapsulated the naive but real excitement of that period of my life, it would have to be those of Budd Boetticher. André Bazin, the editor of *Cahiers du Cinéma*, called Boetticher's film *Seven Men From Now* 'le plus simple et le plus beau western d'après guerre'. It was just one of a string of small-scale Westerns, each starring the almost expressionless yet vivid presence of Randolph Scott and almost always written by Burt Kennedy. They belonged to a period in Hollywood, alas long gone, when a small group of people could find a creative space inside the system. Working at the low-budget end of a popular genre, Boetticher and his team were able to take familiar features of this genre and give them genuinely fresh and inventive inflections. And I liked the fact that they were B-films and therefore ignored by the mainstream critics of national newspapers, whose opinions I didn't much rate anyway. They were films, I felt, with qualities I was discovering for myself with, of course, a little initial help from the French ... and Charles Barr. It was also a world apart from everything I was officially meant to be studying. And to me more important. Although I loved reading particular authors and books, I did the minimum amount of work needed to get through the English and Spanish exams at the end of each summer. At the time, I considered the hours I spent in the Library every day as my passport to another year of film-going. Only later, when I began to make films myself, did I realize how much of what I read had in fact seeped into my life. As I travelled around making cultural documentaries on a range of subjects, particularly in Spain and Latin America, I found the official and unofficial sides of my life at Trinity coming back together again. But when I look back, it was the movies that mattered most. True, I never matched Charles Barr's (alleged) twenty-one films in one long weekend in Belfast – he was always the more frenetic film-goer. The most I could manage was two films a day, every day for three months, while studying for my final exams. If only I'd had to answer questions on Hollywood 1940–60 rather than on English and Spanish literature I'm sure I'd have got a First.

We didn't see just American movies in Dublin. It was a great time for European movie-makers and much of their work (somewhat late and somewhat censored) arrived in the city. Down by the Liffey, the Astor and Corinthian cinemas showed the latest films of Bergman, Fellini, Buñuel, Resnais, Truffaut and Godard ... and it was the work of these film-makers that Pete Bell and I tried to pastiche in our somewhat ambitious (mercifully unfinished) first directorial attempt at making a short fiction film, funded by an £80-grant from the Irish Film Society. The film was shot by a mature fellow student, Michael de Larrabeiti, who before coming to Trinity had once worked as an assistant film cameraman and later went on to become a very successful children's author. We rented a 16mm Bolex camera, discovered a pile of old tracking rails in a Dublin warehouse, found a surreal location in the Dublin Mountains – where a fireplace and chimney breast were all that remained of an abandoned house – dragooned a bunch of friends as actors, dressed them in dinner jackets and ... and ... well, my career as a film-maker was off to a shaky start. Though the film was never completed, at least I was able to bullshit about it during the interview for a trainee post as assistant film editor at the BBC. It probably landed me the job.

It also turned out to be the first and last fiction film I ever made. In the late 1960s I became an arts documentary film-maker at the BBC and have worked in that field ever since. Which is where I come back to my old TCD Spanish professor, 'Ted' Riley. In 1995 I was commissioned to make a sixty-minute film for the BBC 2 series *Bookmark* about the astonishing diversity of popular iconography generated by that great Spanish literary duo, Don Quixote and Sancho Panza. I asked Ted, an acknowledged expert on this subject, to be my advisor. As his Spanish student I'd proved a disappointment, but we got on well while filming, and he really seemed to enjoy the process of editing. And when the film was finished, I sent him a VHS cassette with a short note: 'Dear Ted, Thanks for all your help. Here is the only essay of mine you ever liked!'

Mike Dibb (TCD 1958–62; Spanish and English) has been producing and directing films for television for over forty years on cinema, jazz, art, sport, litera-ture and popular culture. These include the John Berger series, **Ways of Seeing** (BAFTA Award 1972); two films with fellow TCD graduate Ian Gibson, **The Fame and Shame of Salvador Dalí** (1996) and **The Spirit of Lorca** (Gold Award, NY Festival of Film and TV, 1989); **What's Cuba Playing At?** (1985); **In Pursuit of Don Juan** (1989); **The Further Adventures of Don Quixote** (1988/9); and three themed series on the contrasting subjects of 'Play', 'Time' and 'Latin-American Culture'. His most recent feature-length music documentaries include **The Miles Davis Story** (NY EMMY award, 2001), **Tango Maestro – The Life and Music of Astor Piazzolla** (2004) and **Keith Jarrett – The Art of Improvisation** (2005), all now available on DVD.

BEYOND THE DALKEY BUS

edna broderick

I REMEMBER coming to Trinity in October 1958 rather as I remember starting school fourteen years earlier. Both initiations have left anxious reflexes, like a sweaty clutching of satchel or book-bag, although in a sense I have never left school or university – perhaps another sign of unresolved anxiety. In any case, Trinity was the Unknown. I dreaded having to take responsibility for work and life after the controlled conditions of school where I had been a swot and hockey player, where there were timetables, where (eventually) you thought you knew what to do. Two years before, I had already found it hard to make the transition from a small Protestant girls' school in Dún Laoghaire (Glengara Park) to a larger, more academic Protestant girls' school: Alexandra College, then in Earlsfort Terrace near Stephen's Green. Yet unlike UCD, also then in Earlsfort Terrace but belonging to a parallel universe, TCD should have been the known world. My father, T.S. Broderick, was the Professor of Pure Mathematics. And I had switched to 'Alex' because he wanted me to prepare for university by taking Trinity Entrance Scholarship (not possible at Glengara). I did well in the Scholarship exam despite vomiting during one of the papers. This happened to be the first time I was in the same room with my future husband, Michael Longley, although our relationship did not really begin until 1960. On a card she made for our fortieth wedding anniversary our painter-daughter Sarah pictures the romantic moment.

If memory is always based in the present, the images that surface from previous lives are further compromised by mythic or analytical structures also deep-laid. As an academic working in Belfast, I comment on (which means getting involved in) Irish cultural politics: an intensely autobiographical as well as contested field. Here 'identity' looms large, and I am likely to process my Trinity experience according to certain themes. Trinity affected my life long before I became a student there. Our family history was entwined with the politics of the Irish universities, and so with Irish culture wars. In other words, I was a McQuaid victim. In the early 1940s my father, a Catholic from County Cork, left the Church when Archbishop McQuaid renewed the ban on Catholics attending Trinity. By making Trinity forbidden, by accentuating its Otherness, by investing it with the aura of 'mortal sin', McQuaid may have made it seductive to some Catholics (Irish Catholic numbers rose in the 1950s). He certainly kept Trinity exotic in Dublin for another quarter-century, like Alexandria in Egypt. He also precipitated me into the 'minority'. My mother was a Scottish Presbyterian, the mixed marriage being frowned on from both sides. As there were few kirks in south Dublin, my sister and I were brought up 'in' the Church of Ireland (the usual preposition, more ethnic than religious, overstates our allegiance). But to recall mid-twentieth-century Trinity only in terms of the broad sectarian history that has shaped the Irish universities, along with so much else, is to override other cultural inflections. In October 1958 I wasn't thinking about identity politics but worrying about how to talk to people. And as regards 'identity', Trinity was probably then the most fluid place in Ireland.

For too long at Trinity I was shy and fearful, even though the exotic place was in my native city, if a city in which some natives were less native than others, a city in which every Trinity student might be tagged 'West Brit'. Perhaps my lack of a genuine 'minority' background made Trinity stranger than it might otherwise have been. Yet the students whom I found exotic – from posh English schools, from further abroad, even from the North – were themselves discovering or inventing Trinity (and McQuaid's Dublin) as liberatingly foreign. They were forging a milieu that glamorized various permutations of sex, alcohol, creativity and mortal sin. If they left the country after graduating, never or rarely to return, their nostalgia can have a whiff of *Brideshead*. Decades of change to

Trinity, to Ireland, will not revise anyone's Arcadian narrative. But neither can those decades negate my provincial cringe in 1958. For someone who came into College by the Dalkey train or bus, as well as by a particular historical route, it was a special shock to hear RP English so confidently spoken.

Not only Catholic Dublin cringed or bristled at loud voices in public places. One or two Southern Protestant students may themselves have been to posh English schools, but modest Irish day or boarding schools were the norm. Trinity's shrinking 'Anglo-Irish' nucleus mainly depended on families in the professions, business, farming, the Church of Ireland. I recently met Jack Daniels and his wife Sonia (my Alex and Trinity friend Sonia Noyek) in Scotland. I was reminded that I had profiled Jack and Neville Keery in *Trinity News* as twin TCD politicos, who were likely to join the Southern Prod diaspora – and so it had largely proved. As for Northern Prods: Trinity, whatever they made of it, gave them a continuing base in Dublin. Until 1968, when the ban was lifted, McQuaid paradoxically held bits of Protestant Ireland together in an ambiguous Trojan horse at the heart of his diocese. Another unintended consequence was that he kept some cultural lines open between Dublin and Belfast. The Northern contingent, generally from Protestant grammar schools, included working-class beneficiaries of the eleven-plus. This also applied to some English students (the red rag of Trinity privilege kept the red flag flying in the Fabian Society), and indeed the majority of these, as of Irish Protestants, were middle-class. Shades of difference between England and Protestant Ireland, whose encounter at Trinity was perhaps the last echo of a long-reverberating clash, are easier to analyse now than they were to negotiate then. I wasn't the only Dublin student who clung to the safety blanket of friends from school. Students who go to a 'local' university can be trapped between the first world and the second. At one point, when working for *Trinity News*, I would collate gossip reports from 'socialite' parties I hadn't attended, tweaking them into some parodic format. How sad. A whiff of *Vile Bodies*.

But if I associate the English top-dressing at Trinity with irritation and social elitism, I also associate it with challenge and Bohemian style: all epitomized by Players. Perhaps outsiders anywhere are always more likely to make things happen. One example is William (Bill) Oddie, reputed to buy new shirts rather than wash old ones, directing Gay's *Beggars' Opera*. Eloquent and opinionated,

Bill was to become an Anglican priest, then a Catholic convert and editor of *The Catholic Herald*. A postdated whiff of Waugh. I also remember him cooking excellent meals and – scourge of received ideas – pronouncing that American cinema was better than continental cinema. At my very first tutorial, another Eng. Lit. student from England enthused about J.R.R. Tolkien, then an unheard-of cult figure. This was Chris Fettes, who persuaded the malleable tutor (Professor H.O. White) to devote time to *The Hobbit*. Chris was more impressive than Professor White – chiefly notable for the Elizabethan mousetrap with which he illustrated *Hamlet*. When Denis Donoghue reviewed McDowell's and Webb's history of Trinity (1982), his polemic against 'that bizarre institution' included the complaint that he and his colleagues at UCD 'were required to teach thousands of students, while our opposite numbers in Trinity dispensed sherry to their chosen few'.

Sour grapes? R.B.D. French's sherry parties were certainly an institution (when did people stop drinking sherry and start drinking wine?), but so were his wit and his eighteenth-century values. To absorb the latter as well as the sherry, we were asked to write a poem in heroic couplets about Front Square. The class of 1958 arrived in the English Department just too late for Donald Davie, and a bit early for Philip Edwards, who took over from White during our time there. But if we slightly missed out on a new wave in literary studies, there were compensations. The members of staff who most influenced me were two lecturers in English, J.K. Walton and Alec Reid, and Donald Wormell, Professor of Latin. My course was the Latin and English moderatorship, grandly titled 'Ancient and Modern' (a bit like Trinity).

Walton put paid to Trinity dilettanteism, expounding Shakespeare with such exciting rigour that I became a Leavisite, *Scrutiny*-addict, and incurable close reader. Alec Reid shaped my future career in less strictly academic ways. Alec will feature in other people's memoirs: his physical presence and disabilities, the sorrow of his losing his son, his involvement with the theatre, his friendship with Beckett, Trinity's poor treatment of him, his drinking, his inspirational talk. My own special memory is Alec lecturing on poetry. In my first term he recited poems by Louis MacNeice ('Meeting Point') and Edward Thomas so powerfully as to make poetry, and those poets, indelible in my life and work. It can be no coincidence that my first publication was on Thomas, that I have currently returned to him, that I wrote a book on MacNeice, and that I helped organize a conference for MacNeice's centenary in 2007. As for Donald Wormell: in retrospect, his personality and his discipline flow together. Somehow he represents civilization, long perspectives, together with MacNeice's caveat in *Autumn Journal* that the ancient world and its discontents were not really 'so unimaginably different'.

The hub of many parties, Alec linked Trinity's literary, social and theatrical sets. There were great hostings at his and Beatrice's house in Ballybrack. But I was a bit intimidated by Trinity's theatre set, perhaps because Players set such high standards for the rest of the arts, perhaps because I distrusted or envied performative display. Front Square itself was an amphitheatre for show-offs. So I walked around the edge, and hovered between *Trinity News* – more earnest than the would-be Wildean *TCD* – and *Icarus*, the literary magazine of which Alec was the presiding genius. At *Trinity News* I worked with Frances-Jane ffrench, David Butler, who died tragically early, and who introduced me to student and Irish politics, and Bill Oddie again, whose then-Bible was a typographical tome on which *The Guardian* (it had just dropped *Manchester*) based its design. Bill operatically manipulated hot-lead type at the Brunswick Press in Pearse Street. Quaking, I succeeded him as editor. Of seven editorials written against the clock, I chiefly recall the 'feminist' one, though the word was still out of fashion let alone politics. I argued that Trinity discriminated against women students by making them leave College rooms at 6 pm (there were ways round this), by not letting them have rooms themselves, and by excluding them from The Historical Society. After the editorial appeared, I was scolded by Fanny Moran, the Professor of Law. Fanny, whose other f-word was 'formidable' rather than 'feminist', sternly told me that men needed space for themselves away from women. But that, of course, was the point. Women were often absent from where the most crucial education was casually taking place. They missed the all-hours talk in Botany Bay and other quarters. But perhaps the talk missed them.

Rules, if not gender roles, relaxed before I graduated. And I moved into Trinity Hall. It wasn't rooms, but it made life less local and I ceased to be a Dalkey-bus Cinderella. Among other bad habits, I learned to drink half-pints (as women had to then) in O'Neills. In Michael's Botany Bay rooms we drank instant coffee and made awful fries. Sometimes we ate the cheapest things on the menu in Gaj's or the Universal Chinese restaurant – extraordinary in pre-gastro Dublin. I was introduced to the work of contemporary poets, to incessant talk and argument about poetry, to a constantly played record of American poets reading their poems, to *Lady Chatterley* and other banned books. And I met the aspiring poets, Irish, English and American, who published in *Icarus*.

Discussing Irish writers' relation to Ireland, the Dutch critic Joep Leerssen coined the term 'auto-exoticism'. Trinity around 1960 (before both the end of the *Chatterley* ban and the Beatles' first LP) was a hotbed of exoticism, whether auto or mutual. This rubbed off on literature. For instance, the poets Brendan Kennelly and Derek Mahon came from opposite ends of the island and (up to a point) the aesthetic spectrum. If I had never met anybody like Brendan (and still haven't), he also seemed to distil all that Trinity had never been. Their symbiotic relationship endures. Derek parodied Brendan with the couplet: 'Irish poets do your besht / There's great things happening in the Wesht'. Mahon's Belfast Baudelairean entered *Icarus* alongside Kennelly's Kerry neo-Revivalism and the post-Empsonian metaphysics that Michael Leahy stylishly imported from England. Poetry was taken very seriously, and literary Dublin lapped around the Trinity railings. Flann O'Brien addressed the Elizabethan Society, completely sozzled. I wrote my first critical articles for *Icarus*: on the American poets e.e. cummings and Richard Wilbur. Gushingly overstated, I think now. But my real apprenticeship as a critic was learning how to read and judge poems by the poets I met at Trinity. Since all this extends into the present, the picture blurs.

The Trinity stereotype of the Northern Irish student resembled the Oxbridge 'Northern Chemist' but with added Calvinism. Certainly, some of them earned the adjective 'dour'. No wonder poets from the North distanced themselves from their origins by copying Dylan Thomas' lifestyle. Those Trinity Northerners who saw themselves as shedding the marks of barbarous Puritanism in Dionysian Dublin, recoiled all the more whenever unreconstructed barbarians from Queen's visited Trinity – usually packing Dionysian release into twenty-four hours. When I began to teach at Queen's in 1963, it felt like an Ovidian exile. I was sure it couldn't be permanent. Yet, after all, Trinity was where I first met the exotic North: a cultural – rather than political

– antidote to what the essayist Hubert Butler later taught me to see as the self-sequestering, self-censoring behaviour ('don't rock the boat') of the Southern Protestants I had grown up with. And was Trinity itself so civilized? My father, who died in the spring before my finals, worked too hard and was paid too little. A few years ago the editors of Samuel Beckett's letters showed me a letter written a decade before I was born, in which Beckett described meeting my father: 'I talked with Broderick last evening, and liked him. But he is defeated.' I take this to be Beckett's comment on the sclerotic character of Trinity at that time, whether you were Protestant or Catholic.

If things had improved by 1958, it was largely thanks to the post-war English and other invaders, staff as well as students, who hybridized the inbred Irish Protestant ethos. The result was an odd mix of *laissez-faire* decadence and oblique pressure. At Trinity you sank or swam or surfed creative waves. And a place deemed obsolete by history and Denis Donoghue had its *avant-garde* moments – not necessarily a paradox. It's a stretch, but Derek Mahon's most celebrated poem, 'A Disused Shed in Co. Wexford', which takes its symbolism from J.G. Farrell's novel *Troubles*, might well go back to Trinity in 1960, to a hidden compost of endings and beginnings:

> Even now there are places where a thought might grow –
> Peruvian mines, worked out and abandoned
> To a slow clock of condensation,
> An echo trapped for ever, and a flutter of
> Wildflowers in the lift-shaft,
> Indian compounds where the wind dances ...

More practically, a four-year degree, with all summer to catch up (if you wanted to) before the exams, gave us space that today's modularized, 'modernized' universities close down. I may have been more naive than most, but I never saw Trinity as leading to a job or career but as an end in itself. Today, continuous assessment and surveillance leave fewer gaps to fall through, fewer to dream in.

Edna Longley (née Broderick; TCD 1958–62; English) taught for many years in the School of English at Queen's University Belfast, where she is now a Professor Emerita. Her books include **Poetry in the Wars** (1986), **Louis MacNeice: A Study** (1989), **The Living Stream: Literature and Revisionism in Ireland** (1994) and **Poetry & Posterity** (2000). From 1986 to 2003 she was co-editor of **The Irish Review**. She is a member of the Royal Irish Academy and the British Academy.

IRELAND'S TANGIER

damian duggan-ryan

TRINITY COLLEGE, DUBLIN, in the early 1960s … wow! What a great place, and was I ready for it? Oh yes – definitely! I had just spent ten years being beaten through rote-learning lessons at an Irish Catholic boarding school. The Holy Ghost Fathers had done my head in. Rugby was compulsory and if you couldn't sing you had to give out programmes to parents for either *The Mikado* or *The Pirates of Penzance*. My school was a grim place, and it was followed by a fruitless half-year as a medical student at Dublin's Catholic University. Here, the main emphasis was on cutting up dogfish and examining the outer skins of tomatoes, while fantasizing occasionally about white coats, starched nurses' uniforms and stethoscopes.

I needed a change, and Trinity beckoned with its spacious lawns and playing fields, a cobbled front square, the Spartan accommodation in Botany Bay and of course 'Kelly's Book' – that ancient tome written by monks hundreds of years before and known officially as 'The Book of Kells'. I fancied doing a bit of Politics and would accept a smattering of Economics if I had to. My mum was a bit miffed about not now having the prospect of a financially sound doctor in the family. But my greatest obstacle to getting into the 'Protestant' university – as Elizabeth I's fine old place was still thought of in Ireland – was his Eminence the Archbishop of Dublin, John Charles McQuaid. As a Catholic,

I needed his permission to go through the 'Front Gate', and it wasn't forthcoming, so I went anyway.

The Campanile, Front Square, the Great Hall and the Rubrics all impressed me on my first day, and I listened with awed respect to an anarchic old professor who talked disparagingly about 'Communists' and was rumoured to fail students on fearsome whims. There were lots of cheerful English people in the Museum Building lecture theatre, along with dour Protestants from Northern Ireland and a great collection of agreeable visitors from all over the world.

My first tentative attempts at socializing were in a small café on the edge of Botany Bay, where lecturers and some fellow students were dissected and gossiped about. The Junior Dean was spotted coming out of the Rubrics. He looked inoffensive and slightly distanced with horn-rimmed spectacles and a battered hat, but one was warned not to get on the wrong side of him, as he was responsible for disciplining unruly undergraduates with drink taken.

Four years seemed like quite a long haul if you were a teenager, but the short terms meant that there was plenty of time to plan adventures and contemplate the state of the world. For many of us though, the most exciting life experiences started on campus, and right from the beginning there was great variety.

The Players Theatre was a select but powerful magnet for many, while those of us who didn't quite make it onto the boards gossiped about those who did. And all the while, testosterone swilled around with emotions as approaches were made and relationships evolved. Sometimes love or lust might pass in the night, but there were always friendships and many of these were lubricated in The Old Stand and McDaid's and also at The Bailey and Davy Byrnes.

I have a fond memory of the well-oiled Irish playwright, Brendan Behan, holding forth in The Bailey. His audience was a mixture of hearty Trinity boating chaps and a few tentative literary and theatrical Freshers who looked on the swaying Brendan as a fine writer who was now, sadly, succumbing to the *creathur*. We listened open-mouthed as he berated us for God knows what, while some of the Trinity boating chaps coughed irritably before telling the national treasure to 'shut up'. Shortly afterwards he subsided while clutching at a lapel on his traditional suit and then collapsed with a muffled roar onto the floor.

The Reading Room at Trinity had most of what you needed to complete coursework assignments, but it was also a place for intimate discussions and occasional proposals. All in suitably hushed tones, of course, to avoid rebukes from the seriously bespectacled librarians. Occasionally, one might assist tourists in the Front Square who wanted to see 'Kelly's Book'. They were frequently Americans, but there were also awestruck young Europeans, who thought that Dublin was great and Trinity absolutely *fantastique!* and *incroyable!*

The allure of all this continental adulation led me to volunteer to drive the College mini-bus for a Summer School, which attracted all sorts of interesting people – mainly from France and Italy. I can't remember what the Summer School was all about. I knew it was organized by a Protestant bishop's son who worked in the Languages Department, but what got us all singing and dancing together were the parties at Trinity Hall. This was where the Summer School guests stayed, and the raucous late-night shenanigans caused a bit of a flurry because in term-time I think the place was a respectable all-girls hall of residence.

The lecturers were a mixed bunch, but some of them got into the vibe and would join us in The Old Stand. One really together Economics tutor introduced me to Ian Fleming's James Bond stories over a frothy Guinness. I thought they were great at the time, but I was disappointed when someone later pointed out a solitary house where Fleming had lived for a while near a bird sanctuary on Little Tobago. It was quite severe and not at all a fun place. But James Bond and his suave creator didn't quite go with literary currents in McDaid's bar. This was an atmospheric place for serious drinking, where the poet Paddy Kavanagh held court in a cramped corner. He would bellow occasionally and everyone would lower their voices until the great man adjusted his skewed cap and went back to his Guinness.

The Trinity Ball was a much-anticipated treat in May or June, along with sedate tea parties in the Fellows' Garden. I was once invited by an ebullient English student member of the Elizabethan Society to come to one of these garden events, where the Junior Dean and Provost greeted us with thin formal smiles, cream cakes and decent tea from Bewley's. Outside, the traffic flowed intermittently by the railings. There weren't too many cars around in early Sixties Dublin and most of our local traffic was kept in order by a stout garda who stood with his baton at the bottom of Grafton Street. To his right was Jammet's, a cool

French restaurant, which unfortunately was way beyond my meagre budget.

Taking a pass arts degree, or 'passing the arts' was definitely the thing to do, because it meant you could disappear after the Trinity Ball and not return until the autumn term started again in late October. My exams, unfortunately, were in September, which meant that if I wanted to collect my 'moderatorship', which was what they called the degree with honours, I had to come back and do a bit of swotting in late July or early August. It was usually quiet during the summer around Front Square, although you'd surely meet a sympathetic soul if you sat for a while on the steps of one of the buildings, and if nothing happened during the day you could wander up Grafton Street in the evening.

Neary's was where the indigenous theatricals hung out and they could get very philosophical over great quantities of Guinness and Jameson's whiskey. But if you wanted a taste of the Irish ascendancy with a few bob left to spend then it was off down to Davy Byrnes, while for the music and *craic* it had to be O'Donoghues, which was not far from the Shelbourne Hotel on St Stephen's Green. As a sheltered Irish Catholic lad, what I liked best about Trinity was the amazing variety of people who had arrived in the early Sixties – and particularly the girls. They were, I thought, a sophisticated bunch, and I was swiftly smitten by an English landowner's daughter. She seemed pretty sensible and down to earth, but she was bafflingly keen to get into the souls of young Irish writers. Many of the most gorgeous girls gravitated towards Players, where budding directors and other theatricals had the pick of a delectable bunch.

Those of us who weren't quite in the dramatic loop, however, had to be a little more adventurous, and for some of us excitement beckoned with down-to-earth girls from the Jacob's biscuit factory, which was somewhere to the right when you got to the top of Grafton Street. Evelyn, who put creamy white sugar fillings in the Kimberly biscuits, was for me a reincarnation of Molly Bloom. She was a philosopher, who would sit of an evening looking at the moon while mesmerizing myself and others with tales of her impoverished family. Her father, she told us, would frequently get home drunk from the Guinness brewery where he worked as drayman. He would then beat the fear of God and the holy virgin into Evelyn and her mother and the other eight children who all lived together in the basement of a Georgian tenement somewhere off North Great George's Street. Her tales left me in a sort of trance and floundering for years afterwards in the rare literary and booze-fuelled worlds of O'Casey, Behan, Donleavy and Joyce.

For many of us, the night started when the pubs closed and we traipsed off a few hundred yards to wherever the do was that night. There'd usually be some well-heeled host with a place nearby, and as the drink flowed, there'd maybe be ballads in the background and a few scowling poets. Most of these came from Trinity, and they all had fragile egos, but they usually passed out before the end of the night. Visitors from across the water brought fun and variety, but there was also a smattering of Irish people around the Front Square who weren't from the North. Delicate flowers from the Southern Protestant ascendancy and a few inquisitive lads from the Catholic side who had dared to come through the 'Front Gate' in spite of His Holiness the Archbishop.

The Trinity Medical School had a lot of off-the-wall trainees, some of whom went on to infamous episodes with the courts in England. But as students they were a great bunch and I can remember getting knocked out for the count the first time I ever went into a boxing ring with one of them. He then helped me up, patted me on the back and invited me to a party, which was opposite the old hospital in Baggot Street. There were Americans amongst the guests and the girls were ravenous for any bits and pieces we might throw out on the local literati. It was difficult to speak with much authority about Joyce or Donleavy, for they were still banned in Ireland, along with condoms and anyone or thing that might lead good people astray!

One could, however, improvise on the details with promises after a night of passion to visit the very house in Mountjoy Square where O'Casey had lived with a dozen other members of his family in two small rooms. Almost any house would do, as there weren't any commemorative plaques, and then there was the tower at Sandycove where Buck Mulligan did his bit in *Ulysses*. An Irish architect acquired this and opened it to the public during my last year at Trinity. It was a grand occasion, with all sorts of important persons, but the one who held my interest was Joyce's publisher, Sylvia Beech. A diminutive old lady with white hair and sharp, questing eyes. Talking with her was fascinating and you could almost catch the scene as it might have been *circa* 1911 in Paris, and then later as Joyce struggled with his eyes and other medical conditions while his poor daughter went slowly mad.

Getting jobs as extras in movies being made at Ardmore Studios near Bray was a little perk that many of us at Trinity enjoyed. I can't recall how we were recruited, but it must have been via either The Bailey or Players, or maybe even The Old Stand, although we had to make our own way out to the studios. I went with Norbert, a charming *assistant* in the French Department, who had a battered old 2CV.

When we arrived we were told by Henry Hathaway's cockney assistant that the movie we were to work on was Somerset Maugham's *Of Human Bondage* and that the stars were Kim Novak and Laurence Harvey, who didn't appear to be getting on too well. Most of us played serious-looking medical students, and in order to get us looking Edwardian a fourth button was added to the normal three-button tweed sports jackets that most of us wore every day. Harvey smoked cigarettes in a holder off screen and was keen to establish some bonding credibility with the Trinity gang. So he provided a few casks of Guinness and ale and a suitably Bohemian party was enjoyed by all in a basement off Baggot Street during the first week of filming. Kim didn't come, but Larry was cool, and there was a lot of good gossip.

I didn't return to Trinity often after I left in 1964. But when I did, I was sad to find that the cosmopolitan crew I had known from the UK and around the world had vanished, for the Archbishop, or his successor, had relented and Trinity had become an almost entirely Southern Irish Catholic place. Agreeable still, but without the international flavour that had made it an Irish Tangier, exotic and erotic, made exciting by its attractive veneer of debauchery. *Ite missa est.*

Damian Duggan-Ryan (TCD 1960–4; Economics and Political Science) wrote short stories while he was at TCD. He then worked on the **Athens Daily Post** and with several UK tabloids. Harrowing experiences tutoring students and right-side-of-the-brain consultancy work with nuclear scientists, accountants and lawyers, while helping his wife Jean to raise their two children, filled most of the middle years. He has now started scribbling again; a novel is close to completion, and he feels he has finally found a satisfying job that will probably see him out.

NO. 10

sebastian balfour

MANY OF THE ENGLISH STUDENTS who, like me, went to Trinity College Dublin seemed oddballs. And those I keep in touch with remain that way. Whether it was the Trinity experience that made us eccentric or we were attracted to Trinity because we were unconventional remains unclear. We were certainly motivated by beneficial financial terms. Many English students like me got grants that kept us in pocket and ensured a flow of Guinness for at least nine months of the year. We got reimbursed for our air fares, three return flights from England to Dublin at £10 each, the student rate of the time. This sort of state largesse is unimaginable for students today.

A much more important reason for going was that it allowed some of us (or perhaps only me) to escape the niceties or cruelties of class and cultural identities in Britain in the early Sixties. Dublin and TCD offered an environment in which I could evade the ambiguities of my own identity (as long as I steered clear of the Sloane Rangers minority in Trinity). In an English university I might have been nailed as a bit of a cultural outsider. TCD was a good place for misfits like me because it was more multicultural and laid back. I was unlikely to be judged before I raised a glass of beer (even less after I had emptied the sixth pint). I doubt if this was ever a conscious strategy on my part. More likely, it was instinct, honed by experience, which led me to run away from myself to Dublin.

But I was also running away from my schoolboy failures. I had two A levels but had failed O-level Maths. Unlike British universities, TCD judged Latin to be more important than Maths and I had had no problem with Latin. The peculiarity of Trinity's entrance requirements enabled students who had failed, for all sorts of reasons, to conform to entrenched bureaucratic standards to gain a place at a university that still had the status of an elite academic institution.

As in British universities at the time, the first generation of working-class students was beginning to get places in TCD as well, and they brought with them a new cockiness and a total absence of respect for class hierarchies. The cocktail of young working- and middle-class students was intoxicating. It was a blast of fresh air for me. Through them, I learnt to flatten my 'a's and picked up a new language of irony and invective. The late Fifties–early Sixties were a time of sea change in British culture. The post-war generation was throwing off old values and asserting a more complex and multi-class culture. Of course, all new generations challenge their parents' generation. The difference is that cultural change in this period was empowered by a confidence rooted in the early period of the post-war economic boom. Like John Osborne's hero in *Look Back in Anger* we felt scorn for the hypocrisy and backwardness of our elders. Samuel Beckett, Francis Bacon, Tony Hancock, Elvis Presley, Lonnie Donnegan, Billy Fury, and then of course the Beatles were all in their own way challenging deference and received values. This was still a largely cultural rebellion with an as yet inchoate political form that would become more explicit later in the decade. I, for one, lived in a state of political innocence, which made my discovery of politics in 1968 all the more intense. We should not judge that innocence too harshly with the arrogance of historical retrospect.

I was attracted to Ireland also, no doubt like many of the other English students, by its post-colonial exoticism. This was not anything to do with the seductions of paddywackery. It was a more cultural construct than the traditional British stereotype of the Irish because we, or some of us, had read Yeats, Flann O'Brien, O'Casey, Frank O'Connor and others. As a result, I half expected to find wild-eyed, tousled-haired poets in pubs on the Liffey speaking in virtual verse over their Guinness. In the event, the only poets I encountered, apart from Brendan Kennelly, were hard-bitten student poets from Northern Ireland attending their 'Protestant' university. Their speech inflections were not droll and mellifluous in keeping with the Irish model in my head but nervy, ironic, hard-edged, with that rising intonation at the end of a phrase as if they were asking a question. Nevertheless, Dublin promised to be laid back, eccentric, slightly Enlightenment in its manners as well as its architecture. There I could escape the drabness of England where the grey clouds of the post-war period were only just beginning to lift.

But there was another, illusory objective that drove me to TCD. I thought I was good at theatre. The TCD student theatre group, Players, was well known even outside Ireland. It had attracted lots of talented actors and directors, who went on to make distinguished careers. I hoped that Players could develop my 'gift' and lead me on to the stage. Had I gone to an English provincial university, the delusion of talent might have lasted a little longer. In Players, it was destroyed in one day.

Like many other Freshers, I had signed up for an audition, expecting to be recognized as promising new material. We gathered in the tiny auditorium and each of us was called to different parts of the theatre to be tested by the established student actors and directors. I was summoned into the changing room and there a rather sour bearded young man whom I never saw again in Players and who had presumably been drafted in just for the occasion, handed me a large, heavy and open book. 'Act this,' he said, pointing to a line from a play. The line read, 'Never, never, never, never, never.' It could not have carried a more personal message. How could I, a nervous eighteen-year-old ex-schoolboy, holding the Complete Works of Shakespeare in my two hands in a sweaty changing room, act the part of King Lear as he mourned over the dead body of Cordelia? I didn't hear from Players after that.

It was a humbling experience, but I didn't give up. I hung around Players until eventually someone there asked me if I'd like to be a stage-dogsbody with the main responsibility of raising the curtain for a new production. By becoming adept at handling the ropes I got more curtain calls than anyone else had in the past and so I was accepted paternalistically into the outer circle of Players, where I floated around for the rest of my university career. But I had discovered in that first audition that my talent was an illusion far greater than that of the theatre.

Nevertheless, I got to play the odd part, always that of a 'gofer' that makes a fleeting appearance 'and then is heard no more'. One of them was the messenger in a production of Anouilh's *The Lark*, directed by Laurie Howes, in which the role of Joan of Arc was taken by the lovely Nina Boyd. I would run on to the stage, deliver a breathless message about victory (or was it defeat?) and then go back to the same doom-ridden changing room.

It was only in my final year that I landed slightly more significant theatrical roles. I directed, or under-directed, a production of Anouilh's *Antigone* in French. Then I did a production for John Arden. He ran an annual festival of theatre in Dublin, in which Players took part. I brought him the American translation of a short play by Cervantes called the *Altar of Marvels* in case he was interested. It was and still is one of my favourite pieces of Spanish literature. Like *Don Quixote*, its strength lies in its use of irony. Some of the great works of the Spanish arts, including the cinema, were produced at times of censorship. The authors and film directors (such as Berlanga in his wonderful 1963 film *The Executioner*) used irony to fool the censor and convey forbidden ideas to the audience. Cervantes' play is an attack on the anti-Semitism of his time. Arden liked it and, with good reason, hated the translation. So he rewrote the translation, converting its literal and old-fashioned language (which deployed phrases such as 'You rascal', 'Dreadful scoundrel' and so on) into the live register of our times. I directed the play in Players with his backing and I think it went down well. Arden's unpublished translation is still on my shelves and deserves a new outing, as does Cervantes' much-neglected play.

Despite the disappointment of my first foray into the theatre as a Fresher, I didn't think about what my eventual career might become. This was for many of us an incredibly banal pursuit, fit only for boring old farts. Underlying that arrogance about the future was an implicit confidence that we would eventually be able to choose whatever career we wanted. We were at Trinity to discover ourselves and the world beyond. Only the present mattered, that precious suspension of sequence and consequence. By my second year at Trinity I already thought of myself as a bit of an 'existentialist', though I hardly understood what that meant. Later, I used French existentialism to clothe my conceit with intellectual respectability. I even briefly took to smoking a long narrow pipe to give an aura of authority to the pretension. When I got savvier, I took to Gauloises, narrowing my eyes à la Jean-Paul Belmondo as I pretended to inhale the smoke.

In my first year, I lodged at Mrs McGann's in Rathgar, along with other spotty Freshers. She was a no-nonsense sort of woman, who dished out the traditional Irish breakfast and evening tea imperiously. The meals were served by a shy, fair and slightly plump Irish girl whom we all fancied but never dared proposition under the baleful eye of Mrs McGann. The girl would put the plates of fish, chips and mushy peas in front of each of us saying 'Now,' with her soft Irish lilt. The English amongst us joked at what we saw as a bit of Irish folklore and we had endless fun finishing off the phrase with 'and forever, Amen'. Although she gave us a beatific smile in exchange, our mockery probably hurt her Catholic soul.

I went to Dublin a Catholic and became an atheist almost immediately. This was not such a contradiction as it might seem. I was never a deeply religious person and whatever faith I brought with me dropped off like a scarf in the breeze of my first contact with Trinity. Religion had played no part in my decision to go to Dublin in the first place. When I started to read Sartre and Camus and others, my formal religious affiliation made no sense any longer. My godfather, who had contributed financially to my Catholic education and probably saw his role solely as religious mentor, got to hear about my lapse and wrote me a letter in which he urged perseverance in the faith just in case it turned out to be true. If it didn't, I would lose nothing. If it did, I would go to hell (or purgatory, I thought, if I enjoyed life a little less). This was Pascal's bet in disguise.

I went assiduously to all the lectures, and was struck in particular by one of the lecturers, a Miss North, a minute, fragile china doll of an ancient woman (or so it seemed to my youthful eyes) who wore an outsized academic gown and a mortar board perched on the top of her tiny white head. She would lecture for an hour from a great distance about the passions of Racine in a fluting voice that could hardly be heard and in a tone that betrayed little feeling. The approach to literature of many of the staff seems so dated now, as if texts were artefacts without connection to the context in which they were produced. The professors and lecturers were probably quite amenable but they enjoyed such a status in those days that a first-year undergraduate like me hardly dared approach them. If we had that temerity, we usually trotted by their sides taking notes as they strode to their offices, gowns flowing in the breeze.

At Trinity two years later I was feeling more confident and invited one of my professors to my rooms in Front Square for a drink. I served him sherry in an inappropriate glass tumbler and he rambled on about literature, all the while averting his eyes from me. I was shocked to notice that he was trembling. I suspected immediately and instinctively that he wanted to have a lot more than sherry with me. I was acutely embarrassed. But he didn't proposition me and the script never departed from the formal exchange of ideas and platitudes between the great professor and the eager student.

For an undergraduate to have a flat in Front Square was an achievement. But it was not glamorous. After a second year sharing a flat near Trinity with a fellow student, my application for rooms was granted and I was awarded the top floor of No. 10. The flat came with a butler, called a 'skip', who served all the flats in No. 10. This was no luxurious suite, nor was the butler anything like Jeeves. For a start there was no toilet in the whole of No. 10. The nearest one was by the entrance of the adjoining block. Nor was there any running water. The skip was supposed to bring up a tin bucket of water every day. The rooms were capacious. They consisted of two bedrooms, a kitchen (though how can it be described as such as it didn't have running water?) and a spacious living room from where you could see O'Connell Street. I shared the place with mice and cockroaches, who helped to keep it reasonably tidy by consuming the crumbs.

One of the challenges of life in TCD (and indeed in Dublin) in the Sixties was seeking ways of palliating the inconveniences of daily life, especially those to do with bodily fluids of all kinds. Next to women students, who displayed remarkable ingenuity and female solidarity in the matter, the men had an easy time. But we all concocted solutions according to the French tradition of *système D*, the ingenious do-it-yourself system of home-made contraptions to compensate for the absence of technology or the lack of money. A solution to my toilet problem came to me one day as I walked past some scaffolding piled up in Front Square, presumably awaiting erection to renovate the exterior of one of the blocks. I stole a length and laid it from my window ledge to the nearest guttering at the back of the building. The diameter of the piece was wide enough for all men's sizes. For a while the system worked well and I no longer needed to go up and down the stairs in the middle of the night after a binge or fill the bucket in the kitchen to overflowing.

But the warm weather came and one evening after dark I became acutely aware of the stench of urine. Without thinking, I grabbed the scaffolding and threw it out of the window. As it left my hands, I realized I had forgotten a rather important detail. Dr McDowell, the perennial Junior Dean (or JD, as we called him), had his lodgings on the ground floor of No. 10. Stretching from an aperture in his wall right below me to the nearest telegraph pole was his telephone wire. As the piece of scaffolding was about to complete its journey there was a 'twang' and I saw it bounce into the air, off the wire, before falling to the ground with a clatter. The JD has always struck me as indestructible. So, I thought, was his telephone connection. However the next day a telephone engineer was on the scene to repair the broken wire. The engineer looked puzzled as he picked up the length of scaffolding. He glanced at the building to discover if it had come from there but there was no masonry work going on at the back of No. 10. As I ducked out of sight I noticed his gaze had lifted to the heavens – that must be it – a divine urinal.

The JD was a legend. He seemed ancient to a young person like me. Wearing at all times a voluminous scarf and a grey pork pie hat squashed onto his long and greasy hair, he would propel himself at full speed around the College without seeming to move a limb. It was a peculiar JD shuffle, accompanied by the jingle of keys that he'd be carrying around in one hand. He also muttered endlessly to himself and one never quite caught the tenor of his words as he passed. Decades later, I was in the University of London headquarters at Senate House and saw the JD approach me along a dimly lit corridor. I was sure it was a ghost. I stood stock still as the apparition came towards me and blurted out, 'Hello, Dr McDowell,' and he replied as he floated past, 'Hello to you there,' as if he remembered me. He seemed completely unchanged. It made me realize that we are not very adept at judging age when we're young.

No. 10's skip was a lovely Dubliner who was a million miles from being a butler. But he had to wear a uniform of sorts as he worked the different flats. I remember him cleaning up the filthy kitchen after a night of beer, wine and kippers still wearing his suit. But we did talk a lot about the weather and shared jokes while I made him cups of tea. Thankfully he showed no deference. But he was also evasive whenever I thought some serious cleaning needed to be done on the landing and the stairs.

Forty years later, the words 'No. 10' have a legendary aura for some. At the time, it became a magnet of social life. Laurie Howes was one of three friends who were to move in and use the spare room from time to time, paying a gypsy rent that has not yet been fully paid to me. He tells me now that he saw No. 10 as the paradise he longed for. I doubt the TCD authorities knew what was going on or even cared that much. Unfortunately for the rest of us, he also moved in his dart board. One of the more jolly japes practised in No. 10 involved darts. It all started one day when Laurie walked into my bedroom with a dart in his hand. I was in bed with a bad cold. He threw the dart at me, I raised my hand to shield my face, and the dart smashed into one of my fingers – and stuck. From then on, we set out to try to murder each other with those arrows. Laurie's favourite trick was to throw one down the stairwell as I descended, making me leap two stairs at a time to avoid injury to my skull. His aim was appalling (I wouldn't be here to tell the story if it had been better) and the darts tended to thud into the wooden step beside my dancing feet.

Two other friends who moved into No. 10 on this part-time basis were Michael de Larrabeiti, son of a philandering Basque émigré and a long-suffering woman from Battersea, and Tony Rance, who used to patrol TCD and Dublin wearing a medieval-looking cloak that fastened around the neck and flowed behind (this may have been the origin of his nickname Trance). Amongst other things, No. 10 was an almost permanent banquet. One problem with the idea of banqueting was the absence of a long table to accommodate all the revellers. This was finally solved one night when Howes and Larrabeiti went through a trap door into the loft, crawled along the beams under the roof, and let themselves into the rooms of the Elizabethan Society in No. 6 in the next block. We then manhandled a long and narrow 'Elizabethan' table all the way down the stairs and up again to the top of No. 10.

Despite the populist connotations of its name, the Elizabethan Society was by all accounts a rather prim club for female staff and students, rather than a hive of feminism. In contrast, we, men and women, dignified our hedonism by calling ourselves the Rabelaisian Society. The title was not entirely misplaced. The coarse humour and the excesses of our Abbaye de Thélème in No. 10 were a reaction against the decorum and the conventions of the Society next door and beyond. Of course, what happened in No. 10 doesn't approach the orgiastic present. Levels of intoxication and sexual experimentation were lower than contemporary practice among the young generation. In fact it was quite tame in comparison. But it was more creative, even a bit revolutionary. Without realizing it we were perhaps enacting the overthrow of post-war values, rooting out the deference instilled in us and embracing the spontaneous energy that lay beneath it.

One episode clings on in the collective memory of No. 10. Rance's sister came over one year from England to visit him in time for the Trinity Ball. She joined us and our girlfriends in No. 10, where we started a banquet long before the event began. When we finally swayed and tripped our way to the Ball, we managed to smuggle her in without a ticket. Soon, she became drunk out of her mind and started to act outrageously as others ate through the buffet or danced away. She got into a mad tizzy, started to quarrel with people and had to be carried bodily out of the marquee. It was dreadful behaviour of course, but it was not the sodden drunkenness of some young women outside the pubs of London today. Rance's sister was tearing down the old battlements of post-war society in a sort of Dionysian frenzy. Or is this just a fanciful rationalization driven by nostalgia?

These memories of TCD are worn smooth, like precious stones waiting on the mantelpiece to be fondled and passed around. The seams connecting me to the unmemorable experiences of the time are buried. Not even a Proustian stumble on a cobblestone in Front Square will stir them up. Trinity left a deep imprint on me that I have still to fathom. But I never really fulfilled the purpose for which I went there in the first place. I studied fitfully. There were too many distractions. I had to make up for my insouciance years later. Michael de Larrabeiti once told me how his parting with TCD was marked by going down a hill in his vintage Fiat without any brakes. I had an old Austin Devon, which I nicknamed Panurge, after Rabelais' iconoclastic bon viveur. When I left TCD in Panurge and indeed for some of my life afterwards, it was like going up a hill without an accelerator.

Sebastian Balfour (TCD 1960–4; French and Spanish) left Dublin for the US where, with three other graduates from TCD, he sold Yorkshire terrier puppies and vintage Rolls-Royces. Abandoning this lucrative business, he fled to Latin America and eventually spent four years in Mexico. He is now Emeritus Professor of Contemporary Spanish Studies at the London School of Economics and Political Science and has published many books and articles on contemporary Spain, and a much-expanded edition of his political biography **Castro – Profiles in Power** (3rd edition 2009). His latest book on Spain (co-authored with Alejandro Quiroga) is called **The Reinvention of Spain. Nation and Identity since Democracy** (2007).

THE ABSENCE OF WHALES

mary carr

IN MY SECOND YEAR at Trinity I was called into my tutor's rooms. R.B.D. French was a short man who always looked as if he had just been polished. His shoes were the deepest black. And although an outsider might have thought him plain, he wasn't. He was in some way exotic – not familiar, a bird of strange plumage. I often wondered if he minded being my tutor.

'I have been told,' he told me, 'that you have been remiss in attending lectures. I have been told –' … he waited, standing in a patch of sunlight, the ultra-English voice (as I, the part-foreigner, thought) searching for the right pitch, 'I have been told that I must *reprimand* you.' I waited. 'Consider yourself,' said RBD, '… reprimanded. Would you care for a glass of sherry?'

It was a small episode. And it was the heart of Trinity. I took it as a lesson in quality of life, not to mention an entire philosophical thesis on education. RBD was very popular. I am not sure that what he represented can be achieved unless there is beneath you an enormous foundation of privilege. But he deserved that popularity, all the same.

I had first come to the College thinking that I would write down every word spoken in the lecture hall. (I was able to write extremely fast.) I would miss nothing! I learned at once that this was not exactly a great plan. Our respect for the world around us was profound, but the lectures didn't have to be good. And for the most part, they weren't. This in no way diminished the quality of the College; in some weird, old-era fashion it may have enhanced that quality. But there seemed in fact to be a general rule that nothing should be said in the lecture hall that we did not already know. (No doubt the idea was to discourage passivity in our own pursuit of learning.) And so I actually came to miss lectures, quite a few of them.

The novelist Wallace Stegner once wrote that being young is a state of mind. You could be 'young' on holiday in a warm, light place at fifty. I think he was wrong. I remember arriving at Trinity a few months before my eighteenth birthday. The walls at Templeogue, where I had been housed, were solid in a way that walls had never quite managed before; there was a dust and a light on them that existed nowhere else. I remember walking on a beach. I think there were streams moving down across the sand to the ocean. If not, I have imported them in memory. I was so happy that the world was all sun, all water, all air. You could not look at a surface without the potential of it reaching out like a hand.

On a party thrown for my retirement, this year, a colleague of mine said that when he had first gone to College as a young man, he thought that (from time to time) he walked a few inches above the ground. He was really doing that. I was reminded of a scrap of doggerel I'd read somewhere:

> Oh, the townsfolk talk
> To see me walk
> Six inches off the ground!

I never had the same exact idea, never thought about my feet when on the cobbles; but I knew exactly what he was talking about. I remember (I think) every-thing about the first weeks at Trinity. I remember the verses that I read in a book of poetry left in my room; I remember ladders in my stockings on that beach; I remember walking for the first time by the railings near Front Gate. A young woman just ahead of me called out, 'Hellooo, Peter!' in a very pleased voice. A life-time later, I remember. No trivia too trivial. It was all stamped with something.

The glass cases at Front Gate seemed to go deep into the walls; they had an aura, cool, rainy, old, of their own. Was all this Trinity, or age? Of course it was partly age. Being seventeen is not, I believe, an equal-opportunity state of mind; it is much too powerful. But the strange thing (and the thesis of this particular act of memory) is that I don't believe it was just age, or that I would have felt quite the same at another place. Any place. A few months earlier I had expected to enrol at Mt Holyoke College in Massachusetts. Then my family decided to move to Dublin, to avoid taxes. Artists didn't pay taxes in Ireland in those days. I don't know if it's still the same. As it turned out, my family did not move – at least not in the originally planned direction. I did, though. There might have been some degree of pleasure had I gone to Holyoke. But it would not have been the same.

I believe there was something about Trinity and the town that made it possible for feelings such as mine to take hold in a way that could not have happened, not quite as strongly, anywhere else. But what was it, then, about the place? Trinity was certainly beautiful. But I had seen stone before: and no such effect. Or was it the people: or some combination of stone, air, light, history and people?

I understand that from at least a few hundred years BC men and women too have been trying to imagine a perfect society: arguably, a free society. The City on the Hill. Trinity was that, of course. Of course? I know that I felt and was free across that four-year span. But again – why?

When you look at the facts, I was, after all, female. Females at the College in the early 1960s could not have rooms in the grounds, could not eat in the dining halls in the grounds, had to be off the cobbles by some hour – eleven, probably – at night, had to live in digs presided over by an 'adult', and could not join a number of the College societies. The men, in contrast, were restricted by none – not one – of these rules. We were not allowed to join the debating society! We could not debate. How could all this possibly have amounted to a sense of freedom – even if you broke a rule or two (no, three, in my case)? TCD was full of mysteries.

The object of all these rules-for-women was, as I understand it, to keep them away from the men. The men had the ground; the women should be kept remote from it. In its goal of achieving this, the failure of the College was profound.

Leisure. Not being bothered by awkward little requirements such as having to work. Effectively, no work at all. That was part of it. Books. Friends. Beer!

The students that I have taught now for almost three decades have to work hard. They don't have time to read the way we used to read – for the pleasure of it. They do have friends.

Am I advocating a form of higher education in which nobody has to work? In fact, I'm not. I don't believe that is the way to go – any more than I believe that the kind of pressure I see here and now is the way to go either. But that was how it was.

We liked our professors. We liked and respected them, a lot. The nature of the individual did not matter. The respect was really for what they represented – for learning. And I think that may have been a major part of the expansive feeling of those days. We believed we were part of some larger frame that was important and, even better, good.

That spirit is not widely present among the students that I teach now. It is certainly no part of the walls and structure of higher education in New York State. Those who do feel the same, feel this in isolation.

THERE WAS ANOTHER, quite different, occasion with RBD, when I did give offence. From time to time, he would invite his students to his house in the country for tea, complete with ducks' eggs. There were usually about four people in the group. I had been invited and I asked if Laurie Howes could come too. It was the one time I did manage to read my tutor. His face shut. I realized I had made a terrible gaffe. It was not so much that I had presumed to ask for an invitation, but I had walked right past the signs that forbade men and women to be more than jolly friends sitting together in a lecture hall.

I remember talking and talking: sitting in pubs, with everything full of light, drinking and talking. A lot of this with Laurie H. and Sebastian Balfour in particular. It seemed important at the time. It almost certainly was not important. But it *was* a pleasure. I have never thought that surface appearance amounts to much. It is function that matters. I recall arguing that one, all those years ago, in a spotty little ancient wood-smelling pub near Eccles Street. Or was it some other pub? LH was on my side; SB was against. 'If I walked in tomorrow, bald,' I told SB, 'I would still be me.' And SB said, 'If you walked in tomorrow, bald, I would faint.' I had met Laurie in a doorway in another Irish town. I had seen him before, but hadn't spoken with him. He would not tell me directly that it was the right door. He said, 'It's one of them.' The relationship between us started some hours later, when we met again. There was a strange ride back to Dublin, marked by many, many punctures. (Mike Smyth recalls this differently, in terms of exhaust. I recall punctures.) As I remarked above, the months before that Easter had been very good indeed. The months that followed were better.

Laurie produced plays and became an editor. Mike Smyth knew how to *light* plays, and had a sense of humour that was understated even for that day and age. Mike de Larrabeiti wrote short, very witty pieces for *Trinity News*, and frightened people. Fiona Wright walked her bike and me out of Players one early morning when I had stayed too long at some rehearsal. Her innocent arrival on the bike a few minutes earlier rayed out, and provided camouflage. She didn't even know me then. It was a simple act of good will.

Fiona had been told by the Archbishop of Dublin that any Catholic – almost – attending Trinity was committing a sin, and she should go home (to England) at once. I heard later that a Catholic could attend the College and not risk damnation if he or she wanted to be a dentist. But if you didn't care that much for teeth, you were in trouble. (There were no other schools of dentistry available in the town.)

I have one recollection of TCD that apparently nobody shares. It involves the museum building. I remember the skeleton of a whale on the area above the first set of steps. It was suspended from the ceiling (probably impossible, given the height of that area). On my one visit back, I asked about that whale. The staff said they had never seen, never heard of a whale. Absolutely no whale. I have apparently imagined the creature and placed it in the Museum Building. My field of research today is memory.

It seems I have at least one, *big*, false one. I remember it all as a kind of strange, golden, stretched, elastic time. I still think Wallace Stegner was wrong. But in spite of that, I do not believe that my experience of Trinity was due simply to youth: some biochemicals in the brain. I hold that it was the place itself. What I have never been able to do, though, is explain it.

Mary Howes (née Carr; TCD 1960–4; Modern Languages: English and French) took a doctorate in Psychology in 1979, specialization in cognition. She has conducted research into the earliest memories of life, and in 1990 published **The Psychology of Human Cognition: Mainstream and Genevan Traditions.** She published **Human Memory: Structures and Images** in 2006.

ALL THE GOLDEN OLDIES

ian blake

SOME YEARS AGO a complete stranger cornered me at a social event. She asked, in a daunting tone of awed respect, 'Were you *really* at TCD in the early Sixties? When I was there our lecturers were always talking about you all. They called it The Golden Age.' Greatly astonished, not to say embarrassed, I muttered, 'Well, they certainly never let on to us!'

I attended my first lecture on my very first night at TCD. I had arrived in Ireland early that morning and walked from the overnight ferry docked in the heart of Dublin, greeted by a damp grey day, gleaming cobbles and the smell of the Liffey at low water. Passing a gesticulating Grattan at Front Gate, I found I had been allocated one of the new study-bedrooms in the GMB, where I came upon the advertisement for a lecture entitled 'Are Intentions Dispositions?' A string of impressive degrees indicated that the speaker, a professor from a Welsh university, was a distinguished philosopher. And attending lectures was surely what universities were all about?

It was high-profile affair. The Provost and Fellows were present in awe-inspiring robes and gowns. Although 'Are Intentions Dispositions?' was closely and elegantly argued, to judge by the applause at the end of an hour, it left me almost suicidal. I had absolutely no idea what he was getting at, nor even the nature of the problem he had so expertly resolved to the satisfaction of everyone except me. Apart from his opening remarks, in which he thanked TCD for inviting him, I understood not one sentence. He might as well have been speaking in Welsh.

Early schooling, disrupted by the war, had left me without a word of Latin and (to say the least) 'inadequate' French. So any idea of reading English as part of a dual honours Modern Languages degree (with French, German, or Italian) was out of the question. I had enrolled in what was by then dismissively known as 'pass arts' – sad relic of the original prestigious degree where those who came top, 'Respondents', were not disreputable culprits in a divorce, but those privileged to be first to 'dispute' with Fellows and Scholars. I had selected Philosophy as one of my three courses because it was a subject I knew nothing about. If the Welsh professor's *intentions* and *dispositions* were anything to go by, I never would.

As a member of the University I could, I learned, attend any lecture and so, for the next three years, I went to most of the honours English lectures as well as my own. They were terrific – Walton's scholarly detail, Edwards' enthusiasm. Anglo Saxon, brilliantly taught by Pfeiffer, almost convinced me I was not the world's worst linguist. I even have '*thorn*' on my typewriter. It opened up *Beowulf* in a way no translation ever can.

I found TCD philosophy entirely comprehensible, lecturers approachable. Asked whether there was 'a book on dreams', Professor Furlong, after modest throat-clearing, replied with endearing diffidence, 'Um-well, um-yes. Um-mine.' I once suggested to Frank O'Connor that Yeats might have been a more logical poet had he read philosophy. 'Oh Willy wanted to invent *his own philosophical system*.'

Frank O'Connor spiced two memorable lectures with delightful anecdotes. Joyce, he said, ostentatiously placed in the hall of his Paris house a curiously framed etching of what the English called 'Kingstown Harbour' but which had been renamed by the new Irish government, so that when, inevitably, visitors asked, 'What's it framed in?' Joyce could answer 'Cork.' And asked why she had never married Yeats, Maud Gonne replied, so Frank told us, imitating her voice, 'Because Willy is so seelly.' When, in 1916, W.B. entered discreetly with news of Sean MacBride's execution, she was sitting by the fire. 'Go out Willy. Then come in again *and do it properly*!' So he threw open the door and, with wide gestures, proclaimed, 'The English … have shot … the Major!' Whereupon, she threw a suitably dramatic fit of hysterics.

Another memorable lecture was given by Dr Leventhal towards the end of his time, a rather sad and largely ignored figure. (Those who thought his courses dull were unperceptive of a dry scholarly wit. 'Milton's line "link-ed sweetness long drawn out" is the perfect description of the television kiss.') Not until that valedictory lecture were we aware of his long friendship with Samuel Beckett.

Subsequently I became marginally involved in a scheme to build a Samuel Beckett Theatre at St Peter's College, Oxford, the brainchild of Francis Warner, one of the Fellows. He had persuaded the inventor of the geodesic dome to become the architect and a Canadian millionaire to donate a huge sum of money. We all met in Paris at a restaurant where live lobsters swam in tanks keeping fresh for the pot. Beckett was so short-sighted that he had to hold the menu up to his nose. Nobody seemed confident enough to address the great man, who was himself very shy. In desperation, Francis Warner revealed I had been at TCD and Beckett asked whether I knew 'Con Leventhal'. I mentioned his lecture, then added, 'I must be the only one here who knows that you represented Trinity at cricket because I've seen your name in the Pavilion,' which thawed the atmosphere a little. But the theatre was never built. Shortly before signing a final agreement, the millionaire died. His executors (and his widow) firmly declined to honour anything not stipulated in his will.

I'd come to Trinity after National Service, spells as an instructor at the Outward Bound Mountain School at Eskdale, and a job as assistant master at an impeccably run boys' boarding preparatory school in Cheshire. The opportunity to read in a library, which had everything, conferred an intellectual freedom that I had never imagined. Then there was also the chance to write *and be published.* I was co-opted by *TCD Miscellany* at the end of my first term, the time when, under Bruce Arnold's editorship, it transmuted from *Punch*-clone into something more akin to *The Spectator* or *New Statesman.* The first issue was almost entirely devoted to Guinness, I seem to recall. An illustrated article on Modigliani's nudes was very controversial and looked as though it would get us banned. But despite its Arnoldian revamp, *TCD* never quite abandoned its irreverent and humorous legacy. The St Valentine's Day issue was always a sell-out. But now it included pithy political comment, factual articles, well-informed film criticism by Mike Dibb and Peter Bell. And occasional 'scoops'.

A spectacularly cheap charter flight to the USA undercut a rival by a considerable amount. However, posters promoting it at Front Gate were repeatedly torn down and removed, late at night. Peter Ryan, with his Leica, and I waited concealed behind the doors opposite the notice boards. At about 1 am, the rival entrepreneur appeared. Looking round to make sure he was unobserved, he tore down the offending poster. Peter took a series of shots through the letterbox. We published the sequence that Friday. Threats to sue never materialized, even though the 'villain' claimed he had three people prepared to swear that he was playing bridge at the time.

There were always last-minute crises: 'We've been let down. Can you fill a page and let us have it by midday?' On the first occasion, I ostensibly reviewed a book by an 'American academic' who claimed that the only reason Jane Austen's novels were ever printed was to disguise the fact that her money came from running a brothel in Southampton during the Napoleonic War. Under the editor's mystifyingly recherché heading, 'O'Grady Says Blake', I opined, with disdainful condescension, 'Dr Knowlton does once descend to the merely ribald, on page 26, when he says, *Was this Miss Austen's contribution to the war effort?*'

On Saturday morning I was stopped by a very senior member of the English faculty. 'Ian, where *on earth* did you get this dreadful book about Jane Austen!' I'm not sure who was the more embarrassed when I confessed that both the book and the author were entirely imaginary and the whole thing a spoof. Some years later I bumped into Brendan Kennelly who had returned to Trinity as a lecturer. One of his undergraduates had submitted a term essay purporting to demonstrate how evidence of Jane Austen's brothel-keeping could be deduced from certain passages in *Pride and Prejudice*. The culprit eventually confessed that he had plagiarized an old copy of *TCD* he found in his rooms.

On the second occasion the promised article was to have been about 'College Literati'. Could I 'do something by twelve o'clock?' ... 'And Another Muse' consisted of snide comments by one 'Andrew Stone': *Michael Longley ... never likes rising from his armchair by the fire between the months of October and May ... Ian Blake ... a bit grim for Trinity ... has however been known to put on plimsolls before kicking dogs and children ... Rudi Holzapfel can be understood only by his delightful and beautiful wife ...*

That night at a party somebody commiserated, 'This chap Andrew Stone is *very* unfair to *you*.' 'I'm afraid we writers just have to put up with that sort of petty jealousy,' I sighed deprecatingly. 'This novel of Sean Murphy's, you *must* read it. It's astonishingly good. I've met the author who's a good chap.'

Neither Sean Murphy, his novel, nor indeed 'Andrew Stone', ever existed beyond my typewriter. However, considering the longevity of Jane Austen's 'career' as a Madam, it would not surprise me to learn that, even now, assistant librarians are vainly searching for their copyright edition of *A Prancing Faun*, by Andrew Stone.

Founded by Alec Reid, a charismatic junior lecturer, *Icarus,* under a different editor each term, published our 'heavier' writing: early poems of Brendan Kennelly, Derek Mahon and Michael Longley will one day be pounced on by researchers. I have before me *Icarus 41*: Brownlow, Hadman, Graham, Lewis, Longley, Mahon, Sinclair, Sprawson, de Vere White, Webb, an unpublished story by Frank O'Connor and Anthony Weale's affectionately drawn cover and illustrations. *Mr Blake's issue has many interesting and good things... but his typographical innovation ... is not a success.*

The Hist was enormous fun. Committee members in black tie discussed Private Business until 'midnight by the Treasurer's watch', which rarely showed 'midnight' until about 1 pm. I recall travelling to debate at UCG with David Butler, and staying overnight with his Episcopal father; Neville Keery winning the Society's Gold Medal for Oratory; Michael Newcomb as Auditor; representing Irish Universities in the Observer Mace Debating Competition at Exeter University. (Rising to support *Irish* entry to the Common Market, I was informed they had, at the last minute, altered the wording of the motion so that it referred specifically to *England*. Perfidious Albion!)

It was, however, preparing a paper on William Golding for The Phil that brought my first academic 'publication'. I am browsing Hannah's bookshop; the courteous elderly assistant asks, 'What are you working on, sir?' I explain that, were my thesis correct, there must somewhere be a 'source' for *Pincher Martin*.

'I read it as a boy,' he muses. Politely I point out that it has only been published a year or two. He demurs. 'I think it was by "Taffrail"... about 1917 ...' Straight back to the Library catalogue. Commons forgotten as soon as I begin reading, I just *know* there will be a crucial passage. Bingo! Sure enough about the middle of the book, Taffrail's (very different) Pincher Martin is torpedoed.

Professor Edwards encouraged me to write to *Notes and Queries* edited by retiring, scholarly James Maxwell, whom I later met at Balliol. It turned out that we both shared a passion for detective stories. He thought *Death Under Sail* by C.P 'Two Cultures' Snow, the worst detective story ever written, which unenviable record I reckon it still holds.

In my first term, John Jay produced *The Hole* by N.F. Simpson. *The funniest play I have ever seen … a well-acted gem*, according to the anonymous reviewer in *TCD* (as The Visionary, I was the only member of the cast not mentioned in his laudatory notice). The following term Mike Ruggins directed *The Long and The Short and the Tall* by Willis Hall. *Terence Brady is so good these days … He is a pleasure to watch … David O'Clee … is as well nigh perfect as Brady's Bamforth … he looks a corporal and a bastard … Ian Blake … does succeed in being dull, obstinate and elephantine which is as legitimate an interpretation of MacLeish as any I suppose …* At the time I thought it a grudging compliment to my interpretation of the *rôle*. Now? I'm not so sure.

At the Irish Universities Drama Festival in Galway the adjudicator expressed himself 'shocked that a University group has not chosen a more intellectual play'. (Perhaps the original title would have bamboozled him. Oxford University Experimental Theatre Group premiered it at the Edinburgh Festival as *The Disciplines of War*.) However our waiting audience queued right round the theatre. On the way back we were halted by a hunt straddling the road. As we drove off, a top-hatted, Roman-nosed battle-axe riding side-saddle demanded, imperiously 'Have you seen the fox?' Terry Brady called out, 'Yes … it's in the boot.'

In 1963 Mike Ruggins produced my play, *The Meeting*, for the IUDA Festival. A hugely talented cast won *The Irish Times* 'Best Original Play' Award – with their splendid ensemble performance. Ralph Bates, memorable as The Old Man, was judged Best Actor. At the end of that year, more by accident than design, I had the great good fortune to be asked to play Zeal-of-the-Land Busy in Laurie Howes' sparkling production of Ben Johnson's marathon of human folly and hypocrisy, *Bartholomew Fair*.

There it is, always tugging at us, our inheritance not only from Lecture and Library, but from The Hist and The Phil; from *TCD* and *Icarus* … all the

Olympians *now and in time to be*. May not we also *write it out in a verse?* Take a prompt from the shade of W.B. *and say our glory was we had such friends.*

Saturday evening. Trees by the Campanile are in blossom. I am dawdling back from the Library. Except for the Junior Dean in that deplorable hat, Trinity seems deserted. Three lovingly polished horse-drawn cabs, each smartly painted (lilac, green, yellow) discreetly promoting three different Dublin Hotels, wait in Front Square, doors open. Three couples, elegant in evening dress, climb in and clip-clop away across the cobbles through a warm May evening. Not until I was at Balliol was it borne in on me that *our* Trinity could not have been so very different from Oxford in the Twenties. If the past really is another country then perhaps, after all, it was a Golden Age too.

Ian Blake (TCD 1960–4; G.S.) won the Vice-Chancellor's Prize for English Verse, and Silver Medals from The College Historical Society and from the University Philosophical Society. Closely supervised by two black-and-white mogs, he now lives and writes looking over the sea to Skye, in a croft-house a hundred yards from the shore along which he takes his three-mile daily walk up the cliff and back along a single-track road.

CASTAWAY

laurie howes

'GO TO IRELAND,' she said. 'They speak English.' And she didn't mean Belfast. Go to Ireland? What a brilliant idea for a young man from 'sourf' London who had given up on A-level French. And now here I was, standing outside Front Gate. Trinity College Dublin. A postal address to rival the Duke of Wellington's.

My friend Diana had been right. They did speak English in Dublin. Two years earlier in London she (an undergraduate at LSE) had persuaded me I was wrong. It wasn't just 'school swots' and members of the establishment who went 'up' to university (a view, not atypical, of some members of that first British post-war eleven-plus/grammar-school generation, of which I was one). Self-opinionated and a posturing youth, I would continue to read the *Morning Star* (post-Suez and blind to the agony of Hungary), plagiarize Colin Wilson, ride the milk train to Brighton, march from Aldermaston, act the angry young man *and* go to university. I would apply. So much for principle. But which university? Certainly not to London and live at home!

It is strange now to recall that in the Britain of the mid-1950s most people didn't travel outside Britain. Family stories of overseas travel came largely from before 1940 or, more often, as a result of 'the war'. Britain was emerging from the deprivations of the post-war era, the famous London smog was lifting and the first buds, which would blossom into the 'Sixties', were forming. For this London teenager, working hard at being a rebel, these included 'jeans', Elvis, James Dean, Bill Haley, Saturday-night jazz at Chelsea Town Hall and coffee and cigarettes (nothing else!) over a coffin in Le Macabre in the early hours. A new age was coming into being, only we didn't know so at the time.

A school exchange trip to France in 1956 opened my eyes to another world. To those adolescent eyes, first-time France appeared magically different and enticing. I tasted Paris and caught crayfish in Le Lot. I discovered Bill Haley and Sibelius, fell in love and wrote a poem or two. Young French people drank wine, smoked Disque Bleu and rode about in Deux Chevaux. I wanted to drink wine, smoke Disque Bleu and ride a 2CV. I wanted to live in France. The return train journey from Dover engraved the ugliness of the English suburban backside on my mind for ever. I didn't want to live here in one of those little boxes. I wanted real city or real countryside, like in France, and preferably both. But it could never be France in a hundred years. A mild dyslexia (recognized as such much, much later) manifested itself in embarrassingly poor foreign language skills. But they spoke English in Ireland! I would apply to Dublin. And I was to learn that they spoke – and wrote – exceptionally good English in Dublin.

Disregarding the history of the first half of the twentieth century, Baile Átha Cliath, according to my local education authority, was still in 'Britain'; consequently it would provide fees, travel and even a modest grant. If my LEA appeared unconcerned by the political geography of the British Isles this was matched by my own quite remarkable ignorance of the culture and history of the place that would be my home for the next four years. I suspect for quite a few of us from across the water, this lack of historical 'baggage' was both a weakness and a strength. We were, literally, innocents abroad and freed from that deep sense of history, which so often defined and also entrapped many of our Irish friends.

THE DRAB GREYNESS of the city was lifted that first morning by the green of passing buses, soft October sunshine and the cry of seagulls. A city by the sea. It is 1960. My very first day in Dublin. The splendour of the College is echoed by the Bank of Ireland building opposite. Both stand out in contrast to much of the rest of Dublin, which while hinting at grander times, appears faded and shabby. This is a poor country. But a British pound sterling was going to go a long way; Dublin would be a good place to spend a student grant.

Students greeted one another, far too confidently and noisily, as they hurried in through that magnificent Front Gate. A gate within a gate, teasing the viewer with secret glimpses of cobbles, lawns and buildings beyond into another world. And it was another world. A tiny (notionally Protestant) enclave within a much larger Catholic city. Trinity was beyond the Pale (certainly for the Archbishop of Dublin) but at the very same time, stood at the heart of the city. Trinity was a city state, distinct and largely divorced (only that was not permitted either) from the resident Irish population that made up the very non-cosmopolitan Dublin of the early Sixties. Dublin was not Paris. Dublin was very Irish. No one, but no one, emigrated into Ireland, apart from a few artists, tax exiles and of course, Trinity students. The traffic was all one-way. Out. Immigration was not an issue. If you had a black face, like my friend Sammy, from Nigeria, you must be a bishop, a diplomat or, at the very least, a doctor.

Petrified, I found I couldn't go past those voices and into Front Square. So much for the streetwise Londoner. Instead I walked on up Grafton Street, down a side street and ordered my first 'glass' of the dark stuff on Irish soil. It tasted nothing like the pints on the ferry the previous night. It tasted marvellous. It was 10.30 in the morning. I had a place at TCD, a grant and the prospect of four whole years in this fine city without having to work for a living. Well, not in Dublin! Could life be better?

The 'Trinity curse' was precisely this – although few guessed so at the time. Trinity would prove a hard act to follow. Refreshed and emboldened by a second 'glass' I returned to Front Gate and entered. I managed to negotiate the network of paths and find buildings on the way to my first meeting with my tutor, without experiencing that ultimate disgrace for any 'Fresher' – being forced to ask the way.

'Look at the person on your right. Now look at the person on your left. One of you will be here in three years' time (pause); that's called probability theory,' was the way Mr Thornton introduced his subject. I loathed statistics. (And I continue to ask to this day: 'Whatever happened to the other two of us?') Indeed sometimes during that first year I was distinctly unsure of exactly why I had signed up for Economics and Political Science. And then I remembered Diana!

While I thrived on the political theory and philosophy lectures offered by Dr Thornley and Professor Chubb, others proved less engaging. For some reason we budding economists and political scientists were thought to be in need of direct hands-on experience of several million years' worth of Irish geology. This was achieved through the mechanism of tediously passing rock samples from the front to the back of a large lecture theatre for an hour that seemed like a day. To make matters worse these 'vital' lectures in economic geography occurred late on Friday afternoon. We struck on the last lecture of the term. A random insertion of stones, bits of concrete, coal, rusty tins and other 'rocky' items hastily gathered from the College grounds into the carefully planned sequence of samples being circulated created a festive distraction and made this final lecture in an otherwise dull series totally memorable. I continued to have my doubts about what I was studying, which I shared with my long-suffering tutor. Perhaps the more general 'pass' degree with three subjects freely chosen would be better – and no statistics or economic geography. Mr FitzGibbon, a kindly engineer, listened to my concerns and then delivered his memorable advice: 'But it doesn't matter what you read at Trinity. The important thing is … being here!'

And he was right. 'Being here' was far more than simply attending lectures during those remarkably short terms and occasionally venturing into one of the great libraries of the world. Being here was about meeting the rich mixture of people who made up the small (by today's standards) but cosmopolitan and discrete community that was Trinity. The Trinity undergraduate culture was quickly learned. Early in the very first term, as the dark Dublin winter closed in, lunchtimes in the pub tended to lengthen and spill over into the afternoon lecture slot. Later, spring would occasionally permit picnics in St Stephen's Green – and it was a brave student who deserted sunshine, endless conversation and good company for an indifferent lecture. Trinity was 'society' rich. Front Gate burst with notices of every conceivable club and association. Yet another reason for missing the odd lecture! You could try your hand at almost anything and I did. I remember fencing, rowing on the Liffey in the early morning, beagling in the Wicklow Mountains, and playing snooker (badly) and debating in The Hist in that first year. Far more serious and long-lasting was joining Players. Players was one of the more important 'tribes' (along with rugby, rowing, The Hist, The Phil and the 'literati' – not to mention the Elizabethans that shaped our small city state). These tribal loyalties largely determined with whom and where you drank and partied and often with whom you lived. There would be drama festivals in Wexford, Galway and Belfast and as a consequence I discovered another Ireland. Clare and Connemara appeared like the edge of the world. And they were, of course, to our very 'European world' of the Sixties. Equally shocking was Belfast and the treasonable discovery that this Englishman felt far more at home in the Republic.

At my first festival there were parties, music and drinking long into the night. And third- and fourth-year students who actually spoke to us! A heady mix for any Fresher. And at this first festival I meet Mary Carr, a petite North American from New England. I could never decide whether it was that festival, the night spent by the sea after 'accidentally' missing the lift home from the beach party, the port and Guinness on the London-to-Holyhead train, the nights on the Liverpool 'cattle boat' or simply the endless talk, but by the first summer we were what my daughters call 'an item'. Trinity had performed one of its more important higher-education objectives: matchmaking.

Accommodation was always an issue for Trinity students – especially for women who were expected to live in 'approved' and cloistered rooms. Trevor Board, my first 'flatmate' and fellow south Londoner, had at the beginning of the second term secured our early release from the 'cemetery' of our digs in Glasnevin, by announcing his conversion to frugivorianism. Our stern land-lady was having none of that nonsense – especially given the price and scarcity of fruit in Dublin. But that second term was spent in far grimmer lodgings in Ballsbridge. Finding the right 'pad' was clearly part of the challenge of being a student. Returning to Dublin that September we couldn't believe our luck. We discovered Eccles Street (on the less fashionable north side). What a find! Blissfully unaware of its Bloomstown connections, but very aware of the rules prohibiting female students from living with male students in unapproved accommodation, Mike Smith, Trevor Board, Mary and Amajeet Bansel and I moved into two of the 'flats' in Eccles Street. For three further years this 'magic' house secreted away a series of students hiding from the long arm of Miss MacManus, the university's accommodation officer.

Amazing as it now seems, it appears rarely to have crossed the minds of the resident owners, the Synnotts from Cork, that a dozen or so students of different genders might just (occasionally) be up 'to no good'. Except for Molly. Molly was the family 'retainer' and kept the house together. A generous measure of Irish whiskey would remind Mrs Synott to tell us yet again that, as a girl, Molly had fought the Black and Tans in Cork, including the 'taking out' of a British tank. For Molly had guessed. She was as bright as the proverbial button. The day the silk knickers were discovered in a male tenant's bed by Mrs Synnott's prying sister-in-law an unusual quietness settled on the house. The news spread fast. Students closed doors. Would we all be in the street by nightfall?

We were not. Molly intervened quickly (as with the tank?), explaining to her employers that English men were different – especially Trinity students. It was quite normal for someone of 'his class' (i.e. English) to sleep in silk knickers. Somehow Mr and Mrs Synnott accepted this unlikely explanation, which of course confirmed their very worst fears concerning Englishmen. The house breathed again. We all stayed. And we stayed because by then, whatever their doubts concerning our sleeping apparel, we students had become the children they would never have. Like so many of their countrymen, they had married remarkably late. We were part of each other's lives. Thick black stewed tea was always available – and one was expected to drink it! In the front room of the large house Mr Synott's elderly mother lay gently dying for the greater part of our next three years. When she received de Valera's telegram on her hundredth birthday we all gathered around her bed to celebrate. The whiskey was particularly good.

And Mrs Synnott senior, unknowingly, provided me with one of my two major acting opportunities in Dublin. I loved the theatre with a passion and had been a frequent spear carrier in Michael Croft's then-London-based National Youth Theatre. But I was no actor. For some reason she became convinced that I was, of all things, a policeman from her now confused and distant past. But which uniform was I wearing? Irish or British? The Synnotts would never tell me, carefully avoiding answering my question. Given my accent, surely it was a British uniform? However all this did not seem to matter to the strongly Republican Synnotts; all I was required to do was 'call in', mutter a 'Good evening' and she would greet me and go off into a land far beyond. I often asked myself if the policeman's visit in some way concerned Molly and her tank and marvelled (with my new-found knowledge of Irish history) at the ability of these kindly people to forgive us 'Brits', whilst clearly not forgetting their own, still very raw, story.

My other major acting opportunity was in film. Ireland in the early Sixties vied with Italy as the place to make cheap movies and Trinity students were part of the action. £3.50 a day as an extra was tempting; one could even be seduced into missing the odd lecture for that sum. And many of us were. Most memorable for me was *Of Human Bondage* starring Laurence Harvey, Kim Novak and Siobhán McKenna, much of which was filmed in Trinity. Best of all was the shooting of the graduation party at an expensive hotel in the Wicklow Mountains. In Players we used cold tea or cordials for 'drinks'. For some reason the waiters in the real hotel served real drinks! Whatever you wanted. I had never drunk Campari before but have enjoyed it since that day. By around the eighth take the afternoon's filming was abandoned – or at least, that part involving those of us who could barely stand! It was a delight drinking those Camparis, but even better to be paid for doing so. We returned to Dublin and later spent our pay in The Old Stand on Dublin Bay prawns, Guinness – and Camparis.

Mike Smith got rooms in Botany Bay. Did I want to be his 'wife'? I did; I wanted to experience living within the College. Even more important was the prospect for all of us at Eccles Street of having a daytime base, especially in those wet winter months when being 'homeless' in College was not much fun. So I would have a room in College, Mary would have Eccles Street and we would visit one another. It seemed very existential at the time. Botany Bay was luxurious compared to Eccles Street. Rumours that some Trinity accommodation was categorized as 'slum' on the city housing map were clearly untrue. This wasn't. It was refurbished accommodation with new furniture, new gas fires (excellent for toast) and bidets – which solved that perennial problem of where to wash your clothes. And there was the new experience of Commons. Learning how to distribute the jug of 'porter' (which would never quite go round the table twice) called for a certain degree of skill plus self-sacrifice to ensure that friends got two glasses and you and others sadly only one. But sometimes even he who poured (and it was a 'he') got two glasses.

For there were no 'shes' in Commons. There was the Elizabethan Society in No. 6 of course, but where were the women in Trinity? Were they actually members of the University? Yet another rumour had it that they were not. Not only were they fortunately denied the stodge of Commons, they had to be out of College rooms before 10 pm (or was it 6 pm? Memory plays strange tricks). Stories of those rusticated to St Andrew's for the sin of simply drinking coffee with female students in their rooms after the witching hour abounded. (And it is said that, on occasion, female students actually spent the entire night in Players Theatre, following a late rehearsal or other pressing nocturnal activities, before slipping out into the Dublin morning.) For there was to be no sex in Trinity after 10 pm. Sex in the morning, afternoon or early evening was apparently fine. Well it wasn't, because sex did not seem 'officially' to happen in Trinity or indeed in much of Ireland. Contraceptives were banned, their sale outlawed.

But Trinity students are nothing if not inventive. One who must remain nameless displayed considerable entrepreneurial skills by carving out part of the middle section of a rather fine and ancient edition of *L'Histoire de l'Eglise irlandaise* and smuggling in supplies, the book duly passing back and forth to England containing its precious cargo. Just what the penalty would have been for this double crime of smuggling and (would it be blasphemy?) one shudders to think. But it is good to now acknowledge the contribution that the Catholic Church made (if covert) to birth control amongst Trinity students in the early Sixties.

And it was not only contraceptives of which the Irish population were deprived by their theocratic masters. There were the papers 'from across the water'. Buying copies of British Sunday newspapers, especially the *News of the World*, was stimulation for any would-be writer. One was forced to imagine the stories that had been so diligently removed by hand every Sunday morning as the papers entered the country. One always knew when there was a particularly good story because the papers arrived even later than normal in the city centre.

Dublin was indeed a strangely Puritan theocracy and I was learning that Catholic Ireland was not Catholic France. But by now the reality of Ireland had long replaced the adolescent fantasy of France. This was a world very different from secular London or Paris. Being an 'outsider' and non-believer helped, so I didn't have to suffer my Catholic friends' quiet rage at the annual Easter denunciation of Trinity and all who attended her by the Archbishop of Dublin. What did confuse me, though, was that several African and Asian friends, who turned out to be Catholic, reported that they had been encouraged to apply to Trinity *by* their Catholic teachers and priests! The Church clearly moved in mysterious ways; or perhaps they were simply using the same 'atlas' as my local education authority?

And the Archbishop was a real power in the city. This was brought home to me when I rather foolishly accepted the flattering offer of the editorship of the *TCD* magazine in the very last term of my fourth year. Not the best sort of run-in for your finals, especially if you had directed a major Players production in your first term! But the glory of Trinity was that you could, and still pass your exams. My co-editor Jeremy Lewis and I took on the might of the Catholic Church. Well not really, but it was to make a good headline in *The* (then) *Manchester Guardian.* What we learned was the power of the Church over our printers. *TCD* was written and edited weekly and always at the very last minute by a changing bunch of amateurs – we students. The printers, a local Dublin firm, were marvellous, never complaining and always helpful, but they shook their heads in horror when they read our copy and instructions for one edition. It started with censorship. Peter Lennon, a journalist, had written four articles, eventually published by *The Manchester Guardian*, identifying a 'climate of repression' in what he saw as a 'bigoted' and 'crookedly Puritanical Ireland'. He cited the work of the Censorship of Publications Board, the government Film Censor, the repressive climate of control at UCD and, most controversially, the hands-on role of the Archbishop of Dublin, Dr McQuaid. Unable to get the articles published in Ireland, Lennon issued an invitation to anyone willing to publish them uncensored in Ireland free of charge. Jeremy and I rose to the bait. Our printers reluctantly agreed to print – and the story ran for the rest of the term with letters and articles passionately argued on both sides – including one from one of our very own printers.

Whether Damian Duggan-Ryan saw his article 'Celibacy and Servitude' as litmus paper or a red rag, only he knows. This hard-hitting article by an Irish Catholic who had transferred to Trinity from UCD outflanked Lennon's as it attacked the Catholic Church's interference in Irish health policy, particularly those related to sexual matters, birth control and therapeutic abortion. But it was probably his discussion of the Church's attitude to 'The morality of the use of the Tampon', which was seen by the Church (apparently) as 'a grave source of temptation', that did it. Or was it his suggestion that the Church saw the UN as 'a symbol of pagan internationalism' and strongly supported the dictatorships in Spain and Portugal? Together they certainly did it. The printers refused to print.

We were clearly joking weren't we? No way were they going to print the article. 'If we do, we'll close,' they said. Printing it would not only mean loss of business from the Church and its agencies; even worse, they claimed, would be the loss of business from all those other firms and bodies, which would be 'lent on' to support the official line.

We reproduced the article; it was photocopied and inserted by hand into the printed edition. The copy sold out. A blow for the freedom of publication. *TCD* made it into the news section of *The Manchester Guardian*. Our first issue had also been controversial. We had focused on the case brought by James McKeith, bitten four times by a garda dog and beaten by the gardaí whilst protesting outside the US embassy against the US blockade of Cuba. In court it was claimed that the dogs 'savagedly set on the crowds' and 'were out of control'. Given that they also bit one garda and a young apprentice journalist, one Rosemary Gibson, they probably were. The Dublin jury were asked the question: 'Did the gardaí wrongfully set dogs on McKeith?' Their answer was 'No' but they added the rider that the use of dogs by the gardaí 'was wrongful and unnecessary'. They spoke a very subtle English in Dublin!

DURING THAT PERIOD, the *TCD* team was good. Anthony Weale drew wonderfully observed cartoon sketches for articles inside the magazine while Tim Booth produced a collector's item of brilliant black-and-white front covers from the Hodges Figgis Art Gallery with a fresh drawing each week paid for by our advertiser. Ian Whitcomb was the quirky and controversial film and entertainment critic while playboy Ranald Graham was sports editor.

For me as editor, those editions, together with a photo-edition of the College Races (which also sold out by lunchtime), were amongst the high spots of our editorship. As was the frivolous, delightfully juvenile and surreal weekly Rupert Bare column written 'undercover' by Michael de Larrabeiti. Rupert renamed students, and some like Sir Nastian Blather carry their titles to this day. Each week Rupert punctured the pretensions of the mighty (Spike Oldcrum has yet to forgive him) and turned some (relatively unknown) student into a celebrity. Students plucked from the air entered the hall of fame for a week as

Rupert wove and frequently fabricated events, relationships and worse. We had learnt a life skill. When in doubt make it up.

Last but not least there was the weekly personal column. Short, sharp and to the point!

- Wanted. A number of lecturers to staff School of Economics. Pay and conditions bad but guarantee of long term employment, Graduates preferred.
- Five shillings offered for every man found in the Elizabethan rooms. Apply Fiona Wright.
- Coffins wanted. French Faculty.
- Would Sebastian Balfour please return whip. Deborah de Vere White.

As my time at Trinity progressed, lectures improved, although not all. Professor 'Joey' Johnson, a scholar of some years, would read from his notes on International Economics as he had always done. He was also short-sighted. Those of us who remained after answering the obligatory roll call would amuse ourselves by following his lecture notes word by word, even on occasions offering corrections to any errors in the prepared text. These precious sets of lecture notes, purchased for a 'fiver', were religiously passed down from one year to the next. Only the truly dedicated stayed to the end, many preferring to exit on their hands and knees, creeping to and through the door at the far end of the lecture hall. Lectures that started with a full house would end with very few. Word must have got out. One morning a fellow student making his escape was confronted at the exit by a pair of trousers, a gown and the lower body of a very senior member of the College establishment. With commendable presence of mind he turned full circle, crept back and retook his seat. Attendance throughout Joey's lectures improved enormously over the few remaining weeks. Mr FitzGibbon had been right. Thankfully, lectures and the world of scholarship were but a small part of a student's years at Trinity.

Far more important to me was Players. I progressed from 'one-acters' and being an assistant director on major productions like *The Possessed* to the real thing. In 1963 I directed Anouilh's *The Lark* with Nina Boyd in the title role of Jeanne d'Arc. The tiny Players stage was ideally claustrophobic for a production that demanded that almost all the actors sit on stage throughout the entire play facing the audience. My last and most challenging production (given the size of the stage) was Johnson's *Bartholomew Fayre* with Max Stafford-Clark, who came up with the brilliant idea of freezing the actors (Tom Jones style) for the many asides that pepper the play. The result was a play as visually exciting as it was dramatic. Amongst a prodigiously talented cast, the memory of Gill Hanna's marvellous Pigwoman still makes me 'corpse', especially in the shower. But that's how Rupert Bare taught me to write!

By my fourth year Botany Bay with its rather comfortable 'suburban' quality felt increasingly restrictive. I had had enough of this 'cosy' College life. No accommodation being available in Eccles Street (although I remained a constant visitor), I moved into a flat in Merrion Square with Tony Rance, a delightful chain-smoking English Anglo-Catholic with a liking for port. Clothed in his magnificent cloak he could, on a misty evening, be mistaken for a lost cardinal or a Romanian count. He loved to dress up. And I also had taken it into my head to wander around Dublin in my grandfather's old frock-coat. What posers we were! This brief period is memorable for yet more parties, disputes with the ferocious landlady and her daughters and the entertaining sounds from two horses that lived in the backyard inches from my bedroom window. Being an urban child I had never realized that horses farted so much.

And then the world suddenly got even better. Sebastian Balfour suggested that Tony Rance and I 'Box and Cox' the top 'flat' of No. 10 Front Square with him and one other. It had two bedrooms and a large sitting-room with ample sofas for crash-pads. The four of us would split the £2-a-week rent. Still, ten shillings a week each was just about right for a 'slum'. The rumour was true! A lack of running water and the need to descend four flights to the lavatory could be something of a challenge, especially after a hard night. But Sir Nastian solved the problem, His flying urinal (sadly still unpatented) worked a treat consisting as it did of an auxiliary pipe running from the window ledge into the main guttering. It was indeed a joy unbounded to view the city prospect from our top flat rather than descend the darkened and cold stairs. It worked wonderfully for several months until one warm summer's evening he threw it up towards the Dublin stars. It was back to doing the stairs.

Sebastian introduced me to our fourth member. Slightly older than us, with the first signs of thinning hair, he looked somewhere between a hit-man, a young Éamon de Valera and a Jesuit priest. There was something odd about him. Share our precious No. 10 with this stranger? I took an instant dislike to him and we remained the very best of mates for the rest of his life. And Michael de Larrabeiti brought further largesse to our expanding empire. When not in No. 10 he was living unlawfully (according to College rules) with Celia Whitehead at their country retreat in Delgany near Bray. Their accommodation consisted of a sturdy corrugated iron cottage overlooking the sea. It was perfect. For parties, long weekends and especially for extremely long lunches. I believe the record, one memorable Saturday, was twelve hours. The one disadvantage was that whoever was cradling the bucket of Guinness purchased from the one pub some distance from the cottage invariably received a lapful of stout, as Mike's Ford Prefect hit the bottom of the hill and climbed on up through the field to the cottage. But wet knickers were a small price to pay for paradise.

So I spent my last glorious year betwixt and between Eccles Street and No. 10, with the occasional excursion to Delgany. It was a very privileged lifestyle. I was enjoying that powerful combination of 'real' city and 'real' countryside first dreamt of on a train passing through suburban London. It was not France, but they spoke English. And I drank Guinness, smoked Sweet Afton, and Mary and I had a quarter-share with Sebastian in Panurge, a bouncy Austin Devon. (I had of course by then successfully acquired my Irish driving licence, valid throughout Europe and the USA, through the demanding task of handing over one pound at the General Post Office.) Who needed wine, Disque Bleu and a 2CV? I loved Ireland. No. 10 was increasingly becoming our collective 'crash-pad' and 'workshop' for endless planning and plotting on whatever we were all about. Players, TCD, Tony Rance's sister, the Rabelaisian Society, the next meal, and who was going to get the next bottle of port. It was also on occasions starting to get more serious for those of us staring into the pit of finals. Having very carefully avoided mentioning the five-letter word 'study' for so long, some of us realized, with a degree of embarrassment, that we were finally starting to engage, if belatedly, with the world of ideas. This was dangerous stuff and not what was expected of Trinity students.

We were also behaving rather badly. An enduring memory from No. 10 is of our last great collective misdemeanour; the 'borrowing' of a fine long table from No. 6 for our 1964 Trinity Ball dinner party. Planned with military precision, this involved creeping at night through the attics (from No. 10 to No. 6), and 'dropping', secret-agent style, from the ceiling into a darkened and shut Elizabethan Society. When the coast was clear we carried the table out, (past a sleeping JD) and up to our flat in No. 10. On the way we paid a surprise night-time courtesy call to the Chess Society rooms whilst exploring the attic space. Their rooms had been locked and barred as a major competition was going on – so we moved a few vital pieces on several boards thereby opening up the competition hopefully to a rank outsider. Apologies are probably in order. We seated twenty people at our illicit banquet, which preceded the official start of the Ball. The search by the Elizabethans for their missing table continued for some months. Apologies, Fiona Wright.

So did we really lead such shallow lives? Where were the big issues? Where were Vietnam, Cuba, civil rights and the Bomb? And what had happened to that pretentious but concerned London teenager? One reason must be that we 'guest students' were in fact 'castaways' living on someone else's island. So many Trinity students were not of Ireland and could only engage with its concerns, at best, second-hand. And too many of these concerns involved Church and State, where Trinity students were singularly poorly placed to argue a case. We were also living in a society on the edge of Europe. Éire was still culturally neutral. International news focused on JFK, the Pope, Australia and the Congo – something of an odd mix if you were not Irish. The Cold War seemed strangely far away, even in the dark days of the Cuban missile crisis. There were the occasional brave demonstrations by those nurturing a Left agenda, but these were modest on any scale. Trinity was a self-selected 'gulag' and the experience encouraged us to live up our own bottoms. We concentrated on those issues that affected us, often involving women. The fiercely fought battle to allow women to drink Guinness in a pint glass. The right of women to attend meetings of The Hist. The right to publish and be damned. The right to buy uncensored books and newspapers. The right to use contraception. These were not unimportant but they were not the major issues of concern to most students in London and Paris. Or were they?

Meanwhile the 'Sixties' was being fashioned on the larger neighbouring island. As with so many 'colonialists' we were being culturally left behind by our mother countries. Some blamed the dark stuff, others those early Fresher sherry parties. There was one other reason. This was that Trinity in the Sixties could be, and was for many of us, a simply fabulous place to be an undergrad-uate. Most other things seemed not to matter that much; the important thing was being there. Many of us were, rather selfishly, having far too good a time.

The Ball marked the end of the term, the year and, in your fourth year, your life as an undergraduate. Only it didn't. Finals were in September. Very suddenly life was very serious. Desperate attempts were made to discover just what had been covered in all those lectures you hadn't attended. Course reading lists with recommended texts became like gold dust as Trinity was suddenly emptied of all its students, except those with September exams. Soon the tourists would replace the students, offering those left behind the possi-bility of marketing a quick visit to Oscar Wilde's very own room (No. 10) for a pound. And that great Trinity library was rediscovered.

Sebastian handed back the keys to No. 10, the refurbishers moved in and I moved back into a newly vacant room in Eccles Street next door to Mary. I now think back on that long summer as one of my happiest times. Those weeks of quiet and focused study stimulated by cold fear. The top rooms at Eccles Street, or the Library, were both perfect for the task. Money was tight; the grant and any savings gone and there was no question of taking a holiday job as in other years. The one luxury was one bottle of Guinness each evening over a simple meal. I had never before realized the enormous satisfaction of such a life. Perhaps at long last I was becoming a real student?

Six exams in three days in September – and then you could sell all your books to Hodges Figgis! And that hurt. But what were we all going to do? What did you do after you left? We had given it hardly a thought. Why worry? Something would come along, wouldn't it? It did. Somewhere in that euphoric post-exam period a plot was hatched with another American, Chuck Hirsch, and his friend John Roberts. We would travel around South America – the logical follow-on to four years at Trinity! And we would finance the expedition by importing and selling Yorkshire terrier puppies and vintage Rolls-Royces and Bentleys in the USA. By the late autumn of 1964 the five of us, Mary, Sebas-tian, Chuck, John and I, were living in Colorado, in an apartment throbbing with Yorkshire terriers. And Sebastian and I were the only graduate waiters in Denver, Colorado, driving to work (occasionally) in a Rolls-Royce.

So much for principle!

Laurie Howes, (TCD 1960–4; Economics and Political Science) came down and got as far as Costa Rica. He returned to London in 1966 and was married briefly to Mary Carr (qv). In 1973 he married his Anglo-Irish wife Clodagh and in 1974 left London to live deep in the Forest of Dean and teach at the Gloucestershire College of Art and Design. In 1980 he finally got round to his Commencement. He was a member of Clockwork Circus (children's theatre) and Dean Arts, both Gloucestershire-based arts charities for some twenty years. Now retired from what became the University of Gloucestershire, he is finally getting round to cultivating his garden. Some of Dr Thornley's lectures did take root.

Student protests against the US arms blockade on Cuba, 1962. Courtesy of The Irish Times.

FORTY YEARS ON

harriet turton

SINCE MY GREAT AUNT, May Ponsonby, lived in Dublin, she it was whom I consulted about where I should live when I started at Trinity. Living in a house in Ballsbridge with her old butler, she was perhaps not best qualified to advise a young student about lodgings, but she was very well-placed to regale me with appalling tales of the Troubles. The letters she gave me to read from friends whose houses had been burnt down were certainly more moving and vivid than any history book, and so was her own description of the night the IRA came to burn down the Ponsonby house, Kilcooley Abbey in County Tipperary. Her life, and that of her husband, was saved by the same elderly butler, who had the presence of mind to turn off the electricity, then stood at the top of the stairs and blew a hunting horn so that the marauders lost both their bearings and their wits, and ran away.

In fact, Aunt May's solution to the housing problem was to contact cousins who lived in Bray. Any recognition of the need for propinquity to Trinity did not occur to her, but it gave me an interesting insight into the life of an upper-class family of three generations, looked after by a very young girl from Cork, who could hardly read or write, and who seemed to be perpetually petrified. There was much talk about old and better days, and aristocratic connections in that ill-repaired and rather depressing house, but still my cousins provided a quick entrée into other old Irish houses, which seemed to have changed little over the years, except for a considerable shrinkage on the staff front.

The bus into Dublin was the regular form of transport, and quite adequate until the plethora of parties, which mounted up towards the end of that first Michaelmas term. So my cousin, in a generous and trusting fashion, offered to lend me her car when it became obvious that the bus timetable made no effort to fit in with Trinity party hours. The fact that I had never driven a car bothered her not a jot, but she did opine that it might be a sensible precaution for me to buy a driving licence, which was easily done over a post-office counter for the princely sum of five shillings. She then parked somewhere near Duke Street and gave me three minutes on how to start and stop the car, plus a vague idea of changing gear, before rushing off to a hair appointment. On my return from a party later that day, slightly the worse for drink, I could recall absolutely nothing that I had been told earlier. Fortunately, I spotted a solitary stranger across the street and remembering that discretion is the better part of valour, I collared him, and explained my predicament. After a few trial runs up and down dark streets, he considered me sufficiently roadworthy to undertake my maiden journey back to Bray, to return the borrowed car.

Still carless, and buses having outlived their charm, I soon moved into a run-down boarding house in Morehampton Road, and shared a bedroom with Penny Rosier and Caroline Best – which was fine until we all contracted German measles at the same time and were incarcerated together. Our fellow lodgers were desperate commercial travellers who needed a flaskful of Paddy's as a kick-start to get them back on the road each morning.

When the seedy attractions of the boarding house faded, we moved into what proved to be the perfect flat in Harcourt Street, for which five of us paid a pound a head – extraordinarily cheap, even in those days, for four bedrooms and a kitchen, which offered as few facilities as we had culinary talents. The apogee of our gastronomic skills was to cook a swan killed by Peter Moore and Keir Campbell.

OUR CO-TENANT, in another part of the house, was not the sort of tenant of which Harcourt Street might boast today, just as the untidy straggle of Trinity students who dodged in and out would be equally out of place. But we must have been typical. There was a shop across the road where you could buy a single egg, or a single fag, or a slice of butter; and a Salvation Army hostel in St Stephen's where you could have a breakfast that would see you through the day for sixpence. The fact that we qualified for such a meal must say something about our general appearance.

The landlords of this Harcourt Street flat never carried out inspections, and seemed quite unconcerned about the state of the flat, which actually could hardly deteriorate below the condition at which we took on the tenancy. It must have been for this reason that various Scottish friends who rented the flat from us for the Dublin Horse Show, at a somewhat inflated price of £10 a week, decided to keep piglets in the bathroom. These creatures were dutifully fed and watered, before presently being greased with some sort of oil, and concealed in guitar cases for the first big ball of the Horse Show week at the Gresham Hotel. The care with which the piglets were concealed was not matched by their delivery, since the driver of the car in which they were hidden drove straight up the steps of the hotel and into the foyer. The piglets, which it was hoped would scamper and frolic between the legs of the guests, instead took fright and hid under the tables. Our tenants were in the process of trying to catch the livestock when the gardaí arrived, and all parties were carried off to Mountjoy Prison. There they spent a memorable night, cheered by the presence of 'the bugler', a drunken and seemingly permanent resident of the gaol, who banged continuously on the door of his cell, insisting that his newly arrived fellow inmates should not be denied their 'rights'.

Next morning in court things were going badly as my friends were having difficulty in raising bail. One well-meaning supporter, asked how large a guarantee her income might support, replied, 'Daddy gives me £100 a year.' This was considered insufficient by the magistrate. Matters looked increasingly desperate until the door of the courtroom swung open and in walked Desmond Guinness. His surety slightly confused the magistrate, who seemed uncertain as to whether Mr Guinness farmed in Kildare or whether Kildare was his farm. Either way, it was enough to secure the release of our tenants. What became of the piglets I never discovered.

Apart from being a time of high spirits and fun, the early Sixties also witnessed a profound change in sexual morality, due to the appearance of 'the

Pill'. For girls like me, fairly prudish and convent-educated, it created more of a ripple than a roar, but still it caused confusion. I remember being thrilled when a rather good-looking and popular undergraduate asked if I would be his girlfriend. I was at a loss to know whether he was suggesting that we should spend time doing things together, like going to the pictures, or going to bed immediately. Far too embarrassed to ask for clarification, I chose the coward's course, and declined. To this day, I still wonder what he had in mind!

At about the same time, I spent a long summer vacation driving overland in a dormobile with friends, from Trinity to Turkey, all for £35 return. News of the new sexual freedom of both British and Irish girls had obviously preceded us to Istanbul, so that when I went to our driver's bedroom, to collect some clothes I had promised to wash for him, we were both arrested by the hotel manager. Since we spoke no Turkish, and he spoke no English, the grounds for arrest were rather obscure, but one thing led to another, as things tend to do in Turkey, and before we knew what was happening, we were taken to court. The incident was eventually translated into headlines in the foreign section of the *Sunday Express*, the headlines doing justice to any aspiring journalist: 'Blonde ex-deb in Turkish court after bedroom row!' My parents were not amused.

My days in Dublin were a happy mix – the decline of the Anglo-Irish ascendancy together with the stirrings of a new, outward-looking Republic. My son Orlando, as I write, is coming to the end of four apparently happy years at Trinity, with friends across the board, but more Irish than English. Even with forty years between his times and mine, I get the impression that our experiences of Trinity have not been entirely dissimilar. Bells rang when I heard that he had recently had a drink with Dr McDowall, in my days the Junior Dean, and was still trying to leave after a quarter of an hour: 'There wasn't a break in his chatter.' When Orlando brought up the subject of this book, McDowall thought for a moment, and then described our generation as 'remarkable people ... they were so *cultured* – if that isn't too elitist a term'. I don't think it is.

Harriet Bridgeman (née Turton; TCD 1960–4; History of Art) has edited two magazines, **The Masters** and **Discovering Antiques,** and sixteen books, from **The British Eccentric** to **The Encyclopedia of Victoriana.** In 1972 she set up the Bridgeman Art Library, a photographic library of fine art, history and culture, representing 2000 museums, libraries, historic houses and other institutions with offices in London, Paris, Berlin and New York. In 1997 she was awarded the European Women of Achievement Award in the Arts, and in 2005 was voted the IBA International Business Woman of the Year. In 2006 she set up the Artists' Collecting Society for the collection of the Artists' Resale Right. The Bridgeman Art Library is currently running an EU Project on metadata and IP and one of its project partners is a CTS laboratory at TCD.

GHOSTLY RUMBLE AMONG THE DRUMS

derek mahon

AS IF TO MARK its decline from the great days, Trinity took the curious step of appointing the present writer its first 'Writing Fellow' for the academic year 1985–6. I was given 'rooms' the size of a matchbox, which I seldom used, having found a flat in Anglesea Road; also the use of an office in the School of English, overlooking the Provost's Garden. I was to act as 'writer in residence', teach 'creative writing', encourage the *children*, and generally make myself available. It worked out fine in fact and, thanks to Rita, I actually got paid. Rita as in Lewis Gilbert's brilliant film *Educating Rita*. This was made in and around the College, and Trinity earmarked its permission fee for the new Writing Fellowship scheme. The job title was a little puzzling, since it seemed to imply that the real Fellows of the College either didn't or couldn't write, which could hardly be true, now could it? And, as always in these situations, there was reciprocal puzzlement as to my role, with High-Table folk wondering quizzically who was this writing fellow and what did he actually *do?* What I actually did, aside from writing and 'teaching', was to relive in imagination a previous era, the early Sixties, when we were undergraduates and often behaved like idiots. I remembered, for example, crashing the Trinity Ball and lying on the lawn in

Front Square as dawn broke, listening to the birds, while the legitimate dancers paraded out arm-in-arm through Front Gate to breakfast in Jurys off Dame Street, or the Red Bank. I hope nobody else remembers it.

The College remained unchanged in many respects, though whether the same is true today I'm not so sure. A poster would announce 'Dublin University Ladies' Boat Club: Bad Taste Party, Islandbridge: How Low Can You Sink?' And I would be chucklingly back in my own undergraduate years when parties of all kinds were the order of the day and night. Everyone, you will recall, drank as if it was going out of style, at a time when a pint cost 'one and six' or so, a bottle of plonk ten bob, and a bottle of hooch two quid. Much time was spent in O'Neills, The Bailey (the *old* Bailey), The Old Stand and Jammet's back bar, no longer there. Drunkenness, in some circles, was not only commonplace but more or less obligatory; conspicuous sobriety was frowned upon. Nor, contrary to tradition, was it us natives who were the most dedicated practitioners (though we kept abreast) but the Sloane Rangers, the tough fops with silk scarves and snarling red two-seaters. This lot, public-school men who weren't bright enough for Oxford or Cambridge, and posh gels not tall enough for the Brigade of Guards, created noise out of proportion to their numbers, bawling 'Charles!' and 'Miranda!', Brideshead-style, and revving their little roadsters. But you know all this. What you may not know is that some are still in circulation, to be found, little changed, in rackety venues like the Chelsea Arts Club. A 'Fulham Wanderer' will often wear a stringy Trinity tie, as if in mourning for lost youth. By 1985 the air of conscious privilege was already a thing of the past – or rather the most privileged were now the offspring of the Dublin middle class, not English toffs and residual Anglo-Irish gratin as in our time.

Work? I hardly did a hand's turn in four years. Except for Alec Reid, Con Leventhal and others you could count on the fingers of one hand, if you had learnt to count, the faculty was so boring then that exhausted revellers, unshaven and hollow-eyed, some still in dressing-gown and slippers if they lived in rooms, would snore to themselves in a fractious manner throughout morning lectures. Sometimes lecturers themselves would succumb to ennui or hysteria, like the Philosophy don of advanced years who introduced us to Kant. Gazing out of a window at New Square, trying to summarize the *Critique of Pure Reason*, he paused and gradually, quite gently, started shaking with silent laughter as if at some cosmic joke, which perhaps it was. He smacked his thigh, leered at us, and laughed bitterly aloud – a prolonged, self-renewing, slightly crazy laugh, what Beckett calls the *risus purus,* 'the laugh laughing at the laugh'. In which we presently joined, and trailed helplessly from the room.

Trinity, in those days, wasn't much about work, though quite a lot of reading got done. The word meant different things. To the question, 'What are you reading?' one might have replied, depending on context, 'Honours Maths', 'the racing page', or even, in exceptional circumstances, *The Decline and Fall of the Roman Empire.* The old circular Reading Room, presided over by the good-natured Harry Bovanizer (the name was of eighteenth-century Rhenish-Palatine origin), seemed as much a social focus as a locus of serious study. Packed to the doors like a fashionable restaurant, it was used partly as a pick-up joint. Girls dressed up then to go into College, the cobbles playing hell with their high heels. Men dressed up too, sort of, except for slobs like myself who wore the same sweater and jeans for four years. Front Square was like a Dior catwalk, and the two sexes sat in the Reading Room with blurry volumes before them, sizing up the talent out of the corners of their eyes. The air crackled with sexual electricity. On one occasion, a man's voice asked loudly and unchivalrously, 'Gloria Shawe-Taylor' (or something), 'are you playing footsie with me?' Sometimes if 'readers' got out of hand, Harry had to double as a bouncer.

'Rooms' then were available only to men, or 'gentlemen' as we were called, without obvious irony, by porters and skips. The skips, of whom the most famous was Larry Kelly, a thoughtful figure who would not have been out of his depth in diplomatic circles, brought us pitchers of hot water each morning, emptied the ashtrays, and silently pocketed whatever modest gratuity might be lying on the kitchen table – the gratuity indicating that a guest had spent the night. It was these shrewd, tolerant men, in their navy-blue jackets and jockey caps, who really ran the College. Larry, my own skip for a year, knew everything that went on, and the Provost had him in for a glass of Jameson each Friday evening to get the low-down on the week's events. When Larry died a very decent obituary notice appeared in *The Irish Times,* to be followed by a letter of appreciation from an American scholar who had spent a sabbatical year in rooms.

Some of our contemporaries have distinguished themselves in the 'real world', some in private life; and some, alas, are no longer with us. Of those literati who have remained active, a number (in the Arts Faculty at least) started in Players Theatre, or in *Icarus* magazine – published each term and edited in rotation by the writing crowd, a few of whom went on to publish 'seriously' in Dublin proper, London and elsewhere. We look back now on our youthful efforts with horror and shame, as well we might: no question of Swift's 'What a genius I had then!' No, what we had then – Brendan, Rudi, Michael, Edna, Deborah de Vere White and the late, still unappreciated Ronnie Wathen – was time and leisure to make our first mistakes and perhaps to learn from them. Our four undergraduate years, unlike the urgent three elsewhere, developed in us a slower pace of thought (too slow perhaps), a respect for reverie and the *longue durée*, which is one of the luxuries of the artistic life. The late John McGahern, asked what he would do with an Arts Council grant, is said to have replied, 'Stare out of the window,' and we did a lot of that. Dublin then was full of people staring out of windows or into pint glasses. Not any more: the so-called 'Celtic Tiger' years, coinciding with a revised microclimate, have banished sloth, silence and rich inconsequence to the mists of time in the interests of greater 'productivity' and enhanced anxiety levels. People are getting up at six in the morning, for heaven's sake! The College is now a 'campus' and we're no longer graduates but alumni. Where is the pride? The hyphen and semi-colon are in danger. What price the life-enhancing inactivity of yore, its benefits evident only in the longer term?

Things turned *fairly* serious, even for us, with the approach of finals – from which, Dr Owen Sheehy-Skeffington warned us, we would never quite recover. He proved to be right except that it wasn't finals themselves that were traumatic so much as leaving Trinity, which had become, for so many of us, a home from home. To be back again twenty years later, too old now to die young, posing as some sort of temporary academic, gave rise to existential problems at first, to do with self-definition and an alarming sense that, despite having lived for years in London, I'd only been away for a term or two. I liked it when the students called me by my first name; but, try as I might, deep down I knew I was a young man no longer, despite appearances. I'd sit in the Senior Common Room with other fogies, read the *TLS* and *The Spectator* and, refusing the port, sip my after-dinner coffee, thinking of Scott Fitzgerald's *Echoes of the Jazz Age*: 'Now … we summon the proper expression of horror as we look back at our wasted youth. Sometimes, though, there is a ghostly rumble among the drums, an asthmatic whisper in the trombone ... and it all seems rosy and romantic to us who were young then, because we will never feel quite so intensely about our surroundings any more.'

Derek Mahon (TCD 1961–5; G.S.) has held journalistic and academic appointments in London and New York. A member of Aosdána, he has received numerous awards including the Irish Academy of Letters Award, the Scott Moncrieff Translation Prize, and Lannan and Guggenheim Fellowships. His publications include **Night-Crossing** (1968), **Lives** (1972), **The Hudson Letter** (1996), **The Yellow Book** (1997), **Harbour Lights** (Winner of The Irish Times Poetry Now Award, 2006) and many others. He received the David Cohen Prize in 2007 for recognition of a lifetime's achievement in literature.

CRAIC AND CARPE DIEM

a tribute to rosemary gibson (1942–1997) by andy gibb

IN 1959 Rosemary left Africa, the highs of flat-racing Haile Selassie's horses and the lows of enforced elocution lessons and pinafore dresses, to return to her native Dublin to terrorize the staff and inmates of Alexandra College, whence she planned an assault on Trinity with her peripatetic and Gaelic-free education. As an expat, a born rebel and an avid reader she had forgotten – or perhaps never knew – Ireland's draconian rules of admission: Church and State were hand in glove then in the Republic, the list of banned books (and contraceptive devices) long and unforgiving. Elsewhere, *Lady Chatterley's Lover* had been reprinted after an epic trial in 1960, Burrough's *Naked Lunch* and Henry Miller's *Tropic of Cancer* had appeared a year later, some six years after ex-TCD student Donleavy's *Ginger Man* had itself scraped through the literary *cordon sanitaire*. Joyce's *Dubliners* was fine but *Ulysses* still was not. Rosemary was horrified by this and amazed that the Gaelic Athletic Association could ban its members from watching or playing 'foreign or garrison games' (it was, she had to concede, the next most powerful and influential organization after the Catholic Church).

In 1961 Rosemary paid the Gaeilge exemption penalty (Irish entrants were normally required to include Gaelic in their Leaving Cert.) and swept onto the cobbles inside Front Gate, an anarchic vision astride her Vespa scooter flattening all before her, intimidating and all at once enticing. This grinning pekinese-nosed girl with trademark haystack blonde hair, matelot shirt, jeans and boots, was everywhere. Long after her Fresher year, she would materialize at Freshers' evenings, just for the 'craic' and practical-joke opportunities, or maybe it was for the Swimming Club (she was a record-breaking swimmer and diver, typically rejecting an invitation to train for the Olympics).

She made the Coffee Bar at No. 27 her own, Sweet Afton to hand, legs akimbo, a gamine rippling with laughter and madcap antics. Above this conflu-ence of Botany Bay, the Rubrics and New Square sat the Dublin University Central Athletic Committee where 'Pinks' were dispensed to exceptional College sportsmen – and increasingly to women, starting with Hilary Roche as Captain of Sailing and continuing with Rosemary herself, heroine of the Iveagh Baths. This smoky rendezvous for new faces was often bursting at the seams with the old guard, so she would take off through the blue haze to Side Gate for a sand-wich and steaming coffee at Mooney's in Pearse Street, or round past the Burke and Goldsmith statues at Front Gate, over to J.J. Fox's (Cigar Merchants and purveyors of affordable tickets for Lansdowne Road rugby) and on to Slatterys in Suffolk Street. Here in the basement, she fell in with a coterie of would-be writers and thespians, fiercely bright and articulate and intolerant of fools. An ingenue to the core and (as described much later in a *Trinity News* profile) 'uncompli-cated by any previous formal education', Rosemary thrived on the atmosphere. Sue McHarg, Heather Lukes, Ann McFerran, Chris Searle, Mirabel Walker, Nigel Ramage, Hamish McRae and many others were all to pursue successful careers in the media (a term almost unknown then) in a life after Trinity. She was happy to exchange these heady intellectual climes for the spit-and-sawdust embrace of O'Neills on the next corner, where a young Brendan Kennelly was honing his poetic arts before eclipsing the lot of them in the years to follow.

On 23 October 1962, Rosemary was summarily knocked off her ill-fitting middle-class middle-of-the-road liberal perch by a demonstration at the Amer-ican embassy (then in Merrion Square) against the US arms blockade on Cuba, which was to highlight the brinkmanship of Jack and Bobby Kennedy and the fragility of freedom of speech in Ireland. Students bearing placards proclaiming 'No More Hiroshimas' and 'Kennedy No. Kruschev No. Peace Yes' attached them-selves to Dr Noel Browne TD as he attempted to breach the bemused and chaotic cordon of gardaí blocking the path to the embassy door. Rosemary had barely been aware of the looming 'Cuba Missile Crisis' but soon became fearful of the Armageddon meltdown theory implicit in a Third World War. Ignoring her political philistinism, she obeyed her visceral sense of the threats at hand and joined the march. In the ensuing fracas in the Square, in Nassau Street and at Lincoln Gate the gardaí lost control of their dogs and several demonstrators were mauled and bitten, amongst them medical student James ('Jim') McKeith and the ubiquitous Rosemary. Despite the protests of Senators Stanford and Sheehy-Skeffington and with the silence of Ross and Jessop, the government denied garda incompetence or an insidious erosion of civil liberties. Rosemary supported Jim in his attempts to sue the gardaí for £600, but time was cruel and moved on, so people forgot and she herself probably never knew the outcome or saw Jim again. Did he drop out or was he perhaps rusticated? Many of her contemporaries had lost terms of credit or had been sent packing for lesser crimes. The newspaper headlines she and Jim and Dr Browne had enjoyed proved ephemeral, a point not lost on her seventeen years later when, gutsy and strident, she and her husband were beaten up by the police in Leicester Square and had to mount a five-year civil action for justice while totally abandoned by the media.

The Abbey Theatre was lurching toward a 1966 relaunch and Trinity Players Theatre was one of the best things in the city, inhabited as it was by some of the Slatterys crowd and future illuminati with whom Rosemary busked in 1964 on the banks of the Seine in Paris: Mike Bogdin (Bogdanov), Constantin de Goguel, Ranald Graham, Mike Newling, David Loxton and others. At the same time, Belfast-born poets Derek Mahon and Michael Longley were making their mark and winning literary prizes here, there and everywhere, and Hayden Murphy was touting his ground-breaking *Broadsheet* to pub literati.

And then there was the fracas over the debating societies. Admission of women to The Hist and Phil was hotly debated and painstakingly conceded only on a limited basis. Women were outnumbered five to one, endured segregated lunches in the Dining Hall and had to be off campus by sunset or face the wrath of Miss Bramble, Dean of Women Students and sister of TV's old man Steptoe – a rag-and-bone man. Never one to be left out, Rosemary crossdressed as a man and briefly penetrated the inner sanctum of The Hist before being unfrocked and unceremoniously ejected.

This antipathy toward women may have been fuelled by the copious quantities of Dr Collis Browne's cough mixture (precursor of mainstream drugs) consumed in the basement of the GMB, but that might be idle speculation.

Rosemary was omnipresent and omniprescient, poking fun at the pomposity of people and institutions, a walking iconoclast who could at the same time and without loss of logic collude with Simon Morgan, an incorrigible exhibitionist like herself. Simon was a sartorial clothes horse replete with cigarette-holder and Colt revolver, whose parties were guarded by bouncers in battledress behind barbed wire, and guests (except Rosemary) had to pay for admission – and yet people were still gagging to get in. Such was the passion of Simon for guns, gadgets and military equipment, and of Rosemary for craic and pranks that they were probably responsible for Dr Robert McDowall, the Junior Dean, famously scampering off across Front Square in fear of his life, after a gunshot with his name on it shattered his muttered musings.

This may explain why the cynics regarded Rosemary's jumping into a freezing and tidal Liffey in January 1963 to save a drowning dog as self-publicity (it was front-page news). When a few months later she did the same for a pigeon, they felt vindicated and suggested uncharitably that she had chucked the bird overboard herself. She certainly had a penchant for dogs (and underdogs) but her statement at the time of the garda dog affair clearly demonstrated her uncanny knack for being at the centre of things without ever planning it.

In 1963, Rosemary untypically kept a low profile when JFK, Ireland's favourite son, arrived to a tumultuous welcome. Across the land, cemeteries were scoured for distant Kennedy relatives, every Irishman wanted a piece of this rudely handsome man. Gone were memories of Cuba and the Bay of Pigs (and Merrion Square demos), and it was still too early for Vietnam draft-dodgers and protest singers Baez and Dylan to spoil JFK's parade or his post-Dublin proclamation at the Brandenburg Gate, 'Ich bin ein Berliner'. Thousands stood mesmerized on the Bank-of-Ireland steps, the old Irish Parliament opposite TCD, as the president's motorcade swept past, so close they felt they could touch 'yer man'. They could never have guessed his fine head and cheeks, flatteringly coloured by cortisone, were soon to be blown apart.

But inevitably the College-wide party resumed after an introspective and respectful pause. No exception, Rosemary helped fill a bath to the brim with a mixture of spirits on the top floor of No. 10 Front Square, an event that probably took place in the Bacchanalian rooms occupied by Laurie Howes and Sebastian Balfour, and sponsored by a minor aristocrat who later took himself off to the Arctic. This was a big advance on the prim, well-behaved cocktail parties in the Elizabethan Society in No. 6, where things barely took off after gallons of cheap sherry. The high jinks went on. There were all-night parties and funfairs on Lambay Island and Ireland's Eye. At an Islandbridge Boat Club Ball, one of the wags released the handbrake on Nick Rathbone's frog-eye sports car and the revellers watched in drunken disbelief from the balcony as, lights ablaze, it slipped down the jetty and gurgled quietly into the depths of the Liffey. Excess, in behaviour and in expense, was commonplace.

In late 1965, the French television service, RTF, tried surreptitiously to capture this profligacy in action. The three beautiful daughters of Dr Mitchell in Ballsbridge agreed to host a 'typical' party. From RTF's point of view, the sole aim, it later transpired, was to demonstrate and define on film the decadence that was Dublin and its undergraduates. Primed with generous fare from the film-makers, they did not disappoint. And yet these were the same young people who actively lauded Regis Debray and his mentor Che. RTF should rather have been introduced to an affluent George Frangopulous who made a habit of entertaining a dozen of Trinity's most stunning women to dinner, single-handedly and simultaneously, without the concept of ego entering his handsome head; or to whiskey heirs like Hugh Teacher or random heirs like Robert Heale who spent days at Leopardstown, the Curragh or Punchestown, returning only for a wine-tasting in the Kildare Street Club.

But life was not all quirky effete self-indulgence, and Trinity spawned many charities for Third World poverty. Diminutive Ian Angus walked to Belfast annually in around twenty-six hours for the Save The Children Fund and there were money-raising fasts at the foot of Nelson's Pillar. There was even a charity element in the Galloping Gonads Club IV at Trinity Regatta one year. This medical team's name was thought unprintable at the time, so it was switched to The Trogs and they wore leopard-skin loincloths and Beatles wigs in aid of something or other. Rosemary later founded a literacy society for Travellers and adopted waifs and strays by the dozen.

Most years the events of Trinity Week, culminating in the Ball and a last-minute scramble for partners, saw Ulick O'Connor at the College Races;

sportsman, socialite, political meddler and 'full of himself' man of letters; Lord Killanin at the Regatta, future International Olympics Committee Chairman from the Tribe of Galway; Conor Cruise O'Brien at the Garden Party, ex-TCD author, diplomat and UN Representative in the Congo; and of course de Valera popped in quite a few times – last seen as frail elder statesman lifting the turf for Trinity's Berkeley Library site. Rosemary always hoped to see her father's favourite there, Victor Bewley, an admirable Quaker and supplier of the best coffee in town. Who knows, he might even have relished the spectacle of Rosemary with a black bin-liner on her head and shoulders invading the Provost's Garden Party. It was, of course, a dig at the stuffiness of the occasion but great fun nonetheless, ending with a speechless Junior Dean being let into the secret of the identity of this girl with great legs by R.B.D. French, her English tutor from No. 23 (not that RBD knew her well, whispering as he did later at her graduation in the Exam Hall how pleased he was to meet her after all her years of non-attendance). Little wonder that Rosemary went on to be a professional clown and Ireland's first female member of the Magic Circle, or that she gelled so naturally in later life with her Hispanophile cousin and lapsed Methodist Ian Gibson, also a Fifties–Sixties Trinity man and born performer in books and lectures on Lorca and Dalí. No great surprise: they both had 'cojones' aplenty and loved to distract and entertain even if it was often egotistical.

Curiosity and *carpe diem* informed Rosemary's life, though she had never read Horace. When Rosemary invited you back for coffee, you instantly acquired three jobs: firstly, to push her car up and down the first dual carriageway in Ireland as far as Naas where her father Jack, a Protestant County Surgeon, worked in a hospital run by nuns who supported his substitution of hypnosis for anaesthesia; secondly, to help her father distribute his latest invention with the prototype name of 'heat blocks', lumps of turf soaked in sump oil for which the locals were desperate, central heating being still many thermbeats away (at the time of the Torrey Canyon disaster he demonstrated on Blessington reservoir the viability of using these blocks as wicks to burn off an oil slick); thirdly, to assist her dynamo dad in his operating theatre with whatever was needed. If you were lucky, you might get to see *Lawrence of Arabia* in a Phibsborough cinema in the evening, only to be recalled by a crudely etched message suddenly appearing on the screen telling the good doctor to call his hospital.

After her exams in the early summer of 1965, Rosemary blazed a trail to the Berlin Wall, hitch-hiking through the East-German road corridor. She returned fully expecting to have failed those exams but, having passed, she now had to face a world for which she was poorly prepared. She found it all very confusing and turned to Dr Sheehy-Skeffington for wisdom and guidance. He was kind but out of tune with her predicament. Her friend Brendan Kennelly recognized Yeats' 'pilgrim soul' in her and advised accordingly (he was later to supervise her M.Phil. on Patrick Kavanagh, passing her draft on to David Norris with an exasperated note saying, 'This is good but Rosemary is illiterate' [*sic*]). Her favourite Kavanagh line from 'Canal Bank Walk', 'Feed the gaping need of my senses, give me ad lib,' was going to be a hard aspiration to fulfil. She moved on, though she knew she would miss Ireland – 'the leafy-with-love banks, and the green waters of the canal pouring redemption' – but she returned before the decade closed, to have her children in Dublin.

Rosemary Gibson (TCD 1961–5; G.S.) became a social worker after post-graduate studies at the LSE, returning to TCD for an M.Phil. in 1970. She was married to Andrew Gibb (qv) for thirty years, having become a mother in 1970, a professional clown in 1980 and member of the Magic Circle in 1995. She died in 1997; David Norris wrote her obituary in **The Irish Times**.

Rosemary Gibson,
BA Commencements,
Front Square, TCD, 1966.

FIRST IMPRESSIONS

jeremy lewis

IN THE SUMMER of 1961 I was, to our mutual satisfaction, sacked from the advertising agency in Baker Street where I had been working for the past year as a junior trainee of startling ineptitude. I had no idea what to do next, but at some point a well-wisher suggested that although, a couple of years before, I had been rudely rebuffed by my father's Cambridge college, it might be worth my applying to Trinity College Dublin. I knew nothing about Ireland or Trinity, but hurried to the local library to remedy matters at once.

There I discovered that the College of the Holy and Undivided Trinity had been founded towards the end of the sixteenth century by Queen Elizabeth, was loosely modelled on its Cambridge namesake, and numbered among its alumni a gaggle of playwrights including Congreve, Goldsmith, Synge, Wilde and Beckett, and assorted literary men like Swift, Burke, Bishop Berkeley, Bram Stoker and Sheridan le Fanu. I gathered from my well-wisher that it was thought very 'wild', and was inhabited by the tweedy, chinless type of English schoolboy, much given to blowing hunting horns and being sick out of windows from a great height – and that it was possible to gain admission on the strength of O rather than A levels. It sounded like perfection, and I wrote off at once; but I received no acknowledgment from this ancient seat of learning, and turned my mind to other things.

I had long given up any idea of going to university when, in early October, a letter arrived bearing an Irish stamp. Inside was a letter from someone who signed off as the Senior Tutor of Trinity College Dublin: he informed me that he would be delighted to give me a place, that term began next day, and that I should report for duty at once if I wanted to take advantage of his offer. Redemption was suddenly at hand, and I needn't worry about earning my keep for another four years. That evening I set out for Euston, heavily encumbered with luggage, and feeling not unlike a Victorian traveller *en route* for darkest Africa. Despite my Geography A level and the Irish stamp, I wasn't sure whether Dublin was in the North or the Republic. Which part of the island was I heading for? Would I be needing the passport my mother had so carefully packed beneath my underpants?

I settled into a dimly lit compartment of the London-to-Holyhead train, and opened *Mr Sponge's Sporting Tour*. The spirit of adventure, never strong at the best of times, ebbed away in the half-light, and I was engulfed by the same feelings of homesickness that, only a couple of years earlier, had marked me out as the Wettest Boy in the School, sobbing into my copy of the *New Statesman* as the train drew out of Paddington. My only companion was a cheerful, red-faced Irishman in a knobbly white jersey. 'Trinity, eh?' he exclaimed, after examining the labels I had pasted on my suitcases. 'By God,' he said, 'they'll have your guts for garters,' and disappeared in the direction of the bar, chuckling to himself in a gratified manner. He returned shortly after, clutching several bottles of stout and a scotch egg; and as the train hurtled through the Midlands on its way to Anglesey he described with hideous relish the misdeeds of Trinity students, till my head reeled with tales of mass intoxication and the smashing of windows and undergraduates being chased across Dublin by gardaí wielding clubs the size of baseball bats.

At one o'clock we arrived in Holyhead, and I humped my luggage aboard the Dún Laoghaire steamer. The Celtic world lay all about me in the darkness: swarthy, diminutive North Walians in blue jerseys and Wellington boots; beefy red-faced labourers from Roscommon or Mayo, the mud of Coventry or Camden Town still sticking to their boots, tossing down pint after pint of Guinness at the bar and singing songs of a kind I had never heard before; censorious young seminarians in black macs and Homburg-hats, with pursed lips and sunken eyes, thankful to be leaving behind them the soil of heathen England; waxen-featured nuns looking queasy and cross-eyed, but refusing to exchange the smoky, sweaty squalor of the second-class bar for a breath of fresh air on deck. I felt, as I was often to feel in the future, large, blonde, conspicuous and irremediably Anglo-Saxon.

I remember little of the four-hour crossing. Greatly daring, I joined the red-faced labourers at the bar and ordered, in a low mumble, the first of the several thousand pints of Dublin stout that were to flow down my throat over the next four years. I treated myself to a pork pie and a cold sausage roll, washed down with another pint of the same. Like a true Englishman, I disdained the steamed-up lounge with its background chorus of retching and groaning, and strode round and round the deck – noticing as I did so a handsome, strong-featured girl in a corduroy coat, with auburn hair, an exciting-looking bosom and, in one hand, a copy of *The Tin Drum*, which she was incapable of reading in the darkness and the Force Five gale. With her wide mouth and high cheek-bones and hair lashing about her face, she looked like a duplicate Brigitte Bardot who had been parachuted on deck: I fell instantly in love with this radiant apparition, and remained so for the next eighteen months. And at about six on a rainswept, silver-grey morning I caught my first sight of a view that would, in days to come, move me more than once to tears of joy and regret: the delicate, elegant cones of the Dublin hills and the Wicklow Mountains to the south and, to the north, Howth Head and the great sweep of Dublin Bay.

An hour or so later I had trundled into Dublin aboard a foreign-feeling black-and-orange train, examined a notice in Amiens Street Station warning Irish girls about the perils of London life and giving the addresses of priests in Hammersmith and Kentish Town, and deposited my cases in the left-luggage office. I felt hungover, underslept and ruinously indigested: the long night, the Guinness and the pork pie; it was still raining, and, for all its seedy elegance, Dublin seemed to exude a whiff of stale stout and old socks. I wandered into Trinity, and the graceful Georgian squares looked sombre and granitic in the chilly morning light, with the odd unshaven figure groping its way in a dressing-gown, towel over one arm and spongebag in hand, towards the College Baths, where enormous enamel tubs could be found, with claws at each corner and vast copper taps belching boiling water, and the steam-laden air was loud with rugger buggers' voices raised in song. I spotted someone I'd known at school coming towards me and, feeling too reduced to reintroduce myself, I dodged behind a pillar till he had disappeared; I bought a postcard of Front Square – the sky a cobalt blue, the grass a fluorescent lime – and wrote home to the effect that Dublin seemed a hell-hole, and that they should expect me back any moment.

Quite how I spent the rest of that day, God only knows, but at some stage in the proceedings I was allocated digs in Blackrock. Mrs Todd was a grey-haired, garrulous, motherly woman, kindliness made flesh: as I soon discovered, she displayed a positive enthusiasm for washing out our socks and underpants, and hanging them out to dry in the family kitchen, and for cooking us enormous high teas of fried eggs, black pudding, bacon and fried potato bread, with never a glimpse of fresh fruit or veg (these, it seemed, were almost impossible to obtain in the Dublin of the 1960s, and were restricted to the occasional wilting cabbage and tin of carrots in corner shops selling cigarettes, newspapers and the best white bread I had ever eaten, baked by Messrs Johnson, Mooney and O'Brien). The Todds were Protestants, and seemed to regard the establishment of the Republic as a temporary aberration, at the end of which the telephone and pillar boxes could be painted red once more, and normal life resumed. Mr Todd was a silent, genial man who spent his days watching BBC television – coming in on the train that morning, I had been impressed by the outsize television aerials on top of the houses, bending in the direction of Wales like arms stretched out in supplication – and he told me that, far from being kings of Ireland, his family had originated in Teddington, and that their daughter Sylvia had recently landed a job with the Swastika Laundry in St Stephen's Green.

Next morning I took another black-and-orange train into the middle of Dublin, and strolled with a nonchalant, proprietorial air through the back gate of Trinity, past the playing fields, and into the main body of the College. How different it seemed from the day before! The sun was shining; the whiff of stout drifting down Dame Street from the Guinness factory seemed pregnant with raffish promise; the undergraduates looked and sounded delightfully urbane and well turned-out, with tightly waisted tweed jackets, mustard-coloured corduroy trousers and a Woosterish absence of chins much in evidence, and loud, self-confident, reassuringly familiar Home Counties accents cutting imperiously across the alien accents of the Ulstermen and the melodious burrs of the men from the South. I found the Ulstermen particularly baffling, never having come across their kind before, and I assumed at first I must have stumbled on a nest of exiled Glaswegians. Many of them wore green blazers with a boar's head emblazoned on the breast pocket in silver filigree; they had a curiously post-war look, with much Brylcreem in evidence and the gnarled, rather shiny features I remembered from my childhood in London in the 1940s. Beside them – and the equally knobbly, equally diffident Southern Irish – the English looked well-fed, dashing, opulent and (to the native eye, no doubt) intolerably arrogant, overbearing and loud, as they revved up their MGs in the middle of the night, and bayed at one another across the Dublin streets. They also, as I soon learnt, behaved much worse than the Irish, reversing the stereotypes of the fierce, drunken Irishman and the quiet, diffident Anglo-Saxon, and exciting much pursing of the lips and twitching of curtains in what was, for all its flamboyant reputation, an eminently respectable city.

I had enrolled to read History, and after cross-examining a bottle-nosed College porter, togged out in a tail-coat and black jockey's cap, I made my way to a lecture hall in the Museum Building, a draughty mid-Victorian monstrosity swathed in marble acanthus leaves and greatly admired by John Ruskin. My fellow scholars, I was glad to note, included the auburn-haired girl with the exciting-looking bosom who had made such a strong impression on the Holyhead boat – her name, I later discovered, was ffiona, spelt with two small 'ff's – and my future room-mate Ian Whitcomb, who boasted a stammer, prehensile fingers and a rolling gait. Four years later, he crowded our rooms in Botany Bay with agents and impresarios after a song he had written and performed had risen to No. 5 on the American hit parade.

The door of the lecture hall was eventually flung open with a theatrical bang, and a figure bearing a striking resemblance to Ludwig van Beethoven strode on stage. This was T.W. Moody, the Professor of History, and he had come to initiate us into the mysteries of his craft. Clutching the lapels of his gown in either hand, and fixing his gaze on a gargoyle on the ceiling above us, he began to intone in a rich, resonant brogue. 'History,' he informed us, much to our surprise, 'is the past,' and he continued in this vein for the next three-quarters of an hour before disappearing as abruptly as he had entered. As we would soon discover, the work expected of dons and undergraduates, and relations between the two parties, were more reminiscent of eighteenth-century Oxford than contemporary Oxbridge: terms were six weeks long; although we were expected to snooze our way through a certain number of lectures, we were seldom asked to write more than two essays a year, and these were returned (if at all) a term later than that in which they had been written; for English students at least, visits to one's tutor were restricted to a termly call asking for his signature on a form entitling one to discounts on flights between Dublin and London.

In the square outside, we gathered – automatically, it seemed – into little groups, each of us instinctively recognizing that to which he or she belonged: the English public schoolboys, many of them sporting modish suede or corduroy jackets, the green-blazered Ulstermen, and the Catholic Irish, a third of the total, who had received special dispensations from the Archbishop of Dublin to attend this hotbed of Orangemen, West Britons and undesirable aliens from over the water. Additional interest was provided by some Nigerians, looking ill-at-ease in blazers and cavalry-twill trousers with creases so rigid that the trousers would almost certainly have stood up by themselves if called upon to do so; a middle-aged Copt in his ninth year reading agriculture, who made a beeline for the girl with the auburn hair and the bosom; and the occasional American from the Midwest – clad in a beret, black mac, jeans and gym shoes, clutching a copy of *Le Nouvel Observateur* and wearing a smile of goofy benevolence – who had read deeply in J.P. Donleavy's *The Ginger Man*, and had hurried over to Dublin in the hope of re-enacting its hero's fabulous misdeeds.

AFTER LONDON, Dublin seemed engagingly small and rural: I felt as though I had suddenly been thrust into the company of garrulous, weatherbeaten, tweed-clad farmers after consorting with sombre City gents in bowlers, black jackets and chalk-striped trousers. Whereas London buildings were still blackened with grim and grit, their Dublin equivalents, though tending to decrepitude, retained their ruddy, youthful glow; the air was sweet with the whiff of burning peat; while London seemed to stretch on forever, the Dublin hills loomed up at the end of Fitzwilliam Street – that mighty and, as yet, unviolated sweep of Georgian terraced houses – like some gigantic stage prop that had been wheeled out to keep Dubliners' urban aspirations firmly in place.

The great town houses of the Anglo-Irish in Merrion and Fitzwilliam Squares, with their enormous intricate fanlights and Italian plasterwork and huge sash windows, seemed grander and more elegant than anything one might find in Belgravia or Bloomsbury, yet the city had something rancid or rotten about it, as though it had been built on a shifting, unstable compost of straw and horses' messes and dead rats and old tweed jackets and alcoholic beverages. Every now and then, or so we read in the vigorous local papers, the front would fall out of some decrepit Georgian terrace on the north side of the city, crashing into the street and exposing the inmates to view as they were eating a meal or climbing into bed or the bath or straining eagerly forward to pick out *This is Your Life* on a flickering black-and-white television set. The houses round about would be propped up with great triangles made of wood, and life would continue as before. Everywhere was in walking distance, and I liked nothing better than to poke about this beautiful, battered city, strolling down the quays that ran on either side of the Liffey – a diminutive, strong-smelling stream, liked a miniature Thames or Seine, lined with plain-featured merchants' houses and pedimented public buildings – or venturing into spacious, immaculate suburbs inhabited by retired colonial officers and the dentists with which Dublin seemed so richly endowed.

Trinity itself had the look of a large and agreeably coarse-grained Oxbridge college, which had commandeered a large area in the middle of Dublin, within hailing distance of the river in one direction and Grafton Street in another. Designed by Sir William Chambers, the main frontage, which looked up Dame Street towards the Guinness brewery and Christ Church Cathedral, was massive, benign and grey, with a faded blue clock in the middle of its pediment; beneath the clock was the Front Gate, manned at all hours by the porters in jockey caps, where enquiring undergraduates could read notices about Gaelic clubs, hurling matches, a cricket tour of southern England, a meeting of Fianna Fáil students or a debate at which Reginald Maudling would bend his mind to some aspect of British domestic politics. It was here that the loud and hectoring English minority gathered before lunch to look each other up and down before heading off to the pub; among the regulars was the middle-aged Copt, hurrying helpfully forward to relieve the better-looking girls of their heavy loads of books.

Beyond Front Gate was a large, cobbled square that contained, in addition to dons' and undergraduates' rooms leading off staircases, a Church-of-Ireland chapel, an equally elegant Examination Hall, a Hogarthian Dining Hall and, Trinity's answer to King's College Chapel, the great blackened Library, reeking of ancient leatherbound volumes, with its huge barrel-vaulted ceiling, marble busts of Greek philosophers and Irish bishops, and the famous Book of Kells, on one page of which Queen Victoria had thoughtfully signed her name. Towards the back of Front Square stood the Campanile, with allegorical women in helmets at each corner: it came into its own in the summer term, when ticketless undergraduates, wearing dinner jackets, concealed themselves in its heights on the afternoon of the Trinity Ball, letting themselves down on a rope as soon as it was safe to do so and strolling off to join in the merriment. Behind the Campanile were the Rubrics, red-brick late-seventeenth-century buildings with a line of Dutch gables running along the top: they were the oldest buildings in Trinity, and rooms there were sought after by bachelor dons and influential sportsmen. In those days – things have changed greatly since – two or three undergraduates, all male, would share a set of rooms, made of a sitting-room, two bedrooms and a miniature kitchen consisting of a gas ring and a sink: as in an Oxbridge college or the Inns of Court, the sets led off a staircase, at the bottom of which was a lavatory and a black notice board giving the names and floors of the various occupants.

On the other side of Front Square to the Library stood an Edwardian monstrosity, the Graduates' Memorial Building, housing solitary rooms for the lonely or misanthropic, snooker tables, a telephone box, and the reading rooms of the rival debating societies, The Phil and The Hist. Most undergraduates joined one of these self-important bodies in their first term, attending the occasional debate – in which elderly-looking undergraduates wore white bow ties and medals, clutched their lapels and banged gavels – and using the reading rooms to shelter from the rain. These sombre, soporific rooms, with their grimy plate-glass windows and ancient leather armchairs and copies of *Punch* and the *Field* and the *Irish Tatler* in maroon leather folders and steel engravings of Burke and Mr Gladstone, were haunted by aspiring Irish politicians and by trainee clubmen, snoozing the afternoon away with their hands crossed over their paunches and copies of *The Irish Times* covering their faces: the silence was broken only by snores, the sudden grunt of one who was rudely awakened, the buzzing of flies against the glass, the gentle tick of the clock, and an occasional rumble of conversation as two seemingly middle-aged undergraduates – both wearing mud-coloured suits with leather patches on the elbows, and both inclining to corpulence – discussed in measured tones the issues of the day.

Behind the GMB stood Botany Bay, the grimmest of Trinity's three squares. The grass in the middle had been asphalted over and turned into a tennis court, and the buildings themselves were austere and barrack-like, built of Wicklow stone the colour of grey worsted. Altogether more congenial was New Square, which lay behind the Rubrics: it had been built in the 1820s, exuded levity and light, and boasted a grass court in its middle. Between these two squares stood a tiny Greek temple, which housed the University Press. Unlike its more ambitious equivalents in Oxford and Cambridge, it had no aspirations beyond printing the university calendar and examination papers: we liked to believe that it was sporadically raided by undergraduates anxious to learn what lay in store for them. Beyond New Square were the games fields, echoing to hearty cries and the horrid thwack of boot on ball; and between the Library and Nassau Street was the Fellows' Garden, built over after my day for a new library building.

Sealed off from the rest of Dublin by a high stone wall surmounted by sharply pointed iron rails, Trinity was benign, tolerant, indolent and indifferent, a place in which the idle and the industrious, the bright and the astonishingly dim, ex-National Servicemen and Catholic boys and girls from Mayo or County Cork were left to sink or swim together. I came to love it more than any other institution or set of buildings I have ever known, and the genial ambivalence and absence of gravitas that were so strong a feature of Trinity life left me, like so many of its graduates, hopelessly adrift once the gates of Paradise had clanged to behind us.

MY ROOM-MATE, David Shaw, was a keen carouser, and we particularly enjoyed our visits to the Brazen Head, an antique, rather English-looking pub in the maze of streets between St Patrick's Cathedral and the river. It doubled up as a residential hotel, peopled for the most part by elderly gentlemen who had come down in the world – and by Trinity's finest poet, Derek Mahon, who

was rumoured to have lived there for an entire term. Deep inside this dilapi-
dated hostelry was a small, gloomy bar, kippered with smoke and lit only by
a yellowing skylight, in which elderly Irishmen in cloth caps and ankle-length
overcoats spent their evenings drinking Jameson and stout, and singing those
infinitely sad, infinitely moving songs with which the Irish, unlike the English,
are so enviably endowed. I found that these songs were guaranteed to bring
out the goose pimples, and wished, as a very obvious Englishman, that I could
either fade into the furniture, decrepit as it was, or suddenly stumble on a
cache of unexpected Irish ancestors, so enabling me to look the old-timers in
the eye as they sang steadily on about the villainies of England and the suffer-
ings of Ireland.

And, of course, Ireland and its history were beginning to prove wonderfully
seductive. How easily we sympathized with those waves of Normans, Flemings,
Welshmen, English and Scots who, within minutes of their arrival, had become
(or so our lecturers told us) *hiberniores ipsis hibernicis.* Or, having the best of
both worlds, like the angular, weatherbeaten Anglo-Irish one spotted striding
down Grafton Street in riding macs and Old Etonian ties, or like Trinity's own
crop of gaitered clergymen – Irish to the English and English to the Irish! Who
could fail to be moved by Ireland's melancholy, haunted history, by the hieratic
chanting of Synge, by the plangent music of Scán Ó Riada (Ireland's Bartok, and
surely a far greater composer than many of those celebrated in these discordant
times), or even the mighty tub of mediaeval Irish butter – an ancient antecedent
of Kerrygold – that had been dug out of the Bog of Allen and could be seen,
along with Celtic crosses and buckles and shields, in the National Museum of
Ireland. Who could doubt that Yeats was the greatest of poets, or that 'the fore-
most of those that I would hear praised' bore an unmistakeable resemblance to
the girl with the auburn hair and the exciting-looking bosom?

As we began to discover the country about us, our academic aspirations
withered in the undemanding Irish air. Stubbs' *Charters* lay unopened and
unmourned; 'Was Early Irish Society Society Tribal? Discuss' remained a matter
of permanent indifference. The garrulous, genial charms of Dublin pub life
lured us from the paths of virtue, and we staggered home to Blackrock reeking
of stout and excess. Mrs Todd took all this in good part, clapping her hands
together then summoning Mr Todd from the television set as David Shaw,

overcome by alcoholic fumes, slid under the dining table just as she was about to serve us the evening's quota of black pudding and potato bread. We were beginning to find, and lose, our feet: all Ireland, and the future, lay before us.

Adapted from *Playing for Time* (London: Collins, 1987).

Jeremy Lewis (TCD 1961–5; History) worked for many years in publishing, and was a director of Chatto & Windus. Now a freelance writer, he is commissioning editor of **The Oldie**, and editor-at-large of the **Literary Review**. He has written biographies of Cyril Connolly, Tobias Smollett and Allen Lane, and is currently writing a book about the Greene family for publication by Jonathan Cape in 2010. His literary memoirs, **Grub Street Irregular**, were published by HarperCollins in 2008; the two previous volumes, **Playing for Time** and **Kindred Spirits**, are available in Faber's print-on-demand list (www.faberfinds.co.uk).

TURNING CARTWHEELS

deborah de vere white

BEING A CATHOLIC, I needed a 'dispensation' to go to Protestant Trinity College. Dispensations were granted by Archbishop John Charles McQuaid, Primate of All Ireland, who lived beside the convent school I went to in the 1950s. His residence in Killiney overlooked the school grounds and according to legend his secretary would telephone the convent to complain whenever a pupil was seen turning a cartwheel. Perhaps there was a cartwheel rota posted up in the episcopal residence and his staff took turns spying through the windows on our playground during break times.

There was no official method of applying for a dispensation. My father would have to write a letter putting my case as persuasively as he could. Something along the lines of 'My daughter likes the Trinity buildings and has always wanted to study there,' was not going to carry much weight. But we held a trump card: one of my younger brothers wanted to be a doctor – his attendance at the Catholic university UCD (essential if he wanted to work in Catholic Dublin hospitals) would be 'offered up', in compensation for mine. It was a classic Faustian pact.

Two other pupils who also went to Trinity from the same convent were Joyce Blake Kelly, who became president of the Lawrentian Society, an organization that catered for the pastoral needs of Catholic students (named presumably after the saint who was burnt to death on a gridiron, rather than D.H.), and, a few years later, the poet Eavan Boland. Did Eavan's father, who had been president of the United Nations, also write a begging letter to the Archbishop for permission to send his daughter to Trinity? It's hard to imagine.

The early 1960s were vintage years for poetry at Trinity, thanks to that triumvirate of great poets Mike Longley and Derek Mahon, both Northerners, and Brendan Kennelly, a Kerryman. Brendan took part in the only meeting of the Lawrentian Society I ever attended, a poetry reading held during my first term at No. 6 Front Square, the preserve of female students. He had sky-blue eyes, colossal gleaming brow and a voice like shifting shingle – the Poet incarnate. Another poet, Rudi Holtzapfel, shared the billing that night. Rudi had written a poem that included 'a brown moon'. He explained that you could say this sort of thing in poetry – it was poetic license. Afterwards I walked out of No. 6 on air – under a brown moon.

My next poetic revelation came through Alec Reid, a large, tousled albino with an endearing lopsided grin. He paced to and fro in the ground-floor lecture room in the Geography Building, head tilted to one side, as he threw out the big question: What is poetry? Whatever lifts the hairs on the back of your neck while you're shaving? Sends shivers down your spine? Gets lost in translation? For answer he quoted Belloc's 'Tarantella', from start to finish.

> Do you remember an Inn,
> Miranda?
> Do you remember an Inn?
> And the tending and the spreading
> Of the straw for a bedding,
> And the fleas that tease in the High Pyrenees,
> And the wine that tasted of tar? …

It was a hair-raising, spine-tingling, unforgettable performance. Reid gave us one more lecture and then disappeared. I never knew why. A few years after leaving College I had a nightmare that I was being forced to attend a student protest in Front Square when all I wanted to do was be in the Reading Room. This never happened. I had the good luck to be at Trinity before students became politicized by events in Paris in 1968, and the Troubles in the North, which were to overshadow the future lives of students from the province, would not start until the end of the decade. The early Sixties was a period of irresponsibility and innocence, hilariously summed up afterwards by Jeremy Lewis in his autobiographical *Playing for Time*. We were free to concentrate on poetry, or plays, or whatever turned us on. 'Turning on' had a special significance for Trinity-goers thanks to pop star Ian Whitcomb, who was reading History. My future husband, an American, was dead impressed that I knew the singer of the US pop chart hit 'You know you really turn me on'.

Like other Dubliners, I inevitably had a different experience of College life from that of my friends who were mostly from Northern Ireland or England. I felt sorry for girls who lived in Trinity Hall, the austere female residence out in the suburbs, with a driveway and communal dining-room. Only male students had rooms in College; that I took for granted. What I envied were the students who lived in attics and garrets in Fitzwilliam and Merrion Squares, or flats overlooking the canal in Wilton Terrace, or on Pembroke Road – flats filled with stained mugs, stray pyjamas and the sound of Joan Baez; even grotty, formica-fitted flats above groceries in parts of the city that I only ever saw at night represented bohemian living and independence.

Instead I lived with my family on Strand Road, near the scene of the Nausicaa episode in *Ulysses*; Ringsend lay at the far end of the strand and Molly Bloom's Howth was across the bay. A short bus ride took me to Front Gate but what a rotten service it was – the 7, 7A and 8 to Dalkey and ludicrously named Sallynoggin. Occasionally I walked home in the small hours, crept indoors and up to my room – past my parents' open bedroom door. They never gave any indication that they were listening out for me. Perhaps I fool myself that they were.

Having the use of a largish house and garden so near College meant that I could ask friends home and throw subsidized parties. I would have liked those parties to have been wilder than they were. But one must have come close because at 6 am some of us looked out of the living room window and saw Derek Mahon in the garden, turning circles in the tall wet grass. Perhaps he was baying future poems to the dawn.

For the days are long –
From the first milk van
To the last shout in the night,
An eternity …

We hauled him in and up the stairs, past the open bedroom door, and laid him on a bed, like Chatterton.

Sometimes the overlap between College and home life became farcical. At around midnight on one occasion, during a party at the top of a house just off Merrion Square, I was knocking back plonk – and, I suppose, droning on about poetry, while struggling internally with far more carnal preoccupations – when a verbal telegram travelled up the many flights of stairs. 'Terence de Vere White is here for Deborah. He's come to take her home. Tell her her dad's here …' Down I slunk, past entwined couples, smokers squeezed side by side on the stairs, sophisticated drinkers on the landings, and out into the cold air and ignominious Morris Minor. The flip side was I had the use of said Morris whenever I wanted, and no one seemed to worry about what condition I was in when I drove it.

Giving parties in the parental home was not the same thing as throwing parties with friends. One Shrove Tuesday Suzanne Lowry and Hilary Laurie – we often shared tutorials – tossed pancakes for multitudes in rooms in Front Square – the ones shared by Laurie Howes and Sebastian Balfour, I think. At the time I could not even whisk up a batter.

In 1963 during my stint as editor of *TCD*, I heard about the assassination of President Kennedy on my way back from the typesetters. The mood at that night's party in a basement in Lower Mount Street was sombre.

Editing the College magazines, *Icarus* and *TCD*, was a privilege and a delight. I was entranced by the hot metal process – the blocks of type laid in reverse, lead spacing bars, the measuring terms pica and point, and the variety of typefaces with their ornamental colophons and dingbats. This fascination stayed with me and proved useful when I eventually went into journalism and caught the last days of typesetting, page layouts and galley proofs, just before the switchover to computers.

While I was seeing the magazine to bed at the typesetters, my father was doing a similar job a few streets away at *The Irish Times* where he was literary editor. He had no interest in the mechanics of printing but he loved the newspaper world that he had courageously moved to in his forties. He was a solicitor by training but a writer by vocation, rising at five every morning to write his novels. One morning, deciding he did not want to spend another day in a solicitor's office, he walked into *The Irish Times* and asked for a job. He came out an hour later as literary editor and from then on threw himself into producing an excellent, up-to-the-minute book review page every Saturday. His miniscule office was piled high with review copies and any time I looked in he would say, 'See anything you like? Take it, go on, take it.' I'm sure he said the same to everyone who came through the door. There weren't many outlets for publishing poetry in Dublin then, so Trinity poets submitted their poems to *The Irish Times* and many must have seen their work appear on that Saturday page.

With a conspicuous surname like 'de Vere White' anonymity was not an option in a city the size of Dublin. But there were (depending on your point of view) compensations. Coming up to exam time, my father would become thoughtful. 'Imm. Fine's book has just come in on Roman antiquities. Who lectures you on Roman history? Parkes, is it?' Or: 'OUP have produced a handsome volume on Virgil's *Eclogues* – one for Wormell, I think. And there's a lovely little edition of Shakespeare's sonnets – do you think Phillip Edwards would like to have it?' And so on, up to and after my exams. The words, 'That should swing it,' were left unspoken. I hope my lecturers laughed; I still do.

The subject I chose to read, Ancient and Modern, had been devised to give women a qualification to teach Latin. Few girls' schools in Ireland taught both Latin and Greek, and consequently very few women students read Classics. Allowing students to combine a modern language with a classical language got around this difficulty. The Classics School was in the far corner of New Court, next to the playing fields. Far fewer students enrolled in it, compared with the numbers in the English or Modern Language Schools. I felt I had the best of two worlds, one neatly fitted into a couple of small obscure rooms – set texts, dead language, no tricky questions, few students, gowns frequently worn. The other, English Literature, was an amorphous sprawling mass of subject matter and personalities, scattered across the campus, constantly splintering and regrouping; gowns were not in evidence, jeans were. It was Ying and Yang before I'd ever smelled a joss stick. I enjoyed both subjects and I blessed the system that placed exams at the end of the summer vacation, leaving us free to enjoy term times and swot during the summer months when the place was empty.

The buildings, which had made me want to come to Trinity in the first place, never failed to raise my spirits each time I stepped through Front Gate. The city within a city was a model of architectural harmony; the grounds were spacious and Arcadian, cut off from everyday Dublin. In 1964, the year before I left, a young London-based architect, Paul Koralech, won a competition to design a new library for Trinity. His photograph was all over the Irish papers, and I sensed how significant the prize must be for him at the beginning of his career. But the new library, and the other new buildings that followed, necessitated by the growing numbers of students, compromised the unclut-tered spaciousness that went with lounging on lawns and end-of-term garden parties. I'm glad I was there before the place started to change.

A final word about the dispensation and Archbishop McQuaid. I did, of course, lose my faith while I was at Trinity – but not because I was at Trinity. It happened during the term when we were reading 'De Rerum Natura' by Lucretius. Professor Wormell, palms held reverently either side of the lectern, intoned the sonorous Latin:

> Sic rerum summa novatur
> Semper, et inter se mortales mutua vivunt …

Don't worry about mortality, it's all a matter of atoms, atoms we are and unto atoms we shall return, is the gist of Lucretius' message. I was standing in front of a statue of George Bernard Shaw outside the entrance to the National Gallery the moment it happened. GBS had nothing to do with it, I simply stopped believing in God. Or, as McQuaid would have put it, I lost my faith. I should have turned a cartwheel.

Deborah Singmaster (née de Vere White; TCD 1961–5; Ancient and Modern) first taught English in Florence. She then moved to London, where she has edited films, has been Orchid Attendant at Kew, visited China for the 1989 uprising, and has written for architectural journals. She now produces audio guides to walks in London and elsewhere (www.footnotesaudiowalks.co.uk). She is married to an American mathematician, with one daughter, and one grandson, Hector.

REMEMBRANCE OF THINGS PISSED

tom haran

Oft in the still night I remember our wasted youth
Derek Mahon from 'To Eugene Lambe in Heaven'

'I am William Fitzhugh. I was here for Horse Show week in August, and there is only one pub to go to and that is The Bailey. We shall all meet there at lunchtime tomorrow.' Thus said the amiable figure who stood in front of the fireplace of the digs at which I had arrived on a wet October night in 1961. He wore a dark double-breasted suit and an old Etonian tie. His natural authority was beyond challenge and so it was that I first turned left on Grafton Street and entered the open doors of 2–3, Duke Street.

The Bailey, a former Georgian coaching inn with a facade of dark red wood, had a main bar and a back bar entered via a little staircase. The bars were connected internally, but the clientel of each was entirely different. The back bar was used by louche students and the front by even more louche citizens, often of a literary tenue, quietly and courteously marshalled by the patron and former editor of *Envoy*, John Ryan. There was a Fish Bar, managed by the elegant and appropriately named Mr Salmon. Behind was the gentlemen's cloakroom, where, clad in a green ceremonial coat with enormous epaulettes, huge brass buttons and much frogging, Luke held dominion. He would disconcertingly apply a moulting clothes brush to the shoulders of clients standing at the urinal, the while bewailing the frigidity of the economic climate. One learnt that he would desist if tipped fairly regularly. As a guide to the tip expected he placed a shilling piece on a plate on a small table by the door. This coin was found to be glued to the plate and the plate was fastened to the table. The table was assumed to be screwed to the floor. On entering the back bar one felt like a newcomer to a party in progress. There were in fact several parties in progress, not necessarily connected, in fact mutually antagonistic. The dominant faction, in noise made, at least, was a group of English exiles known abusively as the Bloodies. Archie Orr Ewing, with spectrally translucent skin; Peter Rudland, known, for his exhibitionistic flatulence, as the Rifter; Daniel Arthur Swan Corbett, a small swaggering man with little grey teeth that glinted like the inside of an oyster shell; Hamish Riley Smith, who would grab another's crossword puzzle and, amusingly, write 'cunt', 'arse', 'balls', in the vacant boxes.

The Bloodies had a rigid dress code: 'One should dress for Trinity as one would for an end of season point-to-point in North Wales.' They were mildly patronizing and condescending to the native ascendancy but were secretly rather impressed (most of them came from not-very-big houses with little or no land). The ascendants were gratified to encounter such confident exemplars of the maternal culture but were quietly appalled by the crassness and crudity of their separated brethren. Although there was little interaction between the back and the front bars – a conversation between Riley Smith and Patrick Kavanagh is difficult to imagine – I was sitting in the front bar when an older man introduced himself as 'Perkins, Colonel RIC'. He then recounted unlikely military reminiscences in a voice of impossible blimpishness. He ended each sentence with an explosive 'Sah!' I escaped to the back bar where I later learned that Colonel Perkins was in reality the novelist Liam O'Flaherty, author of *The Informer*, whose service as private soldier in the Irish Guards in the Great War had given him a compelling need to irritate young men who spoke with a certain kind of English voice.

Another faction centred around Hamilton Good. Hamilton was a large handsome man with a wide smile of disorganized dentition, unimproved by his habit of opening bottles of stout with his jaws. He was known as the Gaffer, an honorific bestowed upon him at Portora Royal School. One year at Trinity taught him that student life, properly lived, was expensive, so he spent three years planting rubber in Malaya and returned with sufficient 'spondulicks' and a red MGA. In The Bailey he appointed himself master of the revels, demanding explanations for absences from the bar, awarding plaudits or demerits for conduct while drinking or drunk, and issuing invitations to other people's parties. As lunchtime melted into afternoon, the Gaffer would muster a platoon and march them to 'the Funnies' in the Grafton Cinema. This mixture of cartoons and Gaelic newsreel lasted seventy-five minutes, enabling the platoon to be marched back down to The Bailey, re-opened after the holy hour.

My father arrived in Dublin and insisted on seeing 'this Bailey place', which I had mentioned so often. He was persistent so I gauged that 4.30 pm, when the lunchtimers had dispersed and the evening crowd uninstalled, would be the time least freighted with potential for embarrassment. As we entered the back bar, an undispersed David Crumlin-Jones, a Hiberno-Spaniard of vile personal habits and worse appearance, stumbled forward. Crumbling Bones' bleary eyes assessed the situation. I had clearly hooked some old pervert and was conning him for drinks. He would join in the fun.

'Introduce me to your friend,' my father said.

'David, this is my father.'

'Father! That's a good one. We'll take this fool for all he's got,' he whispered deafeningly. 'I'll have a large brandy.' Salvation appeared in the form of the Gaffer coming up the little stairs. And in a suit! God bless him!

'Here is my friend Hamilton Good. I think we should have an early supper in the Fish Bar.'

'Will you join us, Hamilton?' My father did not include Bones in the party.

'A grey pleashure, Doctor.' Then I remembered. The drunken bastard was inclined, if he had been up all night drinking and on to the early houses in the morning, to return to his digs after lunch, bathe, shave, put on his best threads, and go back into action. In the little Fish Bar, the Gaffer tried to engage my father in discussion. Dad tolerated the long silences and the garbled sense. After about three hundred years, Gaffer thanked my father and shambled away. I awaited his response with leaden dread. My father sighed and said the Gaffer was a decent sort underneath. He then recalled a story from his own student days about a Church-of-Ireland rector whose son was at Trinity. Missing a train to his distant parish, he called unheralded at his son's digs. He rang the bell and enquired if John Saunders lived there.

'Indeed he does,' said the careworn landlady. 'Loosen his collar and leave him in the hall.'

The speed with which the news of a party spread was impressive. Standing outside the bar with half a dozen stout in a brown paper bag under one's arm, the message came. 'Party. Basement 27, Pembroke Road. Say Sheilah invited you.' No information was sought or given as to the purpose of the party – a twenty-first birthday, an engagement, a farewell to someone joining a religious order. So many kitchens jammed with non-nationals in overcoats – overcoats on winter nights were regarded as common property, like bicycles in Amsterdam, and it was unwise to disrobe – singing witless rugby songs while the hostess stood aghast or more often nobly trying to feed this mob of unknown choristers. Next to playing the spoons, the Gaffer liked above all to sing. His voice was admired but not always his lyrics ('Dan, Dan, the Lavatory Man'). One night I saw him conduct a group including the usual Bloodies, a Wykehamist, a Malvernian and two Home Counties Old Harrovians in the full-throated singing of 'The Boys of Kilmichael' with the variorum last couplet: 'For the boys of Kilmicheal were waiting with hand grenades, rifles and shot / And the Irish Republican Army made shite of the whole bloody lot.' A profound cultural achievement.

The Trinity Ball took place in late May. The tickets were limited and expensive, but the Ball was popular with Dublin socialites. A front-bar regular had a printing business and on the night of the Ball, tickets with the correct legend, printed on both sides of the card of the correct colour, were sold for 75 per cent of the true price. Other tickets (clearly trial pieces), printed on one side only in the correct colour or printed both sides in the incorrect colour were priced accordingly. One couple, clad in what is best described as 'glad rags' (evening dress was stipulated), set off for the Ball clutching a pair of tickets printed on one side only, wrong colour and mistaken date, which they bought for two shillings. They were successfully admitted. I saw them towards dawn in the Fellows' Garden, dancing with manic energy.

Not all our hours were spent in The Bailey, the Funnies or sliding into parties. Poker games began late and often lasted towards dawn and breakfast in the Wicklow Hotel. These games were played, as all poker should be played, for stakes somewhat beyond the means of the players. One man lost his entire maintenance grant from Gloucestershire County Council on the second day of Michaelmas term. Mild-mannered David Lovell played every night of every term; he consistently respected the mathematical odds and thus supported a wife and child in a London suburb. Rupert Mackson was welcome at every table. He would announce, 'I am going to lose twenty-five pounds and then leave.' Which he always did. Charles Norman, with flashing teeth and a cigarette holder, was a very superior player. He would play at our table until midnight and then take his charm and inevitable winnings, which he would use as grubstake for the really big game with cattle dealers' sons at UCD, at a house in Francis Street.

For many years Dexamphetamine Sulphate or Dexedrine (now known and feared as Speed) was freely available over the counter in pharmacies. Generally it was not used for kicks but as an aid for cramming for exams. After nine months of idleness and debauchery, cerebral processes required a jump-start. Prodigious feats of study were performed: 'Buy a girl a drink, will you? I have just covered nine hundred years of Byzantine history in three hours and the exam is tomorrow.' There were dangers. The little yellow pills made one very talkative. I had a conversation with another user about not very much which lasted two days and the intervening night; a large inroad into the ten days allotted to covering the year's course in three subjects. Later the drug was put on prescription, creating a niche market. Our college connection was the Preacher, a large Ballymoney man, inclined when exhilarated with his own merchandise, potentiated by his native Bushmills, to deliver ear-splitting exhortatory passages from the Good Book. There is a photograph of three law graduates in Commencement garb on the lower steps of the Exam Hall. Two steps up stands the Preacher, his arms spread possessively over his successful clients.

I was not aware of other drugs, until I noticed a young man called Rock, engaged in a profound, necessarily one-sided, conversation with a Yorkshire terrier installed in the pocket of his duffel coat. My companion remarked that Rock was stoned.

'At eleven in the morning, on coffee?'

'No, not drunk, stoned. Marijuana.' In 1964 the word meant nothing to me.

Student politics, or any other kind, were of no concern in the back bar. Although I do recall one act of participation. George Rivers had been drunk for a week. He explained incoherently: 'I have found a well. A deep well.' I saw him that night tottering across Parliament Square, a heavy pail of dry sherry in each hand. George's friend John Wingfield had been elected treasurer of the Fabian Society on the grounds that his public-school background marked him for an idealist and therefore trustworthy with money. John suggested that the subscription fund be invested in a huge barrel of sherry to be kept in the society's rooms and available to the members who judged this an enlightened idea. His friend George then drained the barrel by night.

The Bloodies and a few like them had small private incomes and sports cars. This was a clear initial advantage in the pursuit and conquest of the few indisputably beautiful girls in every year, the principal preoccupation of much of the male student body. Their less affluent rivals were mainly from the Players society, able to offer small parts in dramatic productions, although some productions sufferered. Offers to sew costumes had a low yield.

Sex did occur in Dublin before the Beatles' first LP. Virginities were lost, abandoned, and surrendered, though mostly unwillingly maintained. Condoms, unlike dangerously addictive drugs, were not on sale legally and many students from abroad had baffling and embarrassing moments at chemists' shops. One pharmacist lay on the floor behind the counter begging his customers to go away or he'd have to call the guards. There was a small black market run by Northerners, but not the Preacher who railed against the diabolical use of such things. Young men were scrupulous about their contraceptive obligations. One girl's initiation into carnality was at a definitive juncture in a flat in Morehampton Road when her partner straightened up, buttoned up, drove back to his rooms in College and returned with the proper prophylactic, to conclude what had been interrupted.

Contemporaries at Oxford might have been tempted to acquire a teddy bear and an affected manner of speech in imitation of Sebastian Flyte from *Brideshead Revisited*. The Sebastian who inspired our generation was from a different stable entirely. Sebastian Dangerfield was the protagonist of J.P. Donleavy's *Ginger Man*. A sociopath whose struggle to maintain his dignity in his battles with his wife, landlord, creditors and all the norms of civilized life, formed the text of the novel and the template of attitude and behaviour of his imitators. Dangerfield's fictional example prompted and justified all kinds of deplorable blackguardism, to be recited and relived in the back bar the following morning. The College authorities must have wished, then and later, that Gainor Crist, upon whom the character was modelled, had chosen to attend another seat of learning.

ONE BRIGHT winter afternoon we were sitting with rich dark pints of stout in front of us and a fire blazing at our backs. Old Michael Keenan, the bar manager in a long white coat, approached us.

'Why are you idling by the fire like old men on this fine day? When I was your age I was here and there and lively with it.' When I discovered that one lively week in Michael's lively young life was spent in the General Post Office in 1916, I resolved to get out more. Thus some sunny afternoons found me with my back resting against the second pillar from the right of the College Chapel, a position affording a clear view of Front Square and the people in passage across it. Fiona Pilkington in tight white trousers and boots to the knee and a singular short cloak. Anne Fenton hiding her face behind long strands of fine blonde hair had an attractive loping gait. Judy Monahan's brown eyes glared from beneath a dark fringe as she strode in her tight jeans aggressively across the cobblestones. Judy Russell, beautiful and vague, a prodromal flower child, floated unpurposefully by. Bridget Byrne with dim fair hair and pale blue eyes sauntered past, her admirers demoralized by her failure to notice them.

Rosemary Fisher, fairest of them all, high cheek bones and liquid dark eyes, looked neither to right nor to left, steady in heels on the uneven ground. 'Cool' was a new concept then and she had it to perfection. That she was crushingly shy and acutely short-sighted (as later appeared) may have better explained her demeanour, but did not diminish (and has not, nearly fifty years later) the aesthetic impact of that lovely vision.

HAVING DELIVERED ME to The Bailey, Bill Fitzhugh did not linger there, finding life more engaging in the activities of the nearby university. He later married a fellow student, the beautiful Gilly Ross. He lived a full life of cheerful diligence, raised a happy family and died last year, aged sixty-four. May the wild earth lie lightly on him. I would without doubt have found my own way to Duke Street.

The Bailey was demolished in 1966. I took a brick from the rubble, feeling that the place had had such a large part of me, I was owed a piece of it.

Tom Haran (TCD 1961–6; Medicine, but was invalided out, and later took an arts degree) was the founder and designer of Captain America's Cookhouse and Solomon Grundys. He was for some years assistant editor of **The Dublin Magazine**. In 1992, he gained BA Hons Fine Art (Painting), Central Saint Martins, London, and has worked as a painter and a sculptor since then. His work is in a number of public collections, including the Irish Writers Museum and the James Joyce Tower. His portrait commissions include Rosanna Davison, Anthony Cronin, U2, Derek Mahon, Desmond Guinness and Paddy Tuohy.

FRENCH LEAVE

jacques chuto

IN THE EARLY AFTERNOON of Sunday, 22 October 1961, I drove my Dauphine under the archway of Front Gate in a howling storm. After unloading as best I could in the streaming rain and taking possession of my rooms in the GMB, I went to have a chat with the porter. 'Is this typical Irish weather?' I asked. The man pointed at the lawn in Front Square: 'Look at our grass,' he said. 'See how green it is?' After such an auspicious start, no wonder that, some forty years later, I was to have a hand in the publication of the Complete Works of the nineteenth-century Dublin poet, James Clarence Mangan, who never ventured out of doors without a bulky umbrella protruding from under his cloak.

In 1961, though, I had never heard of Mangan. I was twenty-one and had come to Trinity to be a French *assistant*, as part of an exchange programme between the College and the Ecole Normale Supérieure in Paris. After the three years of strenuous work I had gone through in order to pass the entrance examination to the Ecole, and the year I had spent afterwards recovering as in limbo, my eight months in Trinity proved to be absolute heaven. I discovered that life could be fun.

I did not have many hours to teach. Conversation classes were easy, even though I had to wear a gown, which, to a young Frenchman, looked like something out of the Middle Ages. The classes were mostly informal chat. We talked (at least, *I* did) about politics, literature, cooking, fashion, anything except sex. As I rambled on, I sometimes put my foot in it: I still remember with shame telling a class that the dummies in the shop windows on Grafton Street looked far more elegant and sophisticated than the average Irish girl. Very rude indeed. Still, my female students did not seem to hold it against me. Teaching translation was more arduous and involved marking papers, but I liked it.

The unpleasant part of the job was having to teach French literature to General Studies students. At first, I tried to get out of it by arguing that these were overtime hours about which I had not been told. When he heard me, the head of the French Department, a paunchy middle-aged Frenchman, fairly shook with rage in his small office in No. 35. He spoke of duty and tradition; if I refused to do those hours I would go back to France! It was probably an empty threat and he did not have to begin to carry it out anyway, for a new factor made me take a kinder view of General Studies. After having dinner in Commons for about a week I decided that College food was definitely not my cup of tea, and that having to sit in that lugubrious hall and to wear that medieval gown in order to eat such unpalatable grub was too ridiculous for words. I took to eating out and immediately realized that the overtime money would come in very handy. So I agreed to try and unveil the beauties of Corneille, Beaumarchais, or Proust to students whose French was, in most cases, hopelessly inadequate. Needless to say, my audiences were not always extremely attentive to the niceties of my literary analyses. On one particular occasion, what I had to say on *Hernani* was accompanied by the buzz of rather too many private conversations. When the class was over, a student, who later was to star in several Hammer horror films, Ralph Bates, came up to me. 'Poor Mr Chuto,' he said kindly. ' I don't mind,' I said. And it was true, I didn't mind. All that mattered to me was that Victor Hugo and the other French authors I was supposed to teach saw to it that I was properly fed.

And properly 'watered' as well. Guinness is an acquired taste, they say. I must have acquired it in a former life, then, for I took to the stuff at once. I loved spending the evening in a pub (Slatterys in Suffolk Street, or The Old Stand, or The Bailey) drinking a few pints, smoking a pipe and talking with friends – and improving my English. Draught Guinness in those days was served at the right temperature; it did not taste as though it came straight out of the fridge. The best parties were those where a keg sat in the room like some pagan divinity, and you went to kneel, or at least stoop, in front of it, whenever your faith needed to be revived. On occasion, you did not feel like driving back to College and you spent what was left of the night sleeping on the floor. And then, on waking up, you approached the altar again – a lovely breakfast!

Sometime in March, Michael de Larrabeiti, who had become my best Dublin friend, won a keg of Guinness in some College raffle and about ten of us congregated at his basement flat in Brighton Square, Rathgar, in order to celebrate this piece of luck. Between 7 pm and 2 am we drank our way down to the bottom of the barrel. Yet this was not just a bout of mindless boozing: all the time the keg lasted we kept competing with one another in sparkling witticisms and downright nonsense, re-enacting *con amore* the 'Discourse of the Drinkers' chapter in *Gargantua* (Sebastian Balfour, who was one of the ten, was to found the Rabelaisian Society the following year). Strange to say, I cannot recall whether there were any girls present that night. Probably not.

However, my days in Dublin were not one endless stag party. There were dancing parties as well, and therefore girls, a species with which I had had very little to do till then. I was delighted to discover that I could be attractive to some of them. At the first party I was invited to, and which, for some reason, the Junior Dean, Dr McDowell, graced with his presence, there were two German girls, one of whom was rather large and plain, while the other, who attended some of my classes, was petite and pretty. Unfortunately it was the Valkyrie who clearly found me to her taste and, after a while, emboldened by the alcohol she had imbibed, came to sit in my lap and started kissing me. What was I to do? I had to keep up my countrymen's reputation. So I kissed her back. And there we sat glued to each other for what seemed to be ages, but all the time I was watching the other more petite German girl dance with fellows I now envied and hated, all the time hearing in the background the voice of the Junior Dean stuttering away ('I mean, er – I mean') to a small audience of non-dancing, non-kissing undergraduates. At last, my tormentor muttered she had to go to the bathroom and set me free. As she was away for quite a while (it turned out that she was being disgustingly sick in the bathroom), I could at last ask her pretty friend for a dance, and, one thing leading to another, by the time the Valkyrie reappeared, I and my new conquest were now kissing shamelessly.

I went out with Charlotte for a few weeks until one fateful night. We first attended a very 'stiff' dinner and dance in evening dress, organized by some College society. I remember nothing of that function, except that the floor was beautifully polished and dangerously slippery – we were in the ballroom of the Shelbourne, I think. We left at about midnight and moved on to a party, which I thought would prove more congenial. We went down the steps of an area in Fitzwilliam Square and entered the basement flat. What a shock! In barely fifteen minutes we had moved from a highly civilized, if slightly boring scene to a noisy, smoky, smelly pandemonium in which my dinner jacket and Charlotte's long dress looked definitely out of place. That did not deter an uncouth student, who grabbed hold of the poor lass and started dancing with her wildly. I put up with this for as long as I could and finally went up to my girl and said (in French), 'Come on, darling, time to go.' We put on our coats and got out. Charlotte had already reached the top of the steps and I was beginning to climb when the young savage came rushing into the area. 'You bloody Frenchman!' he yelled. 'Who the hell do you think you are?' And he kicked me. I turned round, absolutely furious, and launched myself at him. As I was slightly higher up he went down and I fell on top of him. And we started fighting on the dirty cement floor in a most undignified manner. The fight did not last long. A sudden glimpse of the student's shirt stained with blood somewhat sobered me up and I disengaged myself and got up. He got up too, his friends whispering into his ear, and I could hear the word 'staff' urgently repeated. Charlotte and I were at last allowed to leave, and I drove her home. I stopped the car outside the house in Rathmines where she rented a room, and kissed her. 'You fought for my sake,' she said in a small voice. She was mistaken: I'd fought that hooligan because he had kicked me, but I did not contradict her. Her gratitude for my supposedly chivalrous deed must have weakened her religious hang-ups (she was a Roman Catholic from Munich, and this was 1962), because, that night, she allowed me to get closer to the goal every healthy young lad sets his sights on. 'This is going a bit too far,' she said when she got out of the car eventually. But I did not think she really meant it and drove back to College well pleased with myself and life in general.

But she *did* mean it, and on the following day she gave me the push. Later in the afternoon, the uncouth student came up to me in Front Square and offered his most abject apologies. 'I didn't know you were staff,' he whimpered. I showed great magnanimity, but feeling noble did not really make up for the fact that I had been jilted.

Some three weeks later, in early March, I was invited to a fancy-dress party thrown by a few Germans who must have been missing their fatherland's carnival. I went as a Caribbean pirate, with the incongruous adjunction of an Afghan fur cap borrowed from my friend Michael. I first called at the dressing room of Players (they were rehearsing Camus' *The Possessed*), where a lovely girl made me up, embellishing me with heavy eyebrows and a fierce moustache. I must have looked decidedly odd driving from College Green to Elgin Road, but fortunately the other drivers were too busy to pay me any attention. It had snowed very heavily on Dublin and the streets were so slippery that applying the brakes a bit too strongly sent the rear of one's vehicle into an alarming skid. Buses were stranded along the kerbs and even in the middle of the road. Still, I managed to make it to my destination. The party was very German. There was German sausage, German wine, and German music. And there was my German girl too. I knew she would be there, of course, and had come in the hope of winning her back. I soon discovered, however, that she had already replaced me. And with whom, or what? A member of the Boat Club! I was appalled at such an utter lack of taste. And although I was glad to perceive, from the way they were dancing together, that the bulky oarsman had not reached any great degree of intimacy with the fickle Fräulein, I could not help feeling ill-treated. So I ate rather more German sausage and drank rather more German wine than I should have, and by the time I left around 2 am I felt both heavy-stomached and light-headed.

The deserted streets were no longer treacherous when I undertook to drive back to College. But I got lost. Without knowing how, I found myself driving along an expanse of water on the other side of which I could see lights, but there was no bridge. Then, I got into what must have been a bus depot. Snow-coated double-deckers towered above me on both sides, and there were no lights or sounds. I suppose I should have been worried but I found the situation extremely funny and drove on and on, and round and round, between those endless rows of identical buses, giggling all the time and repeating to myself, 'Snow was general all over Ireland' (I had been reading *Dubliners*). I have no idea how long I was there, but eventually, and still without knowing how, I found the way out, suddenly recognized a street, and got back to Trinity at last. It was 4 am. I parked the Dauphine near the Campanile, got out, locked the door, and the key ring came undone and the car key dropped and sank into a thick carpet of snow. There was no point in trying to recover it given my condition. So I retired to bed, still giggling, and slept like a log until 10 am, when I got up and went to my car with a bottle of hot water, which I poured unto the snow, which fortunately had not been disturbed (it was Sunday). And, lo and behold, there was my car key! A happy ending, and a return to some kind of normality after a crazy night.

There were other nights and other girls, too, but I will say no more on the subject lest readers should think that my Trinity days were a time of unbroken rakishness. I did some teaching, as I said before, and I read a lot. Having a BA in Classics, English literature was largely unknown territory to me and I made repeated forays into it. Being a member of staff, I had taken 'the oath' (another quaint custom) and was allowed to help myself from the racks of the Library, which students couldn't do at the time. Strange to say, though, I cannot remember exactly which books I read, apart from *Dubliners* and *A Portrait*. I went to the cinema, even though Dublin was far from being a film buff's paradise. In Paris, I went to the Cinémathèque at least twice a week; in Dublin I patronized from time to time suburban houses, which showed old Westerns or horror films, like the Stella in Rathmines or the Ritz ('Always a good show!') in Ballsbridge. It was nothing to write home about and besides, Irish spectators were an infuriating lot: they invariably talked throughout the film and got up before the end to escape the national anthem. As for the Dublin theatres, they do not seem to have seen much of me. I only have two theatrical memories of that time. One is of the Players production of *The Possessed*. I didn't like the play a lot, but found the production very good. Ralph Bates gave an impressive performance as Stavrogin. And surely lovely Jo Van Gyseghem played in it as well, didn't she? The other memory is typically narcissistic. The Modern Languages Society decided to produce Anouilh's *Antigone* in French, and they asked me to play the part of the Chorus. When I was fourteen, at the Jesuit boarding school I attended in Brittany, I had played the part of Antigone's old nurse. Clearly this was a promotion, and I readily agreed. Wearing the dinner jacket that was to be involved in a vulgar fight a few days later, I came on stage occasionally to comment upon the action in long speeches that underlined the inevitability of tragedy. We played three nights in a row to packed houses and I felt exhilarated.

By a strange coincidence, at about the same time, I was commenting upon a tragedy in real life – the Algerian war. In December the College journal *TCD Miscellany* carried an article entitled 'Algeria', which I found totally wrong-headed. I wrote a letter to the editor, which was published in its entirety even though it occupied more than one page. Towards the end of February, the Modern Languages Society asked me to give a talk in French on the same subject.

The meeting took place in camera in a classroom of No. 35; it was chaired by Dr Sheehy-Skeffington. I spoke for about an hour trying to explain to the audience why I thought that Algeria should remain French. I do not think I convinced many of them. I certainly made no impression on the chairman. When I predicted that Algeria under Algerian rule would sink into chaos, the trained controversialist replied that people should be allowed to make their own mistakes. A week later, *TCD* carried a two-page article entitled 'King without a Crown', in which I again expressed my distaste for de Gaulle and his Algerian policy. Such activism made me almost famous. Michael Bogdin (now Bogdanov) ended his column in *Trinity News* with a jocular 'Vive Chuto!' The people at the French embassy, however, were not amused, and they seriously contemplated packing me off to France. Fortunately, the head of the French Department shared my ideas. So it was that the man who in October threatened to send me back to Paris, now pleaded on my behalf, and I stayed on.

I also took part in College politics once. I was having a quiet pint in The Bailey when a girl came up to me and asked would I join her and her friends on a protest demonstration. The Historical Society was holding a meeting that night and the idea was to gatecrash it in order to protest the fact that women were still refused membership of the Society. So off we marched to the GMB, a small group of twenty people or so, only two or three of whom were male, and we entered the room in which the worthy members were gathered. Our entrance caused great consternation. We asked them kindly to proceed with whatever it was that they were doing, but they stubbornly refused, eyeing the female intruders with the kind of distaste that a Taliban might show at the sight of a lock of hair peeping out from under a hijab. They told us to leave and, when we wouldn't be moved, they sent for the Junior Dean. Dr McDowell came stuttering in ('I mean, er – I mean') and took down the names of all the demonstrators (I had to spell mine for him). We left eventually, having made our point, and adjourned to a pub to celebrate our feat of arms. A couple of days later, I was summoned to the Junior Dean's office. 'You might have told me you were a French *assistant*,' he grumbled. 'You didn't ask,' I said. And there the matter ended. I was not punished and women continued to be denied access to The Historical Society. But I still remember with delight that night when I struck a blow for equality between the sexes.

It was a sad day for me (and, I think, for the friends who walked me to the North Wall Quay) when I left Dublin on that sunny day in mid-May to go back to France. The following October I drove through a thick, most unpromising fog to take up my post as French lector in Queen's College, Cambridge. The pay was better, I taught fewer hours (and no General Studies!), but the British students here seemed to be a different breed from those I had so easily mixed with in Dublin, and never made me feel at home. In eight months I was not invited to one single party. I made a few acquaintances but did not keep in touch with any of them. So I worked. I read all Shakespeare's plays, one after another, and wrote a 200-hundred page MA dissertation on the Canadian humorist Stephen Leacock. And all the time I kept wondering why on earth I hadn't applied for another year in TCD.

Jacques Chuto (TCD 1961–2, French assistant as part of his training at the Ecole Normale Supérieure in Paris). Incurably smitten with Ireland, he wrote his doctoral thesis for the Sorbonne on the Irish poet James Clarence Mangan, and co-edited **The Collected Works of James Clarence Mangan** (2003). He has taught English and Irish literature at several universities including Yaoundé (Cameroon), Lille and Paris. He is now happily retired and busy translating Derek Mahon's poetry into French.

JUST FUMBLINGS

john wilkinson

'**UNWISE**,' they said when I told of my plans for a visit to TCD after a forty-year absence. 'All has changed, both Trinity and Dublin. You'll feel a total stranger and will leave disappointed. Don't go! Best cherish those glorious memories of the golden days that were yours in the TCD of the early Sixties.'

So I bought my ticket – Toulouse to Dublin, Aer Lingus – with the lowest of expectations, fully prepared to face the certain sadness my friends had categorically predicted. And there I was, within a few hours, standing before Front Gate, as familiar and friendly as it always had been all those years ago, and through which I had last strolled at the age of twenty – educated (well, degree-bearing, shall I say), Rastignac-like, ready and eager to fight my way through life in the big, wide world outside.

But, ah! Where were the equally familiar and friendly Front Gate porters of yesteryear, so distinguished in their coachmen's uniforms? Oh yes – replaced by security officers. Never mind. A mere detail and sign of the nervous times in which we all now have to live. The rooms I'd booked were fine – No. 6, Front Square, also now provided with a security door at the foot of the staircase; but with running water, hot and cold, and a loo on the same floor. What luxury! No longer the need for Mick, the skip (i.e. College manservant) who daily used to toil up and down bringing us both water for washing and peat for burning in the open grate, giving off both heat and the smell which, as with Proust's lilac, when fleetingly recaptured, at once transports me back to those brilliant days of life in College.

Within minutes I was out and about. Yes, the Fellows' Garden had been translated into a Conference Centre, but no, College Park had not been concreted over. In fact, on that particular hot, late-June day, it was host to hundreds of sprawling, half-naked students relaxing in the sun. The cricket pavilion was now a bar and the pints were flowing fast. So too was the conversation. I joined in. Polite interest turned to evident surprise when I let slip that I'd met Éamon de Valera on that very spot during College Races in Trinity Week all those years before. I was clearly part of history.

Time had certainly moved on, as a glance through the list of College societies clearly showed. Never in the early Sixties, for example, would one have found the Anarchists featuring on it. However it was comforting to see that the musical scene, my scene, was still very much the same – Choral and Orchestral Societies, on whose committees I had served: the Cherry Cup Quartet competition, in which I regularly competed. In those days, however, there was no College Chapel Choir. The choir of St Patrick's Cathedral came into College then, sang the Sunday service and promptly left. That was it!

The keen undergraduate singers of those days joined a select group, the College Singers, which I had the great privilege and pleasure of conducting – regular concerts in the Examination Hall, at St Colomba's, participating in the Dublin Feis Ceoil singing competition, a visit to the Edinburgh Festival Fringe and, memorably, a performance of Gilbert and Sullivan's *Trial by Jury*, which I conducted in the Dining Hall to a packed audience – a combined operation bringing together our band of Singers and the actors from Dublin University Players – notably Anthony Weale, playing the Judge. And I remember long rehearsals on Saturday mornings in No. 5, followed by concerts, followed by parties, lots of parties and lots of fun. The musical events were frequently attended by Charles Acton, the *Irish Times* music critic, and sympathetically written up by him in the next day's columns.

These were the last days of George Henry Phillips Hewson as Professor of Music. 'Daddy' Hewson, already in his eighties, was a legend in his own time. He had sung as a St Patrick's Cathedral chorister in College Chapel in the 1890s;

had been organist at St Patrick's from 1920 to 1960, giving memorable recitals in the difficult days of the 1920s when concerts were few and far between. And this grand old man of Irish music delivered to us his last year of lectures on the history of music, always well attended since it was generally known that he'd never failed anyone at the end-of-year exam. I see him clearly even now in that gloomy room in No. 4, hobbling over to the beaten-up old upright (yes – he had a club-foot! How ever did he cope with an organ pedal board?) and striking up with great verve and panache a flurry of Wagner – one of his favourites.

After his departure his successor Brian Boydell arrived and with him a breath of fresh air in the department – a new concert room in No. 5, complete with a Steinway concert grand, regular lunchtime concerts and lots of warm encouragement to young amateur musicians like myself. A further joy was to participate in the musical life of Dublin beyond College walls. We went to the Gaiety Theatre to sing in Bizet's *Carmen*; we had walk-on parts as Toreadors! With Tibor Paul conducting the RTÉ Orchestra. I played my clarinet with the orchestra of the Royal Irish Academy of Music, and we regularly sang the Sunday Mass at St Bartholomew's church, Ballsbridge, and rubbed shoulders with the lions of the Dublin musical world – John Beckett, John O'Sullivan, David Lee, often meeting in Jammet's back bar, long since disappeared, where we packed in enough liquid refreshment to fuel impassioned debate on music and musicians, good performances and bad.

I cast my eyes further down that alphabetical list of College societies, and choirs and choral societies gave way to the Juggling Society. The thought of Trinity Jugglers amused me almost as much as that of the Trinity Anarchists, both totally foreign concepts to the TCD of the early Sixties (although one could argue, perhaps, that we did indeed juggle in our own way. Frequent juggling in fact with our lectures, with those we knew we had to attend, those we could reasonably risk not attending, and those we could definitely drop with impunity). But imagine my utter bemusement when my eyes eventually focused on the TCD Lesbian, Gay, Bisexual and Transgender Society (the LGBT), with ample evidence of a full membership together with an impressive calendar of events, designed, I imagine, to cater for all those various tastes. What troubled me most, I think, was simply not having the vaguest idea of how on earth I would have reacted had I been faced with the LGBT society on arrival at Trinity in 1961 at the tender age of nineteen. I tried to imagine those stands at the Freshers' Week jamboree.

'Come on! Roll up! Roll up! Are you gay? Bisexual? Interested in Transgenders? No? What the devil are you then?'

Well, yes, good question. What was I then? Certainly one of the 400 or so students who came over each year from the UK to make up the Trinity population of 2000 or so. Equally certainly one of the many who came from the single-sex public schools of the day and whose early sexual experiences, if not orientation, had largely been homosexual. Not exclusively in my case. Holidays at home had brought parties and dances in their wake and there would be occasions for kissing with girls, cuddling, heavy petting, and sometimes more, either in the shrubberies of the various large houses of the hosts, or in the cramped Minis of the guests, depending on the season of the year. But the time spent at a single-sex boys' school between the ages of eight and eighteen gave one far greater scope for sexual activity – forbidden with the housemaster's cane as the supposed deterrent. It didn't deter, unsurprisingly, even if the memories of the beatings were, and still are, painful ones. In hindsight, of course, one realizes that many of those engaging happily in gay sex at school became overnight serial lady-killers at university. Many, yes, but not all, by any means. I for one on reaching Trinity had no idea which way the wind was blowing. Sex with both boys and girls was fun. Why the need to discuss the matter, let alone choose between the two? It never seemed an issue and I imagine I wouldn't have wished to join a society to have it set a seal on my sexuality. And so at Trinity I drifted along, as I'm sure many others did, influenced sometimes by busy heterosexuals like Michael de Larrabeiti, and sometimes by the likes of Carl Bontoft – both of them vivid and challenging characters.

Michael, a mature student some seven years my senior, was already a man of much and varied experience. He'd grown up in the rough and tumble of wartime Battersea and was more or less self-educated. He had worked as a shepherd in Provence and had subsequently turned his hand to photography and, in the summer of 1961, found himself on the back of a motorbike hell-bent for Afghanistan as the official photographer of the 1961 Oxford University Marco Polo Expedition.

His knowledge of women was legendary and he considered it one of his missions to egg me on from the moment he saw me with my lovely new young girlfriend who had suddenly turned up one day to sing soprano with the College Singers. 'Oh, John,' he would say. 'Get a move on! What the hell are you waiting for? She'll get bored.' (Often expressing these thoughts in a South London vernacular too rich to reproduce here.)

How naive I must have seemed to him. No real idea of where I was going. Just fumblings. And such a lovely girl too, also experiencing her first steps in a relationship. An intelligent, musical girl from Rathgar, granddaughter of a former Church-of-Ireland bishop. A girl whom I could take to the Trinity Ball and who could invite me to The Elizabethan Garden Party – a highly prized invitation indeed. And parties, and dinners and drinks with her, and with others too on the side. But as much as Michael urged me on to daring deeds so too I would be listening to that charismatic Carl. Carl, the Senior Sophister, taking many a Junior Freshman like me under his wing.

Carl Hendrik Bonnaventure Bontoft, Vicomte de Saint Quentin, or just plain 'Bon' to his friends. Bon was the only student of the time who had actually 'come out' (not a term then known) and declared he was a homosexual. He was flamboyant, immensely provocative and clearly more than slightly 'over the top' for a lot of people's liking. However he was highly musical, had written a Missa Brevis in memoriam to Pope John XXIII, especially for the College Singers and so it was inevitable that we should spend much time together.

He too, like me, moved in Dublin musical circles and it was largely through and with him that I first became aware of the fact that gays are so often attracted to and by the arts – music, dance, theatre, principally – and will naturally gravitate to those activities. Is it because of a heightened sensitivity, as is sometimes said? So, too, gays will often tend to associate more with Catholicism and High Anglicanism rather than with Protestantism, Methodism and the Low Churches. Perhaps it is because of an attraction to liturgy, ceremony, ritual and vestments? It is difficult to say, but in any event I felt as much at ease in the gay Dublin musical circles as with the gays I befriended both in the choir and congregation of the High Anglican Church of St Bartholomew's, Ballsbridge, whose services I attended most Sundays during the Trinity terms.

There were no Gay Bar Guides in those days but gays naturally found their favourite haunts. Ours was Davy Byrnes and Friday night was the night.

We Trinity students – young, musical and certainly gay-friendly if not openly active, would regularly meet up with a somewhat older generation with similar interests and the drink would flow. 'Time, Gentlemen please!' would be called eventually, armfuls of bottled stout would be bought and we would retire to No. 43 Fitzwilliam Square where beer-stained LPs would be produced, the volume and general level of excitement turned up and litres of drink gulped down. Laughter, heated arguments on the relative merits of the choirs of King's and St John's, Cambridge, and much gay banter until the early hours of Saturday morning. How I ever managed to be in a fit state to begin the 9 am rehearsal with the Singers remains a permanent mystery to me. But yes, of course, there was my lovely soprano girlfriend standing in the front row, smiling, inspiring and encouraging me to greater and greater musical efforts! So much to be thankful for.

Now, forty years on my love of great music, begun at Trinity, has stood the test of time. The ambivalence of my sexuality has long been resolved (in my own good time and without the interference of either undergraduate gay clubs, sexologists, psychiatrists or whatever) and, after four years – supposedly studying French and German – I finally left Trinity on the crest of a wave. Don't get me wrong. The French and German studies were not totally wasted on me. Even if the lectures and syllabuses on the whole failed to inspire me (I'm no academic) I nevertheless developed into an out and out Francophile, have taught French for a living and now live most happily just outside Toulouse. German, too, has had its uses, especially so with its many musical connotations. I so much better appreciate the lieder of Schubert, Schumann, Wolff and the operas of Wagner, for example, with a knowledge of the language.

I left TCD to do a one-year Diploma of Education at St John's, Cambridge – a disappointment, frankly. Cambridge was nothing outside its colleges. My brother had the opposite experience at Bedford College, London. Bedford was without identity and utterly swamped by the size of the metropolis. TCD had the best of both worlds -- a tight collegiate community set in the centre of a small capital city. To pass through that familiar Front Gate was to move instantly from one world to a very different one. And I now realize how much both of those worlds meant and still mean to me.

So my short stroll down memory lane merely confirmed what I had known all along – namely that those far-off Trinity days were indeed golden days, and that the memories of them have continued to be glorious and powerful ones – to this very day and to this very moment.

John Wilkinson (TCD 1961–5; Modern Languages: French and German) went on to became Senior French Master at Marlborough College. He is now the owner of Chai John, Restaurant and Auberge at Le Castera, near Toulouse, France.

MOVING ON

anthony weale

I DON'T KNOW where the time went, but my last visit to Dublin was nearly forty years ago. In 1972, I was there on business, pinstriped and respectable, staying at the Shelbourne, and lunching late in the Oyster Bar, a luxury I'd never previously enjoyed. Even now I feel a bit of a fake admitting that I was on business, and wore a suit, but there it is. As my mother rather loftily remarked, for me it was a choice between that and beachcombing.

It must have been in mid-March that year, when I'd run out of things to say to other dull pinstripers who were in the same bar, that I strolled from the hotel along St Stephen's Green, down Dawson Street, and round to TCD. It was quite late in the afternoon, getting very cold, and the sun was clear and red down Dame Street. I suppose people were thinking about going home, or into the pubs, from the office. There were no students about, spring term having just ended. I inclined my head towards Messrs Goldsmith and Burke, waved towards Mr Grattan, who of course was waving back, muttered something unflattering about a former manager of the Bank of Ireland who had refused me a small loan on many occasions, and for the first time since I graduated seven years before, wheeled right, past the Porter's Lodge, into Front Square.

It didn't seem to have changed very much. I walked round for a look at the new Library, built since I'd left, and didn't think that much of it, in fact thought it distinctly inferior to the lost Provost's Garden. I entered anyway, and went up to the counter. Harry Bovenizer, an assistant librarian who had formerly helped me to track down some of the more obscure and offensive minor works of Swift, was there, transposed from the old building, in the same tight suit and as cheerful as ever. We chatted for a bit and I invited him for a quickie on expenses round at O'Neills, but he was due elsewhere and had to hurry away. I wandered listlessly back towards the Campanile – and whom should I see but Dr W. Fitzroy Pyle, warmly clad in coat and scarf. I trotted up behind him, and asked after his health. By this time, I already knew, he had retired, but he still had a grace-and-favour room in Front Square, and, with his familiar wide smile, he invited me up for a sherry. The room – I can't remember its number, but it was somewhere near Chapel – was very dark and cold: Dr Pyle apparently was obliged to pay for any electricity used, though the room came to him with no other liability. We stood red-nosed in our overcoats looking out of the window over the darkening cobbles, drank manzanilla out of dusty cut glass, and recalled the time when some mountaineering joker had placed a red top hat on the Campanile's lightning conductor. Had I heard, he asked cheerfully, that Dr J.C. McQuaid had recently and unexpectedly retired, on the Pope's instructions. It was very good news, said Dr Pyle, implying it couldn't have happened to a nicer fellow.

Dr Pyle, TCD's genial Senior Tutor, was the first office-bearer of Dublin University that I met, in 1961. At my father's insistence, I called at his room after the family holiday in West Cork, to inquire if my application to take a course at Trinity had been successful. Dr Pyle was very polite, but, beaming widely, ruefully told me that he must deny me a place, since my A-level Latin result simply wasn't up to scratch. However, if I cared to have a stab at TCD's own Latin scholarship examination, that might possibly change things. I carefully refrained from pointing out that I did not plan to read Classics, but English; instead I seized him by the hand and welcomed my second chance. Vigorous cramming in Virgil and Livy by my younger brother, who already had the offer of a classical scholarship at Oxford, got me a distinction six weeks later, a congratulatory postcard from Dr Pyle, and that was that: I was in.

Just about every term at Trinity presented me with the same challenge: where was I going to live? All terms began in the same way. I'd get off the boat from Liverpool at North Wall, and walk up the quays to College. I'd potter about for the day, with a pint here, a pint there, waiting for the evening papers. The fact is that, for reasons that no longer matter, I never had enough money to hold on to a place over the vacation, so each term I had to start again, anxiously checking the letting agents on the first day back, phoning about yet another bed-sitter, and inspecting damp rooms in the company of dismal, pimply clerks. My residential arrangements seemed to go steadily downhill as time went by, so that I spent most of my last year stretched out on a sofa in Front Square, or worse, rolled up in a carpet in Botany Bay.

My only experience of digs, all found, plus a landlady, was in my first term, a Mrs Higgins' place in Belmont Road, Donnybrook. Her house was a shabby supporter of a terrace, with a predictably narrow hall, where I rested my bike until it was stolen, and a bathroom halfway up the stairs, with a gas-fired geyser, which exploded on payment of a shilling, and which frightened me even after I had abandoned it in favour of luxurious and, to digs-dwellers, illicit baths in College. I shared a small bedroom with Dave, a jolly chap from somewhere in the Midlands, I think. In the other bedroom slept Ted, who had a rich Yorkshire accent and had been to Shrewsbury, and a large, red-haired and foul-mouthed Dutchman, who constantly yelled 'Gott Verdomet,' or something like that, and 'F—in' Louis again,' as Mrs Higgins served up the fried black pudding that enriched every meal. My fellow lodgers spent a good deal of leisure time together, and although I drank with them sometimes early on Saturday evenings, after a match, we had few sporting interests in common: I had given up rugger, and though keen to excel at something, had also given up throwing the javelin after nearly killing a groundsman in College Park in my first athletics trial there. In short, the four of us rarely ended up together in the same pub. I was for ever being led astray, mainly in a theatrical direction. I preferred to eat late upstairs at the Paradiso in Westmoreland Street after rehearsals in the little Players Theatre. Ultimately, I would make my solitary way to Donnybrook on foot, via a party if I could find one. Back in Belmont Road, I'd hang about apprehensively before creeping towards Mrs Higgins' house. I always sensed that she was lying in wait for me. The second weekend of that very first term, indeed, she sprang out from the kitchen in her dressing-gown, gripped my biceps and, shaking me vigorously, asked me what on earth my mother would think of me, or of her for that matter, for letting me go to the dogs and me such a promising young man just arrived at the College.

About a week later, at three o'clock one Sunday morning, with the rain falling steadily, I found myself sitting on a park bench. I'd been with new friends in a damp basement somewhere along the Royal Canal, and I was pretty tight, but not so tight as to be free of the anxiety that Mrs Higgins yet again was lurking inside, perhaps in the narrow hallway of her house, behind her yellow net curtains. My bench was almost opposite Mrs H's front door on a patch of grass popular with the dogs of Donnybrook and on this bench I sat, with the rain coursing down my neck, waiting until I became sober enough to enter the house unnoticed. Presently, a noisy and malodorous motor bike drew up, and a garda with the water running off him said, 'Good evening to yeous.' The rain continued to pour down, and the garda's oilskins glistened under the street light. The water dripped from his nose. 'What might yeous be doin' here at this time of the night?'

Oh God, I thought, if it isn't Mrs H, it's the police. Nervously I explained that I lived in digs over the road and confessed that I had been drinking, and that my landlady Mrs Higgins would as we spoke be fidgeting vindictively in bed beside her husband, whom, by the way, I had never clapped eyes on, but whom I knew was called Malcolm, since I'd heard her shouting for him, and that he was probably bald, because recently I'd found an abandoned toupee in the weedy front garden. Mrs Higgins' tongue even now would be flickering in and out like a snake's, and she'd be hissing in anticipation of my return. Consequently I had thought it better that I sit on the bench for a while, until I was confident that I could enter the digs undetected.

The garda swung his leg over his bike, kicked down the stand, shook himself like a retriever, and sat down heavily beside me. 'Would yeous mind if I sat here and we had a bit of craic? It gets awful lonely ridin' around on your own in the rain all night.' It emerged that he had a landlady too, who was quite probably related to Mrs Higgins. 'It's the friggin' husbands I feel sorry for,' said the garda, eliptically.

My second term was disastrous. I found myself sharing a small bed-sitter somewhere near Rathmines with the large Dutchman. I've forgotten exactly how it happened, but his language hadn't improved, and within a few days I realized that I didn't much like living with loud men from the Low Countries. We fell out bitterly and irretrievably early in the term, and I started staying up all night with a congenial actor, John Castle, who trod the creaking boards in the bed-sitter downstairs. He and I would spend the night drinking and laughing, taking off Michael MacLiammóir and other mannered giants of the stage, and when the Dutchman went noisily off in the morning to his Economics lectures, I would retire to bed, and get up very late.

Then there was a lonely third term on my own in a mouldy top-floor room in Upper Mount Street, and another term in a little room with David O'Clee, who was hand in blouse with a very nice girl, which meant I was often asked if I would mind staying away for a bit. And there were two terms sharing a tiny room in Duke Street near Davy Byrnes with Ranald Graham, who wrote poetry in the style of Wallace Stephens and played the blues on the guitar, introducing me to the works of Blind Lemon (who froze to death somewhere), while most days an old lady plucked a harp with a cracked soundbox in the street outside, and a sublimely untalented fiddler in a waterproof punished his instrument by the entrance to The Bailey.

IT WAS AROUND the middle of my academic career that I fell in with Mike Jones, and we took a damp basement flat together in Rathgar Road. The building was owned by an elderly, semi-retired psychiatrist, Dr Melisande Zlotover, who lived in Victorian chaos over our heads. Often, as I returned to our basement, perhaps with a brown paper parcel of clean shirts from the Swastika Laundry, or a lump of calf's liver cheaply acquired, this mysterious woman would be standing at a window on the first floor in a loose, dark garment looking down at me, and would raise her thin hand, letting her fingers move vaguely in my direction. I found her strangely unsettling, like a sparrow trapped in the kitchen. Mike, however, became fascinated by Dr Zlotover, and frequently reported that he had spent the afternoon upstairs in her drawing-room, reclining on oriental rugs, drinking green tea and hoping that the secrets he knew she held about him might be unlocked. Each I thought was as dotty as the other. I'm sure it was under her influence that Mike developed his strong, occasionally ecstatic, social views, and signed up to the Zlotover regime, becoming very opinionated about Swedenborg's angels (one of whom, according to his adviser upstairs, was born after every act of human copulation), about Catholic girls in general, and about the merits of natural foods, avoiding giblets, which were bad for the brain, and insisting that all vegetables should be bought with the mud still on them and steamed, never boiled. Indeed, soon after we moved in, at Mike's instigation we spent a whole Saturday cruising the pubs north of the river hunting for a vegetable steamer. We found one with a rather second-hand look about it at the market in Moore Street, and used it that evening to cook a cabbage, which Mike relished, but I couldn't tell the difference.

About this time he also wrote a gloomy but strangely prophetic play, which told of two innocent young GIs being captured in what I think we still called French Indo-China, cruelly interrogated by a sadistic oriental colonel and his power-crazed mistress, and finally shot, offstage, in proper Aristotelean fashion; this some time before President Johnson sent the first combat troops into Vietnam. It was the year of the trouser-stirring Profumo affair, and even more shocking, of the assassination of President Kennedy. Like most of my generation, I can recall quite clearly where I was when the news came through. A group of us were in the International Bar in Wicklow Street. Norrie Boulting was there, a modest and portly man who had the most sublime tenor voice, perfect for Thomas Moore and Arthur Sullivan, and who regularly used to set light to a double calvados and toss it down in one. Paul Shepherd was there too, a witty, square young hispanophile with an MGB sports car and an American fiancée, Lee, who burst into tears on hearing of the dreadful event, and sobbed bitterly for the rest of the evening. Mike himself erupted, standing like a tribune of the people, I remember, waving his arms about, calling down the wrath of God, in whom he had never previously mentioned any trust, on the perpetrators of the wicked deed, who he felt sure were in the pay of the CIA's J. Edgar Hoover, who the whole world knew was a devilish, right-wing transvestite. I remember feeling it was neither the time nor the place to admit my ignorance on this last point.

The following summer, planning some serious revision for the first part of my finals, I stayed on in Dublin for a month or so. The weather was glorious, and Mike tried to convince me that I should join him in a production of *Twelfth Night* that he planned to stage on the sands at Malahide when the tide was out. He had persuaded Seamus Ford, an old stalwart of the Dublin theatre, with a voice from the bottom of a barrel, to take on Malvolio, on payment of a couple of bottles of gin. Various friends took the other parts, but I declined to have anything to do with it, on the grounds that academic duty called. Mike's normally raw feelings were surprisingly quite unaffected by my refusal to join in, though he insisted that I must come to the performance.

It was a mild evening, the warm sun was sinking and things were running a bit late, when the faint sounds of a lute played on a portable gramophone floated over the sands, and a man with a false beard sitting in a deck chair broke in with music and the food of love. I couldn't be sure what happened after that, since the acoustics were poor and all the performers seemed so far away. Ladies and gentlemen in a bizarre mixture of costumes came and went, tip-toeing unsteadily between the rock pools and seaweed; the occasional familiar phrase floated past on the summer night. We'd reached, I think, that part of the play when Malvolio has found the letter that causes all the trouble, when one of the audience, which was not large, made some remark implying that your man playing the part was not quite sober. Malvolio, standing in a large, dark pool, either treated this remark with the contempt it deserved or simply didn't hear it, but Mike, who I think was playing Sir Toby, came forward, wearing some sort of black cushion on his head, to thank the man in the audience, and to invite him either to put 'em up or to leave. The sun had set by this time, and the light was almost gone. The tide was coming in quite rapidly. Nobody stirred in the small crowd, but the same voice yelled out something about the rest of the cast being pretty much in the same condition. A black-haired Irish girl who I fancy had been acting Olivia came up from the shadows, and pushing her way through the small audience, grabbed the man in a half nelson and said, 'Right, that's it, Tommy, we're off.' Darkness fell, the play was abandoned, and we went back to Dublin in a hired charabanc. Mike hoped I had enjoyed the play, and said that it had been a very moving experience. The tears were running down his face, and he could barely speak for laughing. Seamus Ford had failed to notice that the performance had been aborted, and intoned chunks of *Twelfth Night* from the back of the bus in a low voice.

I have no clear memory of how it happened, but one morning Mike and I woke up in the same cell in the Bridewell. It was cold, smelly and dark. We were roused by a loud clatter of buckets and a banging on the cell door; a large garda carrying two chipped enamel mugs came in yelling at us to 'Come over here and drink this f—in' muck.' It was a perfectly fair description: brown stains all over the walls confirmed that earlier occupants of the same cell had shared the officer's opinion of the refreshments. We passed a cold and shaky morning gloomily sitting on our wooden planks, wondering what had happened. At about half past eleven, there was further clatter and yelling when the same garda burst in, demanded what the hell we were doing there when we should be up in the court in front of His Honour, and chased us down a passageway swinging his boot at us, then up a narrow flight of stairs, and, like moles into the sunlight, into the dock.

The courtroom was very full and warm. A clerk began a reading of the charges, reminding me dimly of being in the back of a black car the night before, with half of Dublin's constabulary trying to sit on my head, and of Mike, standing pale and erect in front of a desk telling a sergeant that while he might not be entirely sober, he had never abused anybody but himself. My own statement, which shamingly was also read out to His Honour, was quite unintelligible. His Honour spoke quietly but to great effect. We students might think it mighty amusing to get drunk, disorderly and objectionable, but he did not. He didn't exactly ask for the black cap, but looked as if he would very much like to. Instead, he gave us a stern lecture on the benefits of study and sobriety, bound us over, and sent us away.

Mike's father was a barrister who quite early in his career had successfully defended a man who anticipated being sent down for the term of his natural life. The generosity of his client knowing no bounds, this unexpected and profitable result enabled Mike's father to throw his wig away, and he settled down to a life of indolent excess. He was an extremely pleasant if taciturn bon viveur, and even when he had descended into a chronic alcoholic fog, he threw splendid parties wherever he happened to be. I can remember him once inviting a few of us to a wonderfully bibulous lunch in Jammet's, which rolled on through holy hour until nearly bedtime; and I can still see him swaying unsteadily on a summer's evening at the front door of a mansion outside Dublin, a glass of something potent in his hand, watching an attempted seduction in the driveway, quietly urging the participants to keep it up, as if he were at the races.

But this unsatisfactory example had an unsettling effect upon Mike, who was creative, highly strung and subject to black care. He meant to be a writer, and, after a number of short, angry plays of a political nature, created a couple of extremely funny revues in his last year at Trinity. He prevailed upon me to produce them, but I had no talent for direction, and I don't think I served him at all well. I tried something terribly clever with set design in the second show, which involved the players heaving a variety of six-foot, five-ply blocks about in the half-light at the end of each sketch, but the blocks were so heavy and unwieldy that the set changes lasted longer than the sketches. To my shame, a more able director ultimately took over the show, polished it up and gave it a short run at the Wexford Festival during the summer. I heard it went quite well, and somebody involved apparently offered Mike some scriptwriting work as a result.

I didn't see Mike again after we left Dublin, though I recently passed to my son the silver hip flask that he gave me on my twenty-first birthday. I became a ten-pound tourist, and emigrated to Australia. While I was there, I saw nobody from Trinity – apart from John Castle on the silver screen in Melbourne, starring in a film with Katherine Hepburn, which hardly counts. Nearly five years later, to miners' strikes and the three-day week, I returned, having missed the best of the Swinging Sixties. While I was hunting for a job, and for somewhere to live with the girl to whom I was about to be married, I bumped into an old friend from Ireland, and went with him to The Grapes in the Brompton Road. He told me what had happened to a host of old acquaintances. Some were directing on the telly, or even in the theatre. Some had grown up into schoolmasters. A particularly good friend had gone into publishing, and had married a dark-eyed girl in a sky-blue coat with a fox fur round her neck, who used to sit with her stockinged feet on my lap to keep them warm as we were tossed about steerage in the wintry Irish Sea on the way to Liverpool. Another was writing Westerns under the name of Nathan Lestrange. I suppose some had even gone into industry, like me, and were never heard of again. But something quite serious had gone wrong for Mike: somebody let him down, and he had jumped off Beachy Head a couple of years before.

Anthony Weale (TCD 1961–5; English) spent most of his working life in the chemical industry, first in synthetic fibres, then running an explosives business in West Africa for some years, then, by way of interlude, on loan to the Foreign Office in Mexico City. He retired after twelve years as ICI's head of government affairs. He is married, with two children and three grandchildren.

THE CORRUGATED COTTAGE

michael de larrabeiti

YOU'RE BOUND to fall in love when you go to college, at least once. That's what I was told. Well, it was six times with me. I fell in love with Dublin, with Trinity College, a corrugated iron cottage, a 1929 Fiat, Harry Bovenizer and the woman I was to marry.

The first sight of Front Square, walking through Front Gate – that was something. Those amazing proportions; the proportions that R.B.D. French, my tutor of English, used as an example of eighteenth-century politeness and decorum. And the rain gleaming on the cobbles, that captivated me too – every stone representing a broken heart, decades of broken hearts.

It had taken me long years to get to Dublin and I was proud of the journey. I had wanted so much to get to Ireland, something to do with my mother's name being Rose Leary I suppose, her father being Ned Leary, one of those Irishmen who had volunteered for the trenches of Flanders and had been mortally wounded in them.

So there I was with a room in Brighton Square – where Joyce was born for Pete's sake – and I drank in Slatterys, O'Neills, The Old Stand, Jammet's, Rice's and a place called Sean Murphy's in the Liberties.

Harry Bovenizer worked in the Reading Room and he didn't look a bit like a librarian. He was tall, at least six feet, broad-shouldered, strong-looking big, practical hands, red cheeked with black hair; handsome like a pirate is hand-some, only he had a shiny old suit on him. He must have started in the library straight from school and just stuck at it. He had good workmates and it wasn't a tiring job, so that left him plenty of energy for getting up to larks evenings and weekends. And he took me under his wing.

His father, Barney, was the gate man at Mount Jerome Cemetery, and the whole family, mother, brother, sister, lived in the gate lodge, a solid square Victorian pile that sank down into the ground. Barney stood in a nook of the lodge at a Dickensian desk and ticked off the corpses as they floated by in their hearses. He had a battered old cap straight on his head with the letters MJ at the front of it. If you went past him and down a steep flight of stairs, you would emerge a different person in a different dimension, welcomed into the warmest sitting-room in Christendom, a room smelling of brewed tea, freshly baked bread and home-made jam. And there stood the mother in her wrap-around apron, and we'd sit there, all of us, and yarn away – never mind the studies, never mind the books.

And then out through the back door into yet another dimension, another world; it was the magic that only occurs in children's books, you were through the looking glass. You had stepped into a living wilderness that was twice as extensive as the dead world of the cemetery up above. Had that territory been on a parchment map there would have been a legend saying, 'Here be dragons.' There were high trees and impenetrable bushes, an Amazonian undergrowth. Half-hidden in the greenery were a couple of wooden sheds where car engines could be winched off their mountings, swung high on chains that glinted with oil. There were old tyres, car seats to sit on, and guns everywhere.

This was Harry's playground, this is where he left Trinity College Library behind him, where he changed costume, where he sat with a rifle on his knee and waited for a rat or a pigeon to appear. There was no noise; Harry's guns had silencers on them. Very good for poaching, he explained; for early in the morn-ings, before work, he would set off out of the city, with his chums Brendan and Liam, in a Volkswagen van, the property of a Chinese doctor, the mystery of whose identity I never solved. They would park out in the woods somewhere, or by a canal or river, and take aim at a line of early-morning rabbits, or a swim of ducks.

'Them rabbits never hear a thing,' Harry would explain, 'they just look at each other, surprised you know, as one by one they fall over, even the ducks never know what hits 'em.'

Then he was back home and into the shiny suit and on the bus to the Library, red face smiling, shouting a cheery 'Hello' to the porters on the gate, the best bit of the day already done and only a bit of work between him and an evening that was full of promise.

I was never up early enough to go on those dawn expeditions but many an evening I sat with Harry and his 'da' when the cemetery closed. It was a corner of heaven on the Rathgar Road; rare moments and the rarest thing about them was that I knew they were rare, and I knew also that I'd better buckle those moments to my heart because I wouldn't get them a second time. Nor should I tell my secret; the world would be jealous of me and come to steal that time away.

And there were some mornings, as I dragged myself from bed in Brighton Square, when I'd hear a thump on the door of my basement flat, and with my mug of tea in my hand I'd open up on the day to find, lying on the steps, the dew and the blood still wet on them, a brace of ducks or a pair of rabbits, thrown from the Chinese doctor's Volkswagen. It made me jubilant to remember, once again, that life was just full of life.

At the end of my first term Barney sold me his old Ford Prefect, he called it Sputnik. Ten pounds, cash. It was black and it had a fuselage like a Spitfire. It had leather seats, a long gear stick and its own peculiar smell, a smell from the early days of machines, a smell of character and substance. It was from a time when cars had their own personalities. I felt rich and proud. I had never had a car, I couldn't even drive.

I had dropped from a large rambling apple tree of a family: three brothers and a sister; uncles and aunts and cousins. None of us had a car, though there was one uncle who drove for a living – Frank – he careered in a yellow newspaper van at speed all over London. He had one of those cowboy jobs, racing past newsstands at fifty miles an hour, throwing out bundles of newspapers without stopping: 'Star, News, Standard,' he used to shout, his voice sounding as rough as a bucketful of tin-tacks from the smoking he did.

'I can't drive,' I said to Harry. 'Only a motorbike and that very badly.'

I got short shrift from him. 'Jesus,' he said, 'don't you worry about a little thing like that … I'll teach you in an afternoon.'

I went into the post office and put a quid on the counter and they gave me a driving licence. I have it still; a fine green harp embossed on it; Dublin CBC, 4 Kildare Street; 7 December 1961.

Harry took me into Phoenix Park one Saturday afternoon and let me drive round and round for an hour, then he took me into the madness of Dublin traffic itself: O'Connell Street, College Green, Pearse Street, Grafton Street, St Stephen's Green.

'Ah, Michael,' he crooned at me from time to time, 'you're a natural.'

I may have been a natural but my hands shook and my stomach was water. It is more than likely that the standard of driving in Dublin these days is better than it was in 1961, I have no idea. All I could think of on the day, as I drove for the very first time, was that in all those cars, buses and lorries and vans, there was not one driver who had taken a test. It was not a thought to be easy with.

By the end of the year I was stepping out with Celia, a tall slim good-looking girl from Devon. She had a graceful upright stance, a low-pitched voice, golden hair and a figure to die for. Eighteen she was, that's all. I saw her that first time striding through the arched portal of Front Gate, her skirt swinging the way skirts swing; tense with life, 'She walked unaware of her own increasing beauty', unaware of her own elegance and the effect it had, 'a flower of good breeding'. So this was why I had come to Dublin.

Heads high in the Ford Prefect we drove south out of the city, down to Bray, a million miles 'them days' from the sophistication of the capital. We went to Greystones and walked along the beach; into Delgany and took stout in the pub. I can remember the drinkers looking at us, the way people look at the lucky ones who still have the bloom of youth on them. We made everyone smile.

Changing the gears we crossed the main road and found a small track heading up a hill, a couple of bungalows, a flock of ducks wandering. The hill became steeper and the Ford only just made it up, bumping and jolting from left to right, the wheels spinning in the dust. Halfway up, on a little flat space we stopped, pulled the brake on and placed a stone behind the rear wheel.

We leant against the car to look at the view. There was nothing to say in such beauty; we simply held hands, happy to be together. The hill dropped away towards to the east. Then a spread of country till the eye came up against the spire of Delgany church, clean and clear in the June sunshine, the trees still, and on the horizon, the sea golden and too bright to look at.

There was a five-barred gate to our left. We went through it, along a cow track, overgrown, the grass knee-high maybe. It led to another plateau where there stood an ugly little cottage built of corrugated iron and painted in a faded grey, a paint that would have come out of the tin faded. The roof was painted in a rusty red, the rust also being a constituent of the paint. And again the view, the view we had seen earlier, beyond Delgany to the sea at Greystones; the sun lower over the water now and the waves of it waiting for the moon.

And so the following autumn, back for my second year, I rented the corru gated cottage, thirty shillings a week. I also shared rooms with Laurie and Sebastian: No. 10 Front Square, ten shillings. Celia had a room in Hatch Place, one pound, sharing with some girls from UCD. We were lordlings, rich on our tiny grants; nobody lived as well as we did, not even the wealthiest of students with the wealthiest of fathers. Not even Gloria 'Double-Back-Action-Breech-Loading-Gore', nor the Bailey boys who spent money on her.

The corrugated cottage was lined with asbestos sheeting. It was furnished with the throw-outs of abandoned bed-sits on the north side of Dublin. There was a double bed, an old Victorian dining table, some chairs with rexine seat covers, cracked crockery and ancient lino on the floor, worn and torn. There was no heating, no water and no lavatory.

But there was a pump at the bottom of the hill, close to the bungalows. I bought a couple of plastic jerry cans and each time we drove by I filled up with water. We had bowls for the washing up and we bathed in College. Harry found me two or three second-hand paraffin stoves and we put new wicks in them. Things were looking good – but there was no lavatory.

I decided on the long drop solution. I borrowed a pick and shovel from Barney at Mount Jerome, cemetery tools, and went out to the back of our cottage, and in the overgrown, head-high weeds that closed us in behind, I dug a square hole about six feet deep. I scrounged or stole timber, four by twos, from a building site in Bray, and shoved them down into each corner, bracing them with struts at strategic points – a hammer-and-nails job, Harry called it.

These uprights rose about six feet above the ground and odds and sods of planks, from various places and painted in many colours, were sawn to length and nailed to the sides. For the roof there was a square of marine ply, painted yellow. The rainbow carsey, we called it. There was a door of sorts, swinging awkwardly on strap hinges, but the seat was the difficult bit.

I only had an old builder's saw. How could I cut a circular hole in a couple of planks of wood and fix them together? Not easy! So I made the hole in our lavatory seat diamond shaped, just four straight lines large enough to accommodate the largest of buttocks. We had proper bog-tosh too, discarding the idea of squares of newspaper hanging on a piece of string, although they might have been more picturesque and more in keeping with the architecture. Finally I purchased one large container of Jeyes fluid and the rainbow carsey was ready for its christening.

The attractions of Delgany were irresistible and, as time went by, we began to spend more and more time there, our friends too. Such meals we had, twenty or more of us, up on that hill, gazing at the view, medieval feasts that lasted from midday till dawn, with our messengers bringing up gallons of Guinness from the village in jerry cans and buckets. And the villagers in their generosity took Celia and me to their hearts, and rather than think unkind thoughts always spoke of us as 'Mr Beatty and his sister'. So the village pub became a haunt and walks on Greystones beach a frequent pleasure, though it was unfortunate that the grass that grew right up to the cottage door was infested with sheep ticks, which burrowed with delight into the skin behind our knees, sucking blood: there was only one remedy – we burnt them off with the bright tips of Sweet Afton cigarettes.

THE RABELAISIAN SOCIETY had been founded by Sebastian Balfour; it had a about half a dozen members, myself amongst them. The movement had been founded with the sole aim of countering the primness of those young ladies who came from the Home Counties; Rabelaisians promoted vulgarity on all possible occasions and in their presence. Sebastian wanted to make sure the English colony at Trinity did not sink into complacency – the English disease. He, together with Laurie, had purchased an old Austin Devon saloon, which he called Panurge. Panurge gave Rabelaisians mobility, and he was a frequent visitor to Delgany.

Perhaps he thought I was too happy, or complacent, in the country. One night, after some hours in the pubs of Dublin, he and Laurie leapt into Panurge and headed south to where Celia and I lay fast asleep in each other's arms, warm and tender in the corrugated cottage. (Sebastian and Laurie had already been responsible for getting me evicted from a room in Mount Street by writing 'Balls to the Landlady' on the front door in green paint. A graffito for which I got the blame.)

CELIA AND I were woken by stones and clumps of grass clattering heavily on the thin sheets of metal that made our roof. The noise went on and on. Celia was scared but I was terrified. After all, I was the man and supposed to do something. Still the noise continued. I could only think that maybe the local Opus Dei and the Sisters of Mary in league with the Jesuits had discovered that Celia was not my sister after all, but something much more sinful. What else could it be?

I still had the pickaxe from the building of the lavatory. I knocked the head of it free and with its handle in my hand I switched on all the lights and went out onto the front step, waving the weapon above my head, my terror making me appear brave.

'You bastards,' I yelled. 'Come up here where I can see you. You'll get this lump of wood round the back of your head. I'll kill the lot of you. I'll get a few boys out here from Dublin will see to the likes of you.'

It was time for Sebastian and Laurie to feel fear now. They could see that I was roused enough to crack their skulls open. Slowly they rose from the grass, helpless in a colossal mirth, clutching tightly to one another in their glee. I was mightily relieved, but I could have killed them in all truth. My whole body was shaking. I had seen myself tarred and feathered and ridden out of town on a rail – another godless sinner returned to the Sodom and Gomorrah that was Trinity College.

But then, it was midsummer's eve. Sebastian and Laurie had brought wine and prawns, cheese and brown bread and grapes and cake: and above all they had brought a record of Mendelssohn's music for *A Midsummer Night's Dream*. We sat outside, the moon was up, surely it must have been, and we played the music a hundred times and raised our glasses to the light on the sea.

And gradually I forgave them, but it took a couple of hours and many a glass of wine.

IN MY LAST TERM I took a walk up the hill behind the cottage and, lost and forlorn, overgrown in a copse, I found a 1926 Fiat; an open tourer, long, solid and sexy with huge wheels and an aluminium body. It was a wreck but I fell in love with it, and here it was, rotting gently in Silver Springs. I found the owner, who had almost forgotten about it, and I bought it for twenty pounds. I must have been crazy; I was crazy. What could I do with it? I was never a mechanic.

I got it towed to Rathgar and found a lock-up garage. When it was time to leave Dublin, Harry got it to the docks for me and it was swung onto the Liverpool boat, handsome in the sky like that, then down majestically into the hold in a rope net.

At Liverpool I was faced with the problem of getting it off the boat and transporting it to London. The crane driver was easy – ten shillings did the trick. The customs' officer was a gift from God. I can see him now, slightly built and stooped in his uniform, buttons of brass, bald, a gentle man with a gentle voice, glasses.

'What a lovely car,' he said. 'So you've been studying at Trinity. Ah, how I wish I could have done that. I would have read English Literature, like you, I think. I love Wordsworth.'

Wordsworth wasn't my favourite but I had a Complete Works with me. I opened my trunk, crammed to the top with books, and dug and scrabbled and came up with the Oxford edition in its blue cover.

'Here,' I said, 'something to read in the evenings.'

His eyes shone with gratitude. 'Wonderful,' he said, waiving the duty on the car.

'Now, how are you going to ship it to London?'

There was a whole Hades of lorry drivers in Liverpool and my customs' officer knew every denizen of its dark spaces. He stood guard over my Fiat while I went, under his direction and bearing his recommendation like the Golden Bough, to a broken-down little office on a street corner. It was painted dirty green, the windows were opaque with dried mud, and on the pavement before it stood a brazier of coke, glowing red. By the brazier stood a shifty-looking fellow whose eyes were so close together he looked like a Cyclops. A captain of skulduggery, his mackintosh was tattered and a racing pink stuck out of its pocket. A grease-stained pork-pie hat was stuck to his head. He was a dealer in contraband. Empty lorries that had off-loaded at the docks drove by him before they went anywhere else, the drivers touting for unofficial cargo. My Fiat was unofficial cargo.

Cyclops' soft lips folded in and out over his broken brown teeth as I told him what I wanted. 'Not easy, a big car like that,' he said. 'Might cost a bit.' I slipped him a couple of quid and stood by the fire, warming my hands. Lorry after lorry came by; the drivers, leaning out of their cab windows, shouted their destinations: 'Newcastle, Sheffield, Carlisle, Southampton, Glasgow.'

'Nah,' Cyclops would yell back. 'Nah.' Or he would give them the good news. 'Pier ten ... a load of cement,' or 'Timber,' or 'Steel girders.' He wrote these loads and destinations down in a grimy red notebook and waited for the drivers to return, lorries loaded now, again leaning out of their cab windows, this time with money in their fists. Then my lorry came and a highwayman leant out of it.

'Car for London,' said Cyclops.

'What car?' he asked and I explained, and the driver smiled; he liked vintage cars. 'A tenner.' We closed the deal.

He was a good man, Val. Back at the docks he talked the crane driver into loading the Fiat for nothing, and that night we slept in a medieval dosshouse, a room so full of beds that you had to climb over them to find your own. There must have been ten sweating men in there, snoring and farting.

I was worried about how to unload the Fiat in London. I had phoned a friend, Angus, and he was to meet me in Blackheath. 'Find a garage with a hydraulic ramp,' I told him, and he did.

The garage foreman was not too happy about the deal but I paid him and he became happy. At last the car was on the ground and in London. I had arranged with another friend to leave the Fiat in his garden; trouble was that his house was on the other side of Shooter's Hill. Shooter's Hill is about two miles long and nearly as steep as Beachy Head.

The garage break-down truck was to do the towing. I had imagined a fixed tow, an iron bar or something. Not a bit of it. The tow was a length of rope, a soft tow. I don't know what came over me. I agreed.

There were no brakes on the Fiat. I wasn't even sure if the steering worked. The tyres were ancient, the canvas visible through the worn rubber, they could have ripped themselves off the rims at any moment. There were no seats either and I was obliged to stand on the girders of the chassis, like a charioteer in Ben Hur, hanging on to the steering wheel to keep upright.

We started off sedately enough, but it was rush hour. There was traffic all around me, drivers hooting, shaking their fists and cursing. Angus drove his Peugeot 403 behind the Fiat and to the side, preventing the outside lane from overtaking, protecting me. We breasted the hill, went slowly over the brow, and then down we went, down and down.

As the two tons of Fiat picked up speed the break-down truck picked up speed also, the driver saving himself. There was no way we could slow down, it was dark and car lights were gleaming and flashing on all sides. Faster and faster we went. Terror made me mindless. I waved at Angus to come alongside, I wanted to get off, I wanted to leap onto his car, never mind the danger. I was going to be killed. Somebody would pull in front of us, the breakdown truck would brake and I would crash into it at full speed and be thrown out under the wheels of a double-decker, squashed on the black tarmac. Was this how my brilliant career was to end? It would be typical of my life, a symbol – speeding downhill with no brakes and out of control. Well, I had learnt something at Trinity – poetry, and only poetry could sum it up: Catullus of course – 'frater, ave atque vale' – 'Hail and farewell, brother.' Adapted from *Spots of Time* (Great Milton: Tallis House, 2006).

Michael de Larrabeiti (TCD 1961–5; English and French) was at various times a camera technician, a tour guide, a roofer and for many years a travel journalist with **The Sunday Times**. He published twelve novels, most famously **The Borrible Trilogy** (2003). He died in 2008.

BANANA SANDWICHES

heather lukes

THERE WAS great rejoicing in my family in England when I heard I had a place at Trinity. It was the year before UCCA was invented and you had to apply to each university separately. I had been tearing my hair out daily with all the form-filling and after a few conditional offers trickled in, I had a definite yes from Trinity. What a relief. Trinity was a big unknown. It had been recommended by the aunt of a friend and I had never set foot in Ireland.

I was worried about being English after reading about the Troubles but I needn't have been. The Irish people I came across were friendly and all-encompassing. Wherever you went, they talked to you. On the buses, in the city pubs and the country, whoever you were, they gloried in conversation. They all seemed so well-read and educated, too. Theatre, cinema, books and poetry, art and architecture, music and song, they did it all. What better place to be a student? It was 1962 and I felt I had landed in an enchanted city.

I had met Sue McHarg at Guildford Tech whilst brushing up our A levels and so we had arranged to meet at Front Gate, as you did, the first day of term. Sue had arrived early and already done a recce when she met me and had wasted no time in fixing us both up with a date for the evening. Digs had been arranged for us though we were on different sides of the river. It cost three pounds, ten shillings a week for a wonderful full breakfast with home-made soda bread, rashers, black pudding and eggs, and an evening meal, which was generally along the lines of boiled bacon and concannon, a mixture of mashed potato and green cabbage, and full slap-up Sunday lunch of a roast and hot pudding swimming in thick custard.

My first digs were miles out, a ninepenny bus ride and far too far to go back every evening for the supper if there was a rehearsal or a party to go to. I always felt safe walking home in the early hours. Sue and I didn't share digs until our second year when we were in Cabra, near Phoenix Park and near enough the slaughter house to hear the cattle groaning their last. Sue and I used to do ballet exercises to warm up in the mornings and the landlord would serve us breakfast on Sunday in his suit without a shirt because, having been worn all week, it was in the wash.

We managed to kid Miss Macmanus, the accommodation officer, that we had found some nice new digs in Sandymount when in fact we'd moved into a flat. Flats were not allowed until your third year. Men had all the rooms in College and women weren't allowed to stay the night. There were many tales of clambering over railings and smuggling in the back of cars. What larks! Our lovely new landlady had moved her family downstairs to the ground floor of a small semi, thereby sacrificing her only bathroom to us. Four of us girls squeezed into the upper floor, but to us it was luxury. The cooker was disguised as a dressing table for the royal visit and the kitchen made to look like a bedroom. What wickedness! We were Judy Russell, Jo Pirie, Sue and me. We felt free. We could cook, we could invite friends round. We showed off our limited skills, which mostly involved shepherd's pie and apple crumble but rose on one occasion to cheese soufflé. We served food straight from the pan and would have to use the same cups for soup, pudding, tea and coffee. Tony Weale was good at shopping and advised us where to buy beef on the bone and he had a habit of helping himself to raw eggs, which he swallowed whole. Judy would mesmerize any male guests with her beauty, her conversation and her rendering of 'The Girl from Ipanema' with a guitar. Any man we brought home would end up worshipping Judy. I can't think why I went on to share with her right through my time at Trinity. Jo was quite a canny one too. She was very much into sharing the chores but her idea of cooking was to say, 'If I put the kettle on will you make the tea?' We had a weekly kitty and agreed generally to go down to Moore Street where there were great bargains to be had, 'tree pence each the mackerel, do ya want anyting love?' The rotten Jo admitted later that when it had been her turn to shop she did go to Moore Street but she got a taxi back and charged it to the kitty. Friends!

Our last and best flat was in Wilton Place, by the canal. It was on the top floor of a Georgian terrace and had views of rooftops. We had a sitting-room with a gas fire, two bedrooms and a bathroom that you reached through a kitchen that wouldn't pass building regulations now. Paula Street, Alice McDowell and Gillie Hanna shared a flat round the corner in Baggot Street. It was a basement that seemed to be under the pavement and the walls were dripping wet. They had concocted a bookcase out of planks of wood and bricks, which was generally much admired.

We ate out at the (Chinese) Universal where a 'special', topped by a fried egg, was six shillings and sixpence. Or we tackled a chunky pork chop, mashed potato and mushrooms balanced on a tiny round table at The Old Stand. After a show we'd go to the Trocadero where the walls were lined with signed photographs of theatre and film stars. We had many teas and buns at Bewley's and on high days and holidays we had lobster at Jurys, or a martini at the Shelbourne.

Not only were women not allowed to live in College when I first arrived but they weren't allowed to eat lunch with the men either. While the men could be tucking into steak-and-kidney pie and treacle tart, we ladies were queueing up in No. 6 for Ryvita and pats of butter floating in a bowl of water. That's just the butter floating, not the Ryvita. Once the Buttery was opened we gathered there and ate off colourful plastic plates.

Money was tight but I boosted my grant by working for the post office or waitressing and managed to go on the odd skiing holiday and buy a typewriter with French accents so I could write my French essays. I was good at saving, I bought cheese scraps and bacon scraps and I made clothes for people with material from Clery's and mended my own shoes with rubber patches you could buy from Woolworths. Sue worked as a disc jockey in a little nightclub called Nobbits and saved pennies in the gas meter by bringing her washing in to The Elizabethan Society where she scrubbed and rinsed it all in a string of basins.

Being theatre-mad I joined Players for five shillings and was in every play I could possibly be in. My first audition was with such famous greats as Ralph

Bates, Gog (Constantin de Goguel) and Roger Cheveley. They hooted with laughter when I said I had played a lot of men's parts at school because I had been at an all-girls' school. What they were mostly laughing at were the words 'men's parts' but I was so innocent I didn't understand. The first time I had ever in my life heard the f-word was from the lips of Jerry Bell up a ladder.

In my first term I was vastly impressed by *The Fire Raisers* directed by Mike Ruggins with a cast that included Ralph Bates, Annabel Brady and Tony Weale. The first time I appeared on the stage in Dublin was in a French play for a modern languages festival with Gillian Crampton and was very chuffed to get 'Heather Lukes was very funny'. That led to the Carnival of Nations with Sue and I doing a silly little dance in silhouette, which was supposed to be French.

My first main production with a speaking part was *The Lark* in February 1963. I was Agnes Sorell, the king's mistress, though I had no experience whatsoever in real life of such a position despite the endearments of Max Stafford-Clark, who offered to enlighten me. Anyway, we girls wore chastity belts in the form of thick elastic 'roll-ons', which were hardly sexy and there was no easily available birth control so although there was much fun and flirting, full-blown sex was not undertaken lightly. I have tried here to follow the advice of the editor of *Women's Way*, a magazine I wrote some articles for in one of my attempts to be a writer. She had sent me out to report on married students and when I came back with my piece she asked, 'Is there any sex in it?' 'Oh, no,' I replied, primly. 'Well can you write some in? You've got about half an hour. We had an article last week about the Pill and we sold out.' Sex sells and it was as true then as it is now, so that hasn't changed.

They say that if you can remember the Sixties you weren't there but Dublin was behind the times: no one ever offered me drugs. The only thing we smoked came in packets of ten or twenty and there were ashtrays in the cinemas. We drank a fair bit and we danced a lot. Judy Russell with her long blonde hair was the nearest any of us got to being a hippy. We dressed quite smartly. We followed a sort of Carnaby Street fashion. We wore knee-length boots in the winter and slingbacks in the summer. Not a trainer in sight. When miniskirts came in we shortened our hems. Sue and I both had pretty little Donald Davis smocks that just about covered our stocking tops. Tights hadn't been invented so sitting prettily was an art. We tripped over the cobbles in tartan capes. We protected our bouffant hairstyles with hairspray and headscarves tied under the chin like the Queen at the races. Yes, we went to the races too.

The year after *The Lark* I was in *Bartholomew Fayre* directed by Laurie Howes. It was brilliant. Despite the small stage we had a two-storey set where someone could chuck rubbish out of the top window shouting, 'Gardez loo!' and a water pump that actually pumped out water. Well, it did if you whispered to Patsy Warwick who was backstage: 'OK Patsy, water please.'

I was in revues with Gill Hanna, Chris Serle, Jo van Geyseghem, Ian Whitcomb and Tony Weale and lovely plays like *The Importance of Being Ernest* and *Charlie's Aunt*. We had a strict rule when rehearsing that anyone arriving late would be fined a penny for every minute and we'd spend any money collected at the end of the production on drink. I was playing Cecily and Ann McFerran was the gorgeous Gwendolin. When she arrived more that twenty minutes late for the rehearsal she fluttered her long eyelashes at Douglas Henderson, the director, shook her cascade of auburn hair and said in her low sexy voice, 'I'm so sorry, Douglas.' 'Oh that's all right,' he said. I was very cross.

I came back early in September to be in plays and stayed on after the summer term to be in plays. The terms were only seven weeks long so not nearly enough time to pack everything in. I loved it all except perhaps the Yeats set of plays, which went down well with many Dubliners but I'm afraid was beyond me. I just used my best poetic sort of voice and tried to keep a straight face when Ian Milton, having banged his sword on the floor in the wings to signify his approach, entered majestically to announce, 'I come to weigh my sword against Cúchulain's,' and held up a mere stump of a sword, broken off at the hilt.

It was like being in the real professional theatre because we got a lot of publicity and there were always photos and reviews in *The Irish Times*, the *Irish Independent* and the evening papers. I have a scrapbook full of yellowing cuttings. Sometimes we went in for competitions organized by *The Irish Times* or *The Sunday Times* and won many awards. We took *The Country Wife* to Bradford, which wasn't a pleasant experience as the set got lost and the student critics didn't like us though Harold Hobson gave us rave reviews.

We went on tour to Wexford during the opera season and squashed into a one-room dormitory at Brown's Hotel. We would walk in through the lounge where there might be a harpsichord playing and go upstairs to the squalor of camp beds, clothes spilling out of suitcases and shared bath towels. Another year we camped in a dusty shed and slept on mats on the floor. The one time we had proper digs in Wexford was when we took *Under Milk Wood*, directed by Mike Bogdanov and not at the festival time. That was a financial disaster but we did have beds and there was warm water in the tap if you got back first after the show. I was replacing Dinah Stabb who had been in its first run at the Players Theatre and was very unsure of all the parts I had to play from cow to chicken to Polly Garter. Hoping for a bit of help from Gillie Hanna I whispered, 'Where do I go next?' 'Haven't a clue,' came the reply.

I WAS terribly excited one day in the autumn term of 1965 when Sue, meeting me at Front Gate said, 'Guess who's the Country Wife?' She had read the newly displayed cast list. A main part at last! It turned out to be a turning point in my life because I married the director, Douglas Henderson and we have been doing plays together now for forty years and, no, it don't seem a day too long!

We decided that the theatre was a bit dodgy and difficult to make a living so we'd better have something to fall back on. We went to Cambridge to do our postgraduate teaching certificates after Trinity and fell back immediately into teaching with theatre being part of our working life and our main hobby.

Back in the good old Dublin days we did have ambitions and we even got into Telefís Éireann in different shows but the big world out there is tough. I lost my lovely place on *Roundabout Now* With Terry Wogan because of my English accent. When I looked into doing a postgraduate teaching certificate in Dublin I discovered that I'd have to learn Irish well enough to teach in Irish if the day should ever come when an edict went out over the land: Thou shalt teach in Irish. When I stayed on for a year in Ireland after marrying Douglas it was difficult to get a job as all married women had babies; they didn't work. So, after all, I was a foreigner, I was English. My love affair with Dublin had to end. I had had a lot of fun, met lots of interesting and some now famous, people, made friends for life including Sue Arnold, Nigel Ramage whom I had met in the Surrey County-Council Grant queue and Ann Heyno who, while studying Psychology, used to test me on personality-analysing questionnaires and declare me far too boring and normal.

For years after leaving Trinity we spotted our old mates from Players frequently on TV and our children were quite used to us exclaiming, 'Oh look, there's Gillie,' 'Stabbie', 'Nigel' (smoking a pipe, 'Ah …! Condor!') or 'Ralphie!' That was Ralph Bates, who despite his rugged good looks became well known as monsters in Hammer films. We also regularly watched Martyn Lewis reading the news on ITV and then BBC, a serious job for someone who had performed mostly in comedies in Players. When our elder son was approaching make-your-mind-up time for a university, we suggested Trinity. 'But I don't want to go on the stage,' he protested. When we asked him what he meant he said he thought Trinity was a drama school.

What a great idea General Studies were! Three subjects that in my case – English, French and Fine Arts – could be linked up at several levels. I really enjoyed comparing Romanticism and Classicism in Art, Music and Literature. The reading list included lots of highly enjoyable novels but we had to smuggle in James Joyce's *Ulysses* as it was banned by the Pope. We had very few lectures and none before midday but they were compulsory. I had the privilege to be taught by greats like Geoff Thurley, Brendan Kennelly and Brian Boydell. We had lively tutorials and I must have worked a bit every now and again for my modest P3 General degree. I do remember sitting in the calm of the Library and trekking backwards and forwards to lectures across College Park and writing essays late into the night. We believed in education for its own sake rather than as a passport to a higher salary. The living was easy. The word 'stress' was never mentioned.

I mingled with high society and went to loads of parties. My scrapbook is also stuffed with invitations to drinks, balls, dances in country houses, clubs and boat-houses. Dublin had been a big, safe playground, an enchanted city where I had the courage to try all kinds of things. I had tasted the high life. I had played at being an actress, presenter, writer, programme-designer, copywriter, cartoonist, model, seamstress, cleaning lady and even a caterer. Our wedding was arranged for December, so as not to clash with any cricket fixtures and the next summer I was going down to Moore Street to buy ripe bananas for banana sandwiches for the First Eleven teas. Does anyone eat banana sandwiches these days?

Heather Lukes (TCD 1962–6; G.S.) married Douglas Henderson (qv) and spent a year in Dublin dabbling in the theatre and writing. She then suffered a PGCE at Homerton College, Cambridge, and a miserable teaching practice, so decided on motherhood instead. Five years later she returned to teaching. She taught English at Badminton School and then at Clifton College Preparatory School. There she became a class teacher, and, in her prime, head of drama. She now thinks her performing days are over, enjoys retirement and is trying to be an artist.

TCD Magazine, *25 May 1966*.

COOKING FOR KENNELLY

mirabel walker

I REMEMBER the four years I spent at Trinity College, not so much for what I did, or read, or studied, but rather in terms of buildings and of friendships. We were fortunate in both. There was seemingly limitless time to make friends, meet boyfriends, discover flat-mates and even get to know one or two of our lecturers.

The handsome eighteenth-century buildings of Trinity and of Dublin we took for granted, as we did so many other aspects of the city. There are buildings there that now I much regret not appreciating more, particularly the Georgian ones around the Liffey. Unbeknownst to us, the pioneering Desmond and Mariga Guinness were then busily campaigning for their protection and beginning to restore some through the Irish Georgian Society, which they revived in 1958 in the face of opposition, bewilderment or plain indifference on the part of most Dubliners, the remainder of the nation, and certainly the rest of the world. Many of these fine buildings, now so prized (and expensive), were then virtually slums, like the houses where Sean O'Casey's *Juno and the Paycock* was set. I wish I had walked round more and looked at their exquisite fanlights and wrought-iron work, their internal staircases and plasterwork, then crumbling and decayed.

Had one explored those buildings, or even been enterprising enough to lease one and live there, we would have learnt so much about Dublin which, in our student bubble, we missed altogether. For a large part of my time at Trinity I was lucky enough to share a flat on the top floor of a spacious house in Merrion Square, No. 79, with Gillie Ross, Liz Bell and Frances Whidborne, three girls who all eventually married their Trinity sweethearts – and all of whom seemed to spend a great deal of time encamped with them in the flat. They were, incidentally, all English; one of the odd things about being in Ireland at Trinity was that I made very few Irish friends there. However I did make great friends with one, Gillie Chance, who lived with her parents in the last wholly family-occupied house in Merrion Square, No. 90. I could see it over the treetops of the Square from the window of my flat and sometimes I was invited across for supper.

No. 90 had great appeal. When you entered it from the Square through a doughty panelled door, with an exceptionally fine brass lock-case; it was like stepping directly into another world, old-fashioned, comfortable, with a sense of continuity, identifiable, like Dublin itself. When I first arrived in Dublin, it seemed like a foreign city where people just happened to speak English but with a more interesting accent and attractive lilt than I had ever come across before (or since). No. 90 seemed to encapsulate the best aspects of it. When I later saw the film *The Dead*, made by John Houston from one of James Joyce's stories, it was reminiscent of that household down to the last detail – the extended family of aunts and cousins, the annual rituals, Christmas and my visits. No. 90 had a complete early-nineteenth-century interior: the encaustic-tiled entrance hall held on one side the consulting rooms of Dr Chance, a prominent Dublin physician, and on the other the waiting room for his patients, which was also the dining-room! The handsome stone staircase, with vivid Turkish carpet runner and brass stair rods, led to the double drawing-room on the first floor with its long sash windows (with mostly original glass) overlooking the Square gardens, where Gillie had been pushed in her pram as a baby.

I used to love going there for dinner. These appeared strangely formal, almost ceremonial after the student meals we knocked up in the cramped kitchen of our flat. After dinner came Mrs Chance's drawing-room ritual of coffee-making in a fiendishly complex apparatus consisting of a glass globe filled with water, which was heated over a spirit lamp and sent hissing and gurgling along a glass tube to shoot up through the coffee grounds in an adjoining glass globe. The resultant sharp strong coffee seemed as delicious as the process by which it was made.

After we left Trinity, Gillie, who like me had read English and Irish literature, became a teacher at Westminster Under School. She was amongst the first of us to get married and her wedding reception was held in that drawing-room in Merrion Square. The guest of honour was Lord Montgomery of Alamein, whose biography Gillie's new husband, Alan Howarth, had just written. 'Monty', small and ferocious-looking, took this opportunity to bark out supposedly amusing observations on the length of the groom's (and his Cambridge friends') hair, this being the time of long hair for chaps, which of course was very un-military.

I had not always been so lucky in accommodation in Dublin as I was with the shared flat in Merrion Square. When I first came to Trinity in 1962 I was billeted in the all-female Trinity Hall, sharing a bedroom with two other girls; it had a turf fire, as did most places in Dublin including shops and bars. This was the room's only attraction. I had not come to University to recreate my school years in an all-girls' boarding school, and as soon as I could, I took myself off to lodgings, in a semi-detached house in Ballsbridge, which, although marginally more liberating, were not much of an improvement. Although I had my own room, our landladies, two harpy-like sisters, were to my mind beyond the Pale: one of their rules being that either the electric fire or the light might be switched on at breakfast, but not both. Every morning began with their marching into the cheerless little dining-room to snap off one or other switch if we'd turned on both at the same time, which of course we had, just to annoy.

From Ballsbridge we would scuttle to the bus stop to get into Trinity for our lectures. Our clear favourites were those given by Geoff Thurley and Brendan Kennelly, whom we regarded more as friends than as teachers. I know I cooked dinner for one (or was it both of them?), and went on a date with one – or the other! Anyway, of the two, who were such stars during my time at Trinity, Brendan was the one with the irresistible voice; this alone would have made us turn up more or less on time for his lectures simply to listen to him, not that (I must admit) we paid him as much attention as we should. I remember him amazed and, though he was much too courteous to actually say so, somewhat appalled by the number and behaviour of the British undergraduates, remarking that 'Front Square was becoming more like Sloane Square'. Which maybe it was.

Would I warm to the Dublin of today? Somehow I don't want to go back and see. I have heard so much about the wave of prosperity (certainly not characteristic of the city I knew), which is said to have engulfed the city and many other parts of Ireland and, in so doing, obliterated much of the individuality and charm. Eccentricity, tradition, beauty, seediness, yes. Affluence? No … I think I am happy to remember Trinity as it was forty years ago.

Mirabel Cecil (née Walker; TCD 1962–6; English) became a journalist and worked for, among other publications, **The Times** and **Country Life**. Her books written with her husband, the historian Hugh Cecil, include **Clever Hearts** (1991), a biography of Desmond and Molly MacCarthy (which won the Duff Cooper Prize and the Marsh Biography Award), and, most recently, **Imperial Marriage** (2005), a biography of Edward and Violet Cecil and Alfred Milner. She has also written **A Kind of Prospero** (1996), the life of her brother, the late Sebastian Walker, who founded the children's book publishers, Walker Books. Her book **Mlinaric on Decorating** (2008) was co-written with David Mlinaric.

LOOK BACK IN AWE

andy gibb

IN MY ANECDOTAGE, it seems to me that my passage to Trinity and to Dublin was down to Yeats and the local vicar's son. The austerity of a minor English public school and the tyranny of an Edwardian father had been broken for me in the late Fifties by a charismatic and camp English teacher whose Harvard Ph.D. on Yeats was still hot off the press. The rich pantheon of Irish writers and poets had been completely foreign to me; but that teacher and his flamboyant histrionics catapulted me to Innisfree, 'my chair was nearest to the fire in every company that talked of love or politics' and I was right there with Cúchulain fighting the waves (I was later to name three giant Alsatian dogs after him, Cúchulain, I mean). This same mentor convinced me that I could get into Oxbridge as an oarsman, others that sitting for a scholarship could obtain me a place: neither option was ever realistic and my farming parents were so out of touch as never to disabuse me in my folly.

The answer came late in my last school year, in the shape of the local vicar's son. This suave and persuasive character was home from TCD, a rising Junior Sophister. For my childhood New-Forest friend Robert Heale and myself, he conjured up the prospect of wild parties, a freedom we could only dream of, and a cornucopia of misfits, mercenaries and missionaries. It was heady stuff, we were hooked and were to apply the very next day. Putty in his hands, we feasted on yet more tales of peers, queers and racketeers – there seemed no end to the possibilities. We had narrowly escaped conscription into the armed forces, now we had the chance to escape across the Irish Sea, forsaking the middle-class straitjacket of English values and dress code (blue jeans were still an American novelty, so Harris Tweed jackets, cavalry twill trousers, brogues and trilbies were the order of the day).

Before boarding the evening mailboat train to Holyhead, we had afternoon tea with Robert's grandmother in the shadow of Marble Arch. Even in those days, there was already something anachronistic and oppressive about her world, and we were both itching to set off on our odyssey. Like other English students, we had generous grants of £300 a year and could not wait to get started. In the event, Robert was to drop out very quickly, when he inherited what was then an obscene amount of money. With the expert assistance of friends and sozzled sychophants, over the next three years he chomped his way through £50,000 on the race courses and in the pubs and clubs of Ireland.

The train from Euston was packed, smoky and alcoholic, a weirdly seductive universe, which was to be replicated on the ferry-cum-cattleboat many hours later. For me, it was the first of thirty such crossings, many of them characterized by rough seas, stout and vomit. A future friend and infamous Trinity VIII cox called Norman Gillette spent many enebriated hours in the cattle section of the boat, surrounded by bovine friends. Robert and I were lucky enough to be adopted by a capable John Kelly (ironically, from my point of view, a future Yeats luminary) and Jim McKeith, an earnest medical student who was shortly to be mauled by a police dog or two while protesting the US arms blockade on Cuba. We were grateful for their savoir-faire style and were happy to be led off the boat at Dún Laoghaire in the small hours, arriving eventually at a Southside flat that John shared with Mike de Larrabeiti, the only man I ever met who had witnessed one of Herr Hitler's doodlebugs landing on a Battersea bus (in fairness, he was a mature student).

Mike's eyes twinkled even at that hour of the morning – no wonder, he was comfortably snuggled up with his beautiful siren, Celia. I forget whether John was already with Christine but the easy-going open house that they offered up to two green lads straight off the boat was infectious. I was familiar with Rimbaud and Baudelaire but, to my virgin eyes, this was hedonism itself, with a splash of bohemian decadence. As dawn seeped through the curtains, it was time to head off across the Liffey to catch a bus to my digs in Clontarf, where four other Freshers were billeted near Bull Wall. Only on the return trip to the city centre was I able to take stock of the idiosyncrasies of my new home. Of Irish history I knew precious little, to my shame (schoolboy history had inexplicably stopped at 1914). But I was shocked to come up against the phallic and triumphalist Nelson Pillar – was the one in Trafalgar Square not enough, I wondered? I was aware that countless Irishmen had enlisted in the British army in two World Wars, risking life and limb for a foreign monarch and legatee of Cromwell. Contradictions were rife, no more so than when I spotted the Swastika Laundry and then an early mainframe computer trundling down O'Connell Street on a horse-drawn trailer, or heard the cries of the fruit-and-veg sellers in Moore Street bouncing off the GPO walls, still pockmarked by bullets from 1916. I asked a garda for the time. He scratched his head and told me it was between three and five. I had clearly entered a baffling new culture. And it was life-blood and exhilarating, despite the poverty staring out from many a Dubliner's face, locals who could barely afford the many picture houses playing double features, or a ring from 'McDowall's by the Pillar' or a loaf from Johnston, Mooney and O'Brien 'who make the best bread'.

As I sauntered down a windswept O'Connell Street on my very first visit to Trinity, I passed Clery's department store (the virtues of whose manager – Denis Guiney – Dr Sheehy-Skeffington would frequently extol) and nipped into a bright and brash Forte's coffee bar resplendent with a chrome jukebox above each table, playing alternately Elvis hits and Telstar. I was ushered in by a tall avuncular doorman sporting epaulettes, military medals, greatcoat and officer-type hat in the company livery. We were to become good friends over the next two years, as I became less naive about life in Dublin and he less in awe of this awkward young Trinity student. Like so many before, I entered the gates of Trinity with my heart in my mouth. The lecture rooms for Mod. Lang. in No. 35 were less awe-inspiring. I had been hoping for something closer to the tiered seating that I later found in the Science buildings and which matched my expectations exactly. As a late entrant in October 1962 and as a General Studies student (the last year for such admissions from the British Isles), I was forced into the Museum Building by the need to take a third subject. Attended by the closest thing to Tyrannosaurus Rex (actually the Great Irish Elk, I recall), this was where exam results were posted and fates sealed accordingly.

Lecturers in my Department were a mixed bag. Dr Sheehy-Skeffington who read fluently from finely chiseled notes was the most impressive, but we sensed he was squeezing his presence with us in between more important parliamentary business, and I was ashamed to learn his father had been executed by the British during the Troubles. Professor Arnould and Miss North lent a certain *ancien siècle* quality to the proceedings and were thought to be elegant but a bit past it as we youngsters strove to curb our mickey-taking tendencies. Dr Loesl was kind and German but highly lampoonable. Dr Thomas was efficient, utilitarian but colourless, only becoming interesting when we heard much later of his work for MI6 during the Second World War. Dr Wright had a fixation with the ceiling, averting her eyes from us as we glazed over – I was never to forgive her for allegedly rejecting Tommy Murtagh's thesis on Simone de Beauvoir, which he was busy polishing in Paris in 1966 when I succeeded him and Mike de Larrabeiti at the Ecole Normale Supérieure. Hughie Shields killed medieval French for me but, despite a charisma-bypass performance at the lectern, he managed to sideline as one of Ireland's best ballad singers. Finally, there was a frisson and freedom in the form of Jean-Paul Pittion, an *assistant* who was one of us, yet wiser and funnier, and who hung out with the undergrads in the Coffee Bar and later in the Buttery.

Marooned as I was in Clontarf for a first term of rigid meal times with a punctilious suburban family, I missed out on the social and political scene, burying myself instead in the likes of *War and Peace* and a fresh look at Yeats, Wilde and GBS. I had already covered at school most of the work expected of us in College and was coasting along to a first-year distinction. On the back of this I was promoted to the honours course without loss of year whereupon I began an inexorable slide into academic mediocrity, landing up with a Third about which no future employer ever enquired or cared. This and the distractions and indulgences of the next three years did not stop Professor Arnould recommending me for a postgrad scholarship in Paris, part of which I spent flirting with Oenology in Dijon, before realizing it was not a gap year and sooner or later I would have to return to the 'real' world. When I did, it was to the world of advertising and 'All because the Lady loves Milk Tray'. Say no more.

We all abandoned our poor landlady after seven weeks: Dave Buchanon to rugby and boxing glory, Denis Wright to poetry and seduction, Andrew Allen to higher mathematics, while a lad called Hamilton chucked in the towel and went home. And I went to Murray's Hotel in Marlborough Street to join new friends and fellow oarsmen, alongside the Pro-Cathedral where a moribund Brendan Behan was allegedly being drip-fed with booze smuggled in by 'friends'. By now, the English Catholics amongst us had sloughed off the shackles of the Christian Brothers, the Jesuits, the Benedictines and other fearsome fraternities, so the half-hearted visits to the Carmelite Church in Grafton Street petered out, unless it was looking like rain. As for me, my religious beliefs had been whipped out of me at school for bunking off chapel, so I was spiritually neutered and thus unbothered by a predominance of one religion or another. I was to be married in an Anglican church in Naas two years before Bernadette Devlin appeared and the Troubles reignited in the North; my best man Pat Stokes was Catholic and I imagine the congregation was as mixed as it could be. Former Boat-Club captain Henry Clarke, on the other hand, risked and lost a safe constituency seat in the North by marrying a Catholic and nobody was more surprised than he. In the early days in the Boat-Club showers at Islandbridge, Pat Stokes received a classic taste of Northern Irish Protestantism when a member of the Senior VIII from those parts alluded to the new 'wogs' in the club. Pat was never a card-carrying Catholic but the insult was not lost on him and came back to him a dozen or so years later when visiting ex-captain Pat Braidwood, who was dying in hospital in a Protestant area of Belfast. Pat walked back through this area in the dark, surrounded by ferocious dogs. Braidwood's last words on the phone were, 'Jesus, Pat, if they'd known you were a Taig, they'd have eaten you alive!'

McQuaid continued annually to excommunicate any Catholic attending Trinity without dispensation. Censorship was still alive and kicking. The oxymoronic ban on contraception and abortion prevailed, relative poverty and ignorance persisted. Mercifully, in those days drugs were few and far between (when my bag was stolen on the way to Murray's there was inconvenience but no paranoia – it contained a small bag of opium, an ambush trophy of my brother's anti-communist army service in the jungles of Malaya). Colourless and illicitly distilled poteen was nevertheless available on the street outside the hotel so I was soon ready with Pat, great-great nephew of Jane Austen and fully lapsed Catholic, to discover the delights of Dublin's pubs, from The Old Stand to The Bailey, from Jammet's back bar to Davy Byrnes. As a natural scientist, Pat had to work harder than arts people like me, and he did so at the back end of College emulating Walton or Rutherford, I forget which. And how often we boarded a number 20 bus with double vision, thinking it was a number 10.

Rowing regattas and exams kept me in Dublin for the early summer of 1963 when John F. Kennedy came to town. On the evening after his triumphal drive through Dublin and past the gates of Trinity, Classics scholar and oarsman Bill Jacques and I were caught liberating a flag commemorating JFK's visit, from Capel Street bridge. I ran like the devil, but Bill was apprehended by a colossus of a garda fresh from the country and appeared before an ex-TCD judge next morning. Fortunately the shared educational provenance worked in his favour. Bill and other rowers were soon to be arrested again after a plate-glass pub door in Eyre Square mysteriously shattered, days after JFK's triumphal visit to Galway. In late November, not long after my room-mate John Roome, a talented organist, had almost burnt us to a cinder with a towel-covered three-bar fire, news came through of Kennedy's assassination in Dallas. To those of us in Murray's canteen for supper it was a chastening and obscene event, whatever our politics. For a long while after, there were few gripes about the food or the morning porridge, as all Dublin went into mourning.

Around my second year, I had demonstrated – at the post-Regatta drinking duels held in The Widows – unsuspected prowess in downing pints of Guinness in seconds. I was therefore selected by *Trinity News*, along with one Kevin Shillington, to drink and sprint at their expense through the thirteen pubs between O'Donoghues of Dubliners fame in Merrion Row and Searsons in Upper Baggot Street. We set a scorching pace for the first three or four pints, slowing to a canter to catch our breath and brain cells and to evacuate the surplus into the Grand Canal at Herbert Place, before the downhill stretch toward Pembroke Road, reaching Searsons just before closing. The so-called Baggot Street Run was accomplished in reasonable time without loss of self-esteem.

Faced by embarrassingly long summer vacations, and penniless after the intensity and expense of Trinity Week, hordes of students converged each year on the pea-canning factories of East Anglia, to live like animals in airless army

Nissen huts and to work like slaves to make a few bob. This they then pissed against the wall of the nearest watering hole, returning to College little better off than when they had embarked. It was here that Pat Braidwood's fate was probably sealed: he was six-foot-six, studying Engineering, a bit of a surveyor and thus perfect material to be a field marker for the crop-spraying bi-planes that disgorged endemically toxic pesticides. A formidable captain of the Boat Club, he was dead within a decade from Hodgkin's disease.

By staying on the clock for seven days and seven nights at Ross Foods' sweatshop, I did manage to leave with a few pounds under my belt. It was enough in different years to get to Moet et Chandon in Epernay to join Alistair Bond and others working there, to visit Pat Stokes and his girlfriend in Sweden and to pursue Rosemary Gibson across the pond to Maine where she was working on dyslexia.

I never really fell in love at Trinity until I met Katharine Nesbitt ('Kaki'), whose family owned Arnotts in Grafton Street and lived in Killiney (not a good enough reason in itself!). She was a good writer, poet and painter, understated in every way, a beauty too with fine dreams. It was my first introduction to middle-class Dublin society and to a Southside nuclear family: patriarch, sophisticated beautiful mother and rival, pre-pledge wayward brother and flowering sister. I was unused to commerce but soon became familiar with names like Findlater, Slazenger and Dunlop. Always close to sailing and the local Royal Yacht Club, Kaki dumped me quite rightly for Belfast scholar and champion sailor Jimmy Nixon after I had the audacity to send her (a real poet) pathetic poesy from Houston. After three weeks bobbing over the Atlantic as a 'greaser' on a Norwegian freighter, I was hopelessly smitten and thought of her every mile of my hitchhiking Kerouac-type trek through thirty-five of the United States and Mexico. When I returned undiplomatically with a Norwegian beauty in tow, she was not impressed (though many predatory Players men were). In any event she had already moved on.

I was once propositioned by a pretty English rose who offered to be my mistress if I would be seen around with her. I was terrified and fascinated by this precocious, emancipated piece of predation and ran a mile. I also stepped out with Kristina Bruggermann with whom I had shared lectures for four years without noticing her grace and beauty. And then there was Rosemary Gibson.

I envied Rosemary her spontaneity and challenging irreverence. And I hated being attracted to her, she was sexy and seductive without realizing it, an unwitting tease, a perennial virgin for whom the Campanile bell was never going to toll. She had everything I sensed I lacked: a free spirit, gutsiness galore, curiosity and a healthy disrespect for authority. By comparison, I felt timid, an appeaser and a hopeless Libran. So I ignored her until she had left. She returned in my final year and I fell under her spell. I was ripe for conversion.

Then the party was over and it was time to get a proper job. In those halcyon days, there was no shortage and the decommissioned admirals of the time who head-hunted for blue-chip companies like De La Rue, GKN, Turner & Newall, Metal Box and British Oxygen beat a path to our door irrespective of our grades. We all played the airfare expenses game, flying once and claiming fivefold. My composure was badly ruffled when the recruitment officer for J. Walter Thompson Advertising, applying the latest sexual stereotyping favoured by Dr Kinsey, asked me to expatiate on my masturbation regime. No need for that at Trinity, I thought. Somehow I did not get that job.

Andrew Gibb (TCD 1962–6; Modern Languages: French and German) left Dublin for Paris to study contemporary literature and to Dijon to follow oenology. He then spent seven-year cycles in advertising and marketing, in teaching, in antiques restoration, in property management and latterly in sustainable development in Papua New Guinea. He was married to Rosemary Gibson (qv) for thirty years.

1964 TCD *Garden Party. Katherine Nesbitt, Andrew Gibb, Prof. R.B.D. French.*
Courtesy of The Irish Times.

RATS, MICE, COFFEE AND BUNS

ann heyno

I ARRIVED at Trinity in October 1962, fresh from boarding school. My headmistress suggested that I try for the newest, Sussex, and one of the oldest, Trinity. I chose Trinity and Trinity accepted me. My father was delighted because my local authority gave me a grant and for the first time in years he didn't have to pay for my education. I even had my ferry fare paid but, as I suffered from sea sickness, my father made up the difference and I had my first taste of Aer Lingus.

I wasn't aware then, as I am now, how privileged I was. Trinity, in those days, had a high percentage of Oxbridge rejects and ex-public-school pupils, and we who went to university represented only 6 per cent of the British population. The government financed us; my fees were paid, so was my board *and* lodging; I had £5 a week spending money and I felt rich and comfortable. It was a different world to the university I work in today.

Why I chose Dublin I will never really know, but from the moment I set foot on Irish soil at Baile Átha Cliath my lifelong love affair with Ireland and everything that's Irish began. I had never been to Ireland before but felt immediately at home. Trinity had arranged digs for me and selected a room-mate. I was to live in the home of Gascott and Mary Symes in County Dublin; they were a respectable family, Protestants as it happened, with a son – Gascott junior. At the time I had little real awareness of the religious tensions that were to dominate the North a few years later. However, having worked in a frozen pea factory in Cleethorpes the previous summer, I picked up a few indications that things in Ireland were a little different from the norms that pertained in England.

Eager to learn as much as I could about the country in which I was soon to be a student, I befriended a fellow worker from Northern Ireland. After a while I asked her what religion she was. She refused to answer me and I soon learnt that one didn't ask this sort of question. At the time I had no idea why. In fact I was so ignorant about the reality of Irish politics that I even harboured a romantic notion that when I arrived in Trinity I would get involved in things and join the IRA. It was becoming obvious to me that I was no longer the Tory I had been brought up to be; nevertheless I realized becoming a member of the IRA wasn't quite the way forward for me, nor was it the way to pursue my dream of improving society.

I arrived at the Symes' respectable home in Sydney Road, Blackrock, a tenpence bus ride from Grafton Street, to find that I was sharing a room with beautiful, blonde, Marianne Alexander from Zanzibar. We got on from the start and lived together at three different addresses for the whole of our time at Trinity. We possessed very different characters and didn't mix a lot socially, but we confided in each other at the end of each day and we drove Mrs Symes mad with our discussions over the dinner table about Kant and Descartes. But she was a wonderful woman and looked after us like a mother. Every night there were two hot-water bottles in our beds: one stone, one rubber.

The year I began at Trinity was the year that the Psychology Department opened, and I was one of its guinea pigs. The faculty was housed in a Georgian terrace in Westland Row, not far from the railway station. We had to climb several flights of stairs to get to the rooms and because it was all just beginning, there was an air of excitement about it, and I remember the Saturday morning sessions spent endlessly experimenting on rats – or was it mice? We were pioneers, starting out together in a new discipline. And I also remember our group coffee and bun sessions in a local café after class: sheer heaven.

It was unfortunate, to my mind, that we did little 'abnormal psychology' though it obviously impinged on my English essays. Geoff Thurley returned my opus on *Wuthering Heights* with 'This is far too Freudian' scrawled on the bottom. Strange that – I didn't know anything about Freud at the time.

I suspect that the little abnormal psychology we did at Trinity was probably very unconventional by today's standards. Indeed, in my final year, one of my lecturers suggested I take some mescaline so I could discover how it felt to be psychotic. I declined. I was approaching finals and I was afraid that I might disturb my equilibrium. It was probably a well-intentioned suggestion and an example of the innocence and naivety of the times.

But I enjoyed the work and I made good, lifelong friends doing it. The camaraderie was extraordinary. And yet I was fascinated by the indignation of those students from the North who protested at the idea that it might be possible to argue that God did not exist. I was even more taken aback by the Irish Catholic student, in my year, who was excommunicated because he came to Trinity. Not only that but he had to work all night in a flour factory to support himself through university. Once more I was made to realize how fortunate I was.

But, in truth, the academic work was only the backdrop. The heart of our experience was the life of Trinity – the buzz. It was Players, it was writing for TCD. It was the social life, it was the falling in love and the heartache that followed, the Trinity Ball, parties in country houses, driving back through country lanes in the mist of the early hours, and it was discovering the magic of Howth Head and Killarney. And there was the Wexford Opera Festival, Achill Island, the beauty of Connemara, and seeing Bob Dylan on his 1966 tour and not appreciating the importance of it. And above all meeting people wherever you went who were laid back and oozing an irresistible charm. All that, in my mind, was TCD, something that would have been a wonderment in anyone's life, and certainly was in mine.

And there were so many young men at Trinity and they all seemed so damned attractive. I had never seen anything like it. I had been educated at Cheltenham Ladies College and there we didn't do boys. We were banned from the part of town that the boys' college frequented. For me Trinity was like discovering an oasis in a desert. A sexual awakening. I remember walking through Front Gate the very first time to discover a line of stalls advertising various societies – I think that's what they were doing. Whatever it was I had eyes only for the men. One in particular was the gorgeous Roland Brinton, with his dark hair and dashing good looks. He was throwing a party and without any ado invited me. Life at Trinity had begun.

It was dark at the party, there was loud music and we were all squeezed into a tiny room. I soon found myself sitting on the floor with a Jean-Paul Belmondo lookalike called Mike Newling. Mike was nineteen or twenty going on thirty-five. His chat-up line was professional. In fact it was so good that I failed to recognize it as such. I was bewitched. 'I'm writing a review,' he said, 'would you like to be in it?' Would I like to be in it! I was flattered, I was excited and I was seduced. That party was the beginning of a four-year relationship with Players, Trinity's own special theatre. But sadly, that tiny stage in No. 3, just to the right of Front Gate, had disappeared the last time I visited Dublin.

My boyfriend at the time was a medical student at Guy's Hospital, and from time to time I would fly over to pay a short visit to him in London. My parents knew nothing of these visits and I went in fear of being found out. At Dublin airport J.P. Donleavy came up to me: 'Aren't you the girl from TCD?' (I had interviewed him the day before for the *TCD Miscellany*). I was flattered. We chatted and eventually walked onto the plane together. As we crossed the tarmac I spotted the television cameras, there, of course, for Donleavy. I had visions of my parents seeing me on television leaving Ireland for London.

'My parents don't know I'm going to London,' I said lamely. 'May I hide behind you?' J.P. was a proper gent. 'Why of course,' he said. So I left Ireland using the legendary Donleavy as camouflage. On the journey we sat together and he was charming, and quietly spoken, as different from his central character, Sebastian Dangerfield, as he could have been. I thoroughly enjoyed his company and hope that he did mine. At Heathrow he continued to be the perfect gentleman and gave me a lift into central London, where I went hot-foot to my boyfriend to regale him with my literary adventure, and also make him regret that he was not at Trinity.

As my fourth year drew to its close I began to think about work. I knew I wanted to be a journalist but I had done nothing about getting a job. Some of my fellow students had got themselves interviews with Thompson Regional Newspapers, but for some reason I hadn't bothered. The day before the interviews I rang 'your man' and apologized for being late. 'I'm just about to have a bath,' he said, 'but come up to the hotel in about an hour and I'll see you.'

So it worked. In September 1966 I started as a graduate trainee on the *Stockport Express*, near Manchester. Stockport was some shock after Dublin.

It had been miniskirts in Trinity but Stockport couldn't handle that and I was shouted at in the street and stared at – and worse. I soldiered on as a journalist, then became a part-time teacher and then trained as a student counsellor at the University of Westminster, where I have been since 1979, running the service since 1985. Student life in 2008 is very different from student life in 1966. Over forty years on and I feel the sense of lightness has gone. I return to Ireland from time to time and the magic remains but I also notice huge changes.

When I received the email asking me to contribute to this collection of Trinity reminiscences I was in the middle of preparing a paper on student suicide for an international congress. It was an important paper and I was feeling anxious. The request from former Trinity friends was a welcome diversion from a subject that I find myself writing and talking about quite a lot these days. Reflecting about what I was going to write brought back the heady excitement of youth and the thrill of the experience. It also made me reflect further on why so many of today's students are depressed and why student suicide and suicide prevention has become one of my areas of expertise.

Being a student in the Sixties, especially at Trinity, was without external pressure. There was a certain amount of peer pressure to compete socially, to act, to write, to look good, but I don't remember there being much pressure to achieve academically. I don't remember it mattering too much what sort of degree we got. We had a vast freedom to enjoy what we learnt. Our time outside studying helped prepare us for work. It taught us to be creative, to think on our feet and to learn fast.

When I eventually presented my paper on student suicide at the international congress I met a young woman who had done her Ph.D. at Trinity, in the Psychology Department, where I had famously toiled. I was delighted to learn that the Psychology Department was thriving. It had moved from Westland Row to purpose built premises inside the main campus. Excellent! No more rats or mice, followed by coffee and buns on a Saturday morning. Yes, it is excellent, and in a way, it's a pity too.

Ann Heyno (TCD 1962–6; G.S.) worked for ten years in journalism, including freelancing for BBC radio's **Woman's Hour** and co-presenting a school's television programme, while teaching English and remedial reading. This led her to train as a counsellor. She is currently head of the Counselling and Advice Service and director of Student Support Services at the University of Westminster, where she has been for twenty-nine years. She taught counselling at Birkbeck, University of London, for nineteen years. She is now about to launch into a new career as an independent consultant.

AN AGE OF INNOCENCE

gill hanna

WHY weren't we revolting? Weren't students the world over in ferment? Weren't American flags being burnt in the streets? Weren't civil disobedience and mass demonstrations breaking out everywhere? Why weren't we involved in all this turmoil?

Because we went to Dublin in 1963 and graduated in 1967.

Because, although we didn't know it, we were living in an Age of Innocence.

Because we didn't know we were on the edge of a precipice of convulsive political change.

Because we were young, golden, carefree; living and studying surrounded by natural and architectural beauty, cushioned by privilege, even if we didn't have any money, and awash in Powers whiskey and Guinness.

Because we were the last generation of students before the Vietnam War, before the Troubles, before Paris 1968, the Prague spring and well before feminism.

Because we were having a good time.

The power of all that hindsight might make the glitter in that golden era look like fool's gold, but how were we to know at the time that we were living in a space the size of the eye of a needle between the horrors of the Second World War, the difficult recovery that followed and the convulsions to come?

We were not committed in the way the next generation of students would be. My greatest 'struggle' in my first year was trying to work out how to get out of Trinity Hall and into a flat. I wasn't alone. There were five of us who realized after the first week that our parents had persuaded us into a dreadful mistake and condemned us to a year of finger-wagging and infantilism; we asked could we leave and were firmly told no. Pain of rustication, scandal, no refund of the fees. The following year we shared a flat in Rathmines, only semi-legal in university terms as it was supposed to be digs, which meant breakfast, but the landlady was as happy as we were for her not to bother, and we self-consciously referred to ourselves as The Group, once we had read the Mary McCarthy novel. We could never work out who was going to turn into which character in the book. I don't think we ever did.

And can it be that our greatest sense of outrage was expressed when Dylan went electric? Or that one my most indelible memories is of feeling smug and superior because we were played the latest Beatles single a good week or two before anyone else heard it while we were in a professional recording studio doing sound effects for *Under Milk Wood*?

Those cataclysmic events of the Sixties created an abyss between what went before and what came after. And certainly for me, sitting finals in September 1967, the whole four years in Trinity were bathed in the innocence and ignorance of the 'before' era. We were busy trying to be cool, exercising our late-teenage discovery of ourselves as a new phenomenon – dolly birds and dedicated followers of fashion. We were the first post-war generation to have the opportunity to be obsessed by fashion and appearance and whose obsession was catered for by the new shopping. Among our greatest worries were: do you think this miniskirt is too short, did you see the new Mary Quant dresses in Nova, how can we get hold of that dark-purple Biba eyeshadow? And of course the classic female Sixties mantra: 'Did you read Katherine Whitehorne's article on Being a Slut?'

We were part of a tidal wave of social change that we weren't even aware of – coming out of the austerity and deprivation of the immediate post-war decade, which our parents had struggled through and which I for one, had barely noticed. Low-key hedonism (low-key because we didn't have the money for a higher key) ruled our daily strolls in and out of Front Gate.

For me, there was never really any question of going to any other university. When your father, uncles, godfathers (and where were the mothers, though it never occurred to me to wonder about that at the time) have all paraded their youth through that formidable stone arch, there's really no other option. Of course in one respect it was bound to turn out badly. I was always going to be a disappointment to the older generation. *I* was never going to be in the College boxing team, nor captain of cricket and hockey. No, as it turned out, my low-key hedonism meant that I was more likely to be found in Bewley's with a coffee and a slice or two of barmbrack, or The Old Stand, which is where I discovered that all Dublin pubs appeared to have an electric kettle on the bar so when it was cold you could have a hot whiskey at any hour of the day (except of course during the holy hour when you'd have to retire to Jammet's back bar for Guinness).

But the city of Dublin and its surroundings were not discoveries for me. My mother was a Dubliner. I had been spending holidays with my grand-parents in Terenure and Glendalough all my life; we'd had many picnics and swims at Brittas Bay, I'd been to the Theatre Royal where you saw a film and a stage show on the same bill, and I was an old hand at the spiral staircase up the inside of Nelson's Pillar in O'Connell Street from where you could see all the way to the Wicklow Mountains. Nor was I terrified at the idea of leaving home – having just lived in Paris for a year pretending to be studying at the Sorbonne. In fact I was working in a laundry during the day, and at night drinking rum and coke with a bunch of expatriate American poker players among whom was a guy who claimed to have been a drummer with the Count Basie band. How cool was *that*?

The first sign, had we known what to look for, the first inkling that all was not well in this paradise of sex and drugs and rock 'n' roll (actually I had quite a lot of rock and roll, very few drugs and even less sex but that's another story) should have been the assassination of John Kennedy. Walking down Grafton Street to a rehearsal of, was it, *Bartholomew Fayre*? – the hoardings of the news-paper sellers ('Heddlermail!') screaming, 'President of the United States assas-sinated.' And while it was a tragedy that we took personally – he was so young, so handsome, so glamorous, he somehow represented us, despite the fact that he ruled on the other side of the Atlantic Ocean – it was so far away, and didn't seem to have any expanding meaning that might affect our lives.

What then?

Falling instantly and unrequitedly in love with a tanned vision with blonde hair and a dark-blue corduroy jacket who had just come back from a year's VSO in Africa.

Excruciating social terror at balls in country mansions where I never had the right long dress and spent most of the evening hiding in the lavatory because I was afraid no one would ask me to dance.

Swimming naked in freezing lakes in the Wicklow Mountains.

Champagne and Guinness parties the Boat Club used to throw in Trinity Week.

Falling unrequitedly in love again, this time with another blonde vision who was taller, more ascetic and drove a powder-blue Bubble car.

The pleasure of walking all day in the Wicklow Mountains, getting caught in a rainstorm and being literally soaked to the skin.

Sitting on T.P McKenna's knee at two in the morning in the after-hours bar in White's Hotel.

The Group's twenty-first birthday ball when we hired the Crystal ballroom, had two bands, and made everyone come in Victorian dress and fill in dance cards.

The apprehension of checking the Rupert Bare column in *TCD* every week: the first page you turned to. Panic and shame if you were mentioned, social death if you weren't.

The Beatles. The Rolling Stones. The Kinks. Dylan.

Finally, at the last minute, in the last weeks of my last term, having sex in a peat bog somewhere near Glendalough.

And yet there were more rumbles of the world we would inhabit later on if we had looked up from that glass of Guinness for five minutes. There may have been some or many who did. I wasn't one of them. Foreshadows of the eruptions to come … Living by then, 1966, at a rather posh address in Ballsbridge, was it Wellington Crescent, doing my ironing and listening to … oh no it can't be … *Mrs Dale's Diary* … (there goes what small shred of street cred. I might have possessed. *No one* under the age of sixty-five listened to *Mrs Dale*. What on earth did I think I was doing? And surely it was too soon for postmodern irony. In my own defence, there wasn't much else to listen to, even Radio One didn't exist until 1967). The news announced that Nelson's Pillar in Dublin had been blown up. So of course I unplugged the iron, jumped on a bus and roared off to see the subsequently infamous Stump. I remember thinking, how sad, now I'll never be able to climb up it again, how elegant it had looked poised there in the middle of O'Connell Street, and it never crossed my mind to wonder what this act meant in the context of Irish history. At that point I think I was under the impression that the IRA consisted of a half-dozen grumpy old men who occasionally lobbed small bombs into pillar-boxes just for the hell of it.

And what about the poor man who sat with his stall and leaflets trying to get us to sign his petition demanding a students' union? How superior I felt to all that sort of strident clamouring. We didn't need a students' union. *We* attended a university that treated us as adults and would discuss grievances with us in an atmosphere of calm attention.

Actually, ludicrous as it may sound, there was some truth to that particular delusion. In the last year of Modern Languages, the Department required the study of a 'Special Subject' for an exam that would be part of finals and would consist of just one question to be answered – a sort of mini-thesis under exam conditions. At the beginning of the year they produced a list of possible topics to choose from. Among the most exciting was something like 'the development of the cedilla from Old French to the present day'. So we staged a very mild-mannered mutiny and went to the wonderful Owen Sheehy-Skeffington (Skeff), our professor, and told him we thought we'd been offered a very dull set of options. He cautiously agreed and asked us what would we care to study instead. French surrealism, we said. Right you are, he replied, and I will be your tutor and set the exam. Who needed all that shouting at Front Gate when you could get what you wanted by talking man-to-man (*sic*) to Skeff?

And how did I miss the fact that Skeff himself was part of an heroic family, that his father had been shot by the Brits in 1917? Or if I knew it, that it seemed to be part of a romantic past and nothing to do with an ever more urgent political present? I did at least recognize his own heroism in another context when I heard him speak, as one of the Trinity senators, in the Senate on the use of corporal punishment as sanctioned in the new Christian Brothers' rule book. The old rule book had specifically outlawed the use of the tawse, an implement of chastisement I had never seen but believed to be a short stick of lead covered with leather. The new rule book omitted that particular clause and Skeff's argument was that by omitting it, the Brothers were tacitly being granted permission to use it. I think he spoke for over two hours. He lost the vote in the Senate but his admiring students recognized him as the hero of the debate. Appropriate somehow that he died in 1970 as the decade came to a close.

The line of continuity/discontinuity between the selves we once were and the selves we are now and perhaps too, the selves we thought we were, can follow the seemingly natural curve of a life so that one phase runs logically into the next; or can run in fault lines, bisecting or chopping up a life into irreconcilable chunks. In its simplest version it's looking at someone and thinking: 'Well of course it makes sense that *he* would have ended up writing bestselling books', or 'Whoever would have thought that *she* would spend her life growing carrots in Connemara?'

For me, those events whose explosion coincided with my immediate post-Trinity life, did indeed cause a fault line that meant the self who was a student in Dublin in the mid-Sixties was a quite different self from the one who spent most of the Seventies and Eighties involved in left-wing and feminist politics in some form or another, and used to feel burning shame looking back at that student self and think, 'How self-indulgent, how unaware.' How embarrassing. I used to be utterly dismissive, furiously critical when I remembered that student self for being so thoughtless, so self-obsessed, so careless.

Now though, maybe it's time to be kinder. Yes, it was a careless and in many ways blinkered life I led, but instead of castigating myself, shouldn't I be grateful for it?

Grateful that Trinity at the time seemed to want to attract students of Life as much as the syllabus? That the obsession with results had not hit the student body in the stultifying way it seems to these days? That what I learned in those four years was as much to do with the people I met as what I was taught in lectures? Grateful that for four years I was able to live the life that one should live when young: with a certain kind of innocence and in an unrepeatable atmosphere of optimism?

We didn't have to worry about global warming, HIV/AIDS, international terrorism, adventurist wars. I think we can be excused for not engaging in the wider world because the wider world seemed to be looking after itself. It wasn't apathy that stopped us revolting. The era of Great Causes was yet to come.

Another era and The Group, turning sixty, decided to stage a rerun of the famous Crystal Ballroom party. How hilarious to find that we couldn't afford it. No ballroom, no bands, no dance cards, no sit-down meals. All way beyond our means. Whether this speaks of rampant inflation or our lack of financial success in the intervening years, who can say. But it was great craic anyway.

Gillian Hanna (TCD 1964–8; Modern Languages: French and Italian) has always been an actress (her last film was Roman Polanski's **Oliver Twist**, 2005) and a translator of plays from French and Italian (Dario Fo's **Accidental Death of an Anarchist, Elizabeth: Almost by Chance a Woman**, and with Franca Rame, **A Common Woman**, all published by Methuen). She was a founder member of the feminist theatre company The Monstrous Regiment. She lives in Dungeness, Kent.

THE TRINITY IDYLL

Douglas Henderson

I **ARRIVED** in Dublin on the Liverpool ferry with a couple of friends, somewhat apprehensive like most English people, knowing little of life in Ireland (or anywhere else, for that matter). Those of us who have been to Trinity are asked regularly why we went there. In my case, my headmaster and Latin teacher were both TCD men, so it did not strike me as remotely odd to be applying there. Further, in those heady days, the English counties were quite happy to give you a full grant (fees and maintenance), so there was no reason not to apply. So TCD it was, to read Latin and French (called rather magnificently 'Ancient and Modern Languages and Literature').

TCD's link with Oxford and Cambridge goes back a long way. My earliest introduction to it was the Oxford, Cambridge and TCD skiing party, which I joined at the end of my first term. It was 400-strong, and we set off on our own train from Victoria and fetched up in Zermatt. I think even the train itself went on the ferry in those days. Here I learned, on a fortnight's holiday, not only to ski but to play poker (a skill that has often come in handy). The organizers were brilliant and the holiday was breathtakingly cheap (I think it was £42 for a fortnight, with full board, lessons, ski hire, the lot). Zermatt had suffered absolutely terrible publicity the previous year, when several people had died from typhus or some such. The organizers astutely recognized that the resort would therefore, the following year, be not only the cleanest resort in the world but also the cheapest. Add to that the buying power of a 400-strong party in the very first week of the skiing season, and you begin to understand why it was so cheap.

It took no time at all to discover that those English notions that Irish people were obsessed by religion and politics and would be highly resentful of anybody with an English accent turned out to be completely unfounded. Not once in four years did I come across any hostility whatsoever. Indeed, it became clear that Irish charm and hospitality is every bit as wonderful and generous as the tourist adverts say it is. Add to that the magnificent city that Dublin was in those days (somewhat internationalized in recent years, but in the Sixties very distinctive and would have been recognizable to James Joyce); not least the architecture with those magnificent squares, city terraces and wide streets.

I started in digs in Cabra recommended to me by Frazer Williams. I can't remember the exact price but it seemed absurdly cheap for bed, breakfast and evening meal, and lunch on Sundays. Unlike most universities, where you start in College and then graduate to your own flat, rooms in the College were so prized that you usually graduated to them only in your third year. Luckily, Nigel Ramage – a year above me – was looking for someone to share rooms, and he was eligible for them in his third year, so for years two and three I shared rooms in No. 4. I reckoned we had the shortest address that would reach us from anywhere in the world: 4 TCD, Ireland.

Being so close to Players, our rooms became a veritable Clapham Junction of comings and goings, or were used as a general dumping ground. We rarely had a quiet night in, partly because we usually rehearsed most nights, but also because we had such a constant stream of visitors. I do remember returning one evening to find Bridget Byrne and Geoff Thurley lying comfortably by our gas fire. They assured me they were discussing Wordsworth; looked more like Uganda to me.

Players was one of my spiritual homes (I was chairman in my final year), and my other was cricket. But, though I would not claim that academic study was my first priority, I look back on many of the lecturers with fond affection and admiration. Professor Wormell with his erudite and inspiring lectures on Horace, John Luce expounding the tricky writer Juvenal to us with, forgive the pun, wonderful lucidity, Professor Arnould on philology, Sheehy-Skeffington and his superb lectures on French phonetics. The latter told us on day one that his intention was to make us sound like educated Parisians, and the first thing we had to do was to learn the following sentence by heart: 'Bonsoir, Jacques, me disait-il toujours et peu après, humblement, il se taisait.' This apparently contains every sound in the French language, and every week we drilled in each different sound. It sounds tedious, but it was inspiring.

I shared these French lectures with Gill Hanna, Paula Street and Ruth Ludgate (and, of course, many others). Gill was particularly alarming to sit near for exams (we sat in alphabetical order). By the time I had read all the questions, decided I couldn't answer any of them, and had a good stretch, I would look round to see that Gillie had already written about ten pages, scribbling away furiously. She was a formidable linguist, Italian being her other subject. We were very close friends, and I spent a memorable and boozy Christmas at her home in Croydon (at least, it was memorable only until mid-afternoon, after which I don't remember very much at all).

We had the great advantage of having our exams in mid-September, which meant that we could get on with the serious business of Players, cricket and social life during the University term, which ended in May, and then get down to academic study and revision during June, July and August. I do remember one fellow student in French (happily, I can't remember his name), who delayed this study/revision process until 1 September, announcing that he would be studying all of the Molière on day one of his programme, all the Corneille on day two (etc). An ambitious programme of revision and one which I seem to remember did not produce success on examination day.

I remember having a piece of luck through academic sloth. I had not been at the lecture when it was announced that sections of 'La Chanson de Roland' would be examined in detail. I therefore revised all of it, and emerged from the exam saying how simple that had been, to be met with fury by fellow examinees, who said that several questions had been asked on sections that they had been told would not be examined in detail. Another examination hiccup occurred in my finals in Latin where we all had that ghastly nightmare of being presented with the wrong exam paper, on a subject (Roman History, I think) that none of us had revised for weeks, expecting to do so a couple of days later.

Happily, the probably dreadful marks were upgraded to take account of this administrative blunder.

Finally, in my *viva voce* following my Latin finals, the extraordinarily erudite panel grilled me on the essay I had written on an obscure Roman historian, one Quintus Fabius Pictor. I began to answer their questions, but soon a lengthy discussion ensued among the panellists themselves about the importance of Mr Q.F.P., and ended only when the delightful Professor of Greek, W.B. Stanford, announced, 'I'm very sorry, but I've never even heard of this Quintus Fabius Pictor.'

One of the delights of TCD was that you were part of a capital-city culture, whether in Players or in cricket. You weren't just part of an enclosed university scene. In cricket, we played in the Leinster League, which was mostly of a very good standard, and much higher than most English people assume. It was difficult for us to win the League, not just because the opposition was mostly very strong, but because the points system told against us. Normally, everybody played everybody twice in the season, but clearly TCD couldn't do that, terms being so short, so we played everybody just once and had our points doubled, but with a substantial penalty deduction.

Nevertheless, we did win the League in 1966.

In my final year I was captain and we rounded off the season with our traditional tour of southern England, where we proceeded to lose the first three matches but to win the last four in style, the highlight being a dramatic run-chase at Finchley.

In my early years at TCD, I was greatly helped by older and no doubt wiser heads, who took me in hand because I was so obviously green. One of them was Norrie Boulting, who took me under his generous and humorous wing. As well as introducing me to the social life of Trinity, he also – as editor of *TCD Miscellany* – invited me to write a weekly column on the doings of the cricket team. It just so happened that I had something of a golden year in 1965, and my columns rather too frequently mentioned my own name. However, it started me on a lifetime of writing up cricket matches, which I continue to do in retirement for *The Times* and *Wisden*.

Another such student was Ian Whitcomb, who one year returned triumphant and distinctly enriched from a trip to the USA where one of his records reached No. 5 in the charts. He decided he would treat several of us to a day at the races. We set off in a grand limousine and were treated like royalty all day.

We were rather proud of our civilized form of social life and despised the 'bring a bottle, slop around and vomit' style we encountered on visiting other universities.

Parties were mostly given by individuals or groups, and guests dressed up fairly smartly. For twenty-first birthday parties (eighteen had not been invented as the age of majority), groups of half a dozen or more gathered their flimsy finances together, borrowed or even rented grand venues such as country houses, had a live band, and produced a decent meal for a few hundred fellow students. We dressed up in dinner jackets and danced till dawn. It was all rather Brideshead really, except that not many of us had the kind of cash the Oxford set could muster.

Which brings me to Players, far and away the central part of my life at Trinity. The Players group when I arrived was flourishing. Once again, it was partly because Players was as much part of the capital city theatre scene as was the Abbey Theatre (then lodged at the Queen's Theatre nearby): every production was reviewed by the main newspaper and periodical critics and so standards had to be good or we would be savaged. In my second year, I did my first Trinity production, of *The Importance of Being Ernest*, with a formidable cast. Michael Mackenzie, room-mate of Max Stafford-Clark, was a superbly smooth Algernon, with Nigel Ramage as a very lively Jack. The love interest was supplied by a touchingly innocent Heather Lukes as Cecily, and she has been my love interest ever since. Ann McFerran, now the well-known and prolific journalist, played the glamorous and languid Gwendolen. Michael Jones gave one of his funniest performances as The Revd Canon Chasuble opposite the delightfully prim Miss Prism of Mia Swales, and the almost definitive Lady Bracknell was Gill Hanna. It was a very happy experience and set me on a lifetime of directing plays.

The Country Wife was chosen more or less at random. We were well into term and the production had to open in about five weeks. Though I had been asked to direct that term's major production, I still hadn't chosen a play. I plucked a volume of Restoration comedies from my bookshelf, opened the book at random, and chose to do Wycherley's very funny and pretty scandalous comedy. We had rave notices, especially in *The Irish Times*, and the production was selected for *The Sunday Times* NUS student drama finals in Bradford. Our experience there was not so happy: the student reviewers didn't like it at all, though Harold Hobson of *The Sunday Times* did. It hadn't helped that the set got lost in a railway siding and had to be put up in enormous haste, nor that a production brilliantly designed (by John Gardner) for a tiny 77-seat theatre had, very unexpectedly, to be transferred to a 900-seat auditorium with quite different stage dimensions. It was a very humbling experience.

I shall cut to *Under Milk Wood* in my final year, when I was chairman. At the end of the previous academic year there had been a bank strike, and Jerry Bell – who alas died very prematurely of cancer – had had difficulty as treasurer in keeping track of the finances. In short, when I took over in September, I discovered that Players, with no subsidy and no financial backing at all, was in debt to the tune of the normal entire annual turnover. I chose *Under Milk Wood* as a sure-fire box-office winner. We played it for four weeks rather than the customary two, and then later transferred it for a week to the Gate. This did the trick in restoring the finances. Brilliantly directed by Mike Bogdin (now Bogdanov), who had graduated just before I arrived, it was a very striking production. So striking that Mike, in the manner of opera directors, has been hawking around the same production ever since. It was somewhat alarming to go to Bath twenty years later to watch the play that was billed as 'after Michael Bogdanov's original production' to find that not only was it virtually identical to ours in every way, down to the last movement, but the person playing 'my' parts looked alarmingly like me!

A transfer to Wexford was less successful, but it was happily funded not by Players, but by a 'secret backer', which turned out to be Mike himself. In the Wexford Opera House, seating 1000-plus, the largest house we played to was one hundred people on the Friday night. The most bizarre experience was going out onstage for a midweek matinée, having been assured by the marketing man that we had a full house, mostly of schoolchildren. The production was such that all actors remained onstage throughout the performance. It seemed a bit quiet for a full house before the curtain went up and, when it did, you didn't have to look but just to feel that there wasn't a single person there. Being very professional, we soldiered on, even though Martyn Lewis seemed about to crack and eventually we heard the rustle of a crisp packet from the back of the house. There were eighteen schoolchildren there, it turned out. The marketing man had sold the wrong afternoon.

By 1967 it was time to move on. We didn't really want to go back too soon and shatter the Trinity idyll. But Dublin and Trinity, however transformed (and however expensive), remain places of wonder. The Sixties was an inspiring period and it was also an inspirational time in our lives. We are both very grateful to have had the chance to experience such a place and such a time.

Douglas Henderson (TCD 1963–7; Latin and French) took a teaching course at Cambridge, and was subsequently appointed at Clifton College, Bristol, in 1968 to teach Latin and English, and remained there until his retirement in 2003. He was Master in charge of cricket for most of that period, and director of drama, Senior Housemaster and Senior Master. He continued to direct plays, with about forty productions both at the College and at the Bristol Arts Centre. He is currently the schools' cricket columnist for **The Times** and for the **Wisden Almanack**.

IN SEARCH OF AN AUTHOR

rock brynner

IN THE SHARP October night, careering over the cobblestones beneath the pungent decks of peat smoke that reflected the amber streetlamps, I recognized our route in from the airport as the garrulous cabbie barrelled down O'Connell Street (where, I noticed, *Lady Chatterley's Lover* was playing in a hole-in-the-wall theatre near the cinema where *Goldfinger* had just opened) and over the bridge, curling left around Trinity, with a right swerve up Dawson Street and a twist around the Green to Abbotsford Road and beyond, unto the distant reaches of Rathmines and Rathgar. Months before, in my dorm-room at Yale, I had traced this very route on the map of Dublin taped to the wall, which also charted the perambulations of Dedalus and Dangerfield as well as the erstwhile residences of Beckett, Yeats, and Behan. At seventeen, my literary *haj* had just begun.

In Dawson Street that night I saw a tall, gaunt figure that resembled a rolled-up carpet leaning against a lamppost, the spitting image of Watt. His fingers were dancing a manic jig before his eyes, absorbing all his attention as I watched him through the rear window. Months later, leaving The Bailey with Ranald Graham, I saw him again. He was deaf, Ranald explained, and was often seen talking to himself in sign language.

Dublin was crawling with a spectacular array of dedicated eccentrics in 1964, all of whom I have transported in my heart around the world. The

Stomping Lady, beneath her clotted tangle of hair, kicking sideways high up in the air with every step, shouting, 'Spot Spot!' Not far from McDaid's, a shrivelled old soul sat on a stoop beside a cow, selling fresh milk; I saw her only once. And at Trinity there was Judge Kelly, 'With his baggy pants and bloodshot eyes,' Ranald recalled in a story published recently, 'loitering around the toilets between Players and the Main Gate. His bladder range was limited. Rumoured to have been a High Court judge until one day he sentenced a student to death for riding a bicycle without lights.'

The IRA was an emeritus society in those days: the brave and honoured patriots who had delivered the Republic from enslavement, like then-President de Valera himself. When, in 1966, Nelson's Pillar was bombed in commemoration of 1916, it seemed like a quaint prank, and any further violence was unimaginable. Those who would kill and die for the next thirty years were mostly children then; some probably rose up out of the packs of scruffy street kids who swarmed O'Connell Street at night with menacing pleas for six pence or for a single two-pence Woodbine from the barrel of loose cigarettes at the news shop. They were fuelled with fearless vitality, carving streams through the crowds of cinema-goers who rushed to the pubs before closing. The scruffy kids are in their fifties today, at least those who survived the borstals, jails and combustible poteen.

One evening near the Strand, after my third pilgrimage to Martello Tower, a shocking figure climbed upstairs on the bus and sat just in front of me. His head was huge and grotesquely misshapen, evoking massive waves of sympathy and revulsion. Before long, as the middle-aged man rose clumsily to disembark, he offered me a friendly smile. Years later, when I learned about 'the elephant man' John Merrick, I finally made some sense of that gentle, distorted figure now long gone, surely, like the Dublin I've loved fiercely ever since.

Dublin was composed of overlapping odours, a shifting panoply that assaulted one's whole face, against a steady background of stale ale. The restaurants vented their curried fumes and deep-fried stink all over the passers-by; and of course Bewley's, whose overwhelming blend of aromas, together with the words 'Oriental Cafés', delivered a fleeting exotic adventure to the pedestrians and motorists who jolted down Grafton Street. The butchers' shops and horse butchers, who kept their street fronts open in winter for the free chill, pervaded the public air with the stench of offal and blood, while the bakeries provided the inimitable fragrance of soda bread. Even the horse-drawn milk truck spread a creamy scent, highlighted with horse lather. A walk down the high street could quell an appetite for an hour or two, but so could one whiff of a piss-stained street corner. And on the morning after any major game, vomit was pooled near most of the sewer drains.

Among the hustlers and roustabouts, beggars and buskers, brawlers and mysterious tinkers, poets and musicians, there was one figure I sought most of all during the four years I spent studying 'Mental and Moral Science' and never set eyes upon.

It wasn't Beckett. I had already met him in Paris, near his flat in Boulevard St Jacques, thanks to a friend of mine named Georges Belmont (a post-Resistance pseudonym), who had met Sam at the Ecole Normale Supérieure in 1927, about the time he first met Joyce; Georges then returned with him to teach French at Trinity. Nor was it Donleavy, whom I encountered near the Green *circa* 1965, wearing plus fours and walking his beagles, and boasting about Balthazar. It wasn't Seamus Heaney, who was still living in Belfast when he published his first book of poems in 1965. And it wasn't any of the upcoming young writers championed by Alan Figgis at Hodges Figgis at 56/58 Dawson Street, Est. 1768.

No, the author I had come to Dublin to find was far more elusive. There were those who thought he didn't exist at all. And if he *was* passing through, he was sure to flee before long, from – as Joyce put it – 'Ireland, who always sent / Her writers and artists to banishment.'

The writer I was there seeking was … myself. But I was years too early. The dough had not yet risen, the oven was barely warm, and I was still – to put it precisely – half-baked. Life, of course, would take care of that deficiency, as only life can do. But for the time being, search as I might, the author I hoped to become could not be found anywhere between Dún Laoghaire and Howth Castle and environs.

Rock Brynner (TCD 1964–8; Mental and Moral Science) is a historian and novelist, and the author of numerous books and plays. After leaving TCD, he performed his one-character play **Opium**, adapted from Jean Cocteau, in Dublin, London, and on Broadway (1970). His first novel, **The Ballad of Habit and Accident** (1981), opens at Trinity College. His second novel, **The Doomsday Report** (1998), confronted the threat of climate change. He has also written **Yul, A Memoir of Father and Son** (1989), and **Empire and Odyssey: The Brynners in Far East Russia and Beyond** (2006). **Dark Remedy: The Impact of Thalidomide and Its Revival as a Vital Medicine** (2001) is the first complete history of thalidomide. His latest book is **Fire Beneath Our Feet: The Crisis That Produced the U.S. Constitution** (forthcoming, 2009).

FINDING A VOICE

fawzia salama

IT WAS a cold October morning. The sky was grey and a soft drizzle made me feel anxious. I sat on a bench outside a church in Fairview, waiting for my compatriot and friend Marie, she being a Christian Copt who went to church on Sundays. I was new to Ireland, dependent on my friend's good will and seniority. There was a funeral in my heart mourning the Cairo sun. From my place on the bench I looked at the low-rise houses, doors closed, curtains drawn. Amid the silence, I missed home. I missed the bustling neighbourhood, the multi-storey blocks with colourful open shutters to allow the sun in. There was no sun in Dublin, only rain, drizzle, and shop signs written in a strange language.

After church, Marie took me to her digs. The door opened and a strong smell of cabbage assaulted my senses. Mrs McCloskey, the proprietor, was on the phone telling a friend that she had been cooking a bit of dinner for poor wee Marie. Mrs McCloskey was short and plump. She had red hair and small piercing eyes. She wore an apron and a shy smile. We sat down, and then she busied herself watching TV.

She took me by surprise when she suddenly went on her knees as she glimpsed the image of the Pope on the screen. Her eyes glistened as she told Marie that His Holiness might visit Ireland. She did not talk to me much and asked me if I had been to Mass. Marie told her I was not Christian. The visit ended quickly. She was sorry she had no more rooms to rent. A few days later, I found a bed-sit in Clontarf with Mrs Van Dael.

I went to Trinity on Monday morning. Going through Front Gate was and still is unforgettable. The sight of Burke and Goldsmith as I took my first steps at the gate ushered a new mode of feeling for years to come. As the years went by, taking a slow walk in Front Square, then sitting at the steps of Chapel and watching the starlings come home to roost in the eaves of Examination Hall, I saw day fade into night. This became part of the spirit of place, and an intimate solitary action, which consolidated my sense of belonging.

That first year at Trinity was a turning point in my life and in my development as a human being inching towards independence and maturity, struggling to find a voice. Making that leap across the culture divide proved much harder than I had anticipated. I was painfully timid and inexperienced. At twenty-two, I had never been out of Egypt, or even out of the neighbourhood where I had been born and brought up.

This process started when I met Philip Edwards, who was then head of English and in charge of my qualifying programme prior to admitting me to the graduate studies programme. Sitting opposite him, my throat was dry as I introduced myself. I addressed him as 'Professor'. He laughed and said, 'This makes me feel very old, why don't you just call me Philip.' You could have knocked me down with a feather. Up to that point in my personal history, a professor was a demi-god. Egyptian professors behaved that way and expected to be approached with caution and deference. In fact, and in spite of his request, I never dared to address him as Philip, though I always think of him as that. For more than forty years, and among my prize possessions I have kept informal handwritten notes from him commending me on some written work. I consider my interaction with him as the starting point of my liberation.

A few months after that first meeting, after many meetings and informal discussions, he set a date for my graduate exam. The old Reading Room had become a boundary within which I lived, worked, and thought about my place in this new order. I was a dreamer not a swotter. I agonized over that. I wrote short poems during the day, and took dancing classes two evenings a week. Some mornings when I did not feel much like studying I would look around the Reading Room, at the semi-circular structure with its dark wood, bookshelves, desks and students on chairs. I drew caricature images of my unsuspecting colleagues as they pored over notes and leaflets. There were times when I experienced moments of sheer panic and despair lest I should fail. I had graduated in Cairo with distinction but here it was a different ball game. There were no texts to memorize, or notes to give you guidance. There were books Philip suggested I read and think about, and endless opportunities to read other books, talk, and listen. I had found my way to Greene's second-hand bookshop. I bought books I wanted to read and others I wanted to keep.

Suddenly, it seemed, it was exam time. On the morning of the exam, Philip Edwards sat me down in a room with a desk. I had all my notebooks with me. He asked me if I needed tea or coffee, then handed me a sheet with a whole lot of questions and simply asked me to deal with three at random. With hindsight, I think he just wanted to define my areas of interest. He left me for three hours exactly. He never asked to take my books and notes away. There was no notion that I might be tempted to cheat. I consider this to have been the starting point of my intellectual freedom and my recognition of it.

I passed the exam. Soon after, I started my work on the short stories of D.H. Lawrence, and a long association with the man from Kerry, Brendan Kennelly, a poet with blue eyes and a captivating smile, who supervised my work on the thesis.

Anglo-Irish literature was in vogue. Many foreign graduate students came to Trinity to take a diploma in Anglo-Irish literature. I met Dagmar from Sweden, and Ila from Pakistan who had trouble with the letter *V*, and Banarji from Bengal. I also met Kate Murphy, a 32-year-old American who became my friend, confidante and mentor. And I met Paul Scanlon, a Canadian who became associated in my mind with danger and tragedy. He was there for a year. And a story went around the Egyptian student community about a love affair between Paul and Fatima. She was a member of a group of Egyptian teachers who came to obtain a higher diploma in education. I shall never know why she tried to commit suicide when the time came for returning to Egypt with her fellow students.

I became close to Kate. She knew that I was an aspiring writer and that my timidity was my worst enemy. She suggested that we both join Frank O'Connor's creative-writing class. We did. And we were given short-story writing assignments. He was an exceptionally modest man, an excellent teacher, who had intuition and great communication skills. He invited us to his apartment where we met his very young American wife.

What Frank O'Connor taught me about short-story writing remained with me over the years as the basic tools I apply when reading or writing short stories. The story I wrote for a class assignment was included in my first short-story collection. It was slightly modified and translated into Arabic for publication in 1986. In class, Kate had to step in to read my story in my place because when I stood up to read it I looked traumatized. She alone knew how timid I was, and she stepped in to rescue me.

When she went back to the States, I felt desolate. We exchanged letters for a long while.

I started to beat my timidity when I surprised myself by saying no in situations that challenged my sense of identity. In a seminar, someone said that my name was too difficult to remember. He looked at me and said, 'I shall call you Françoise.' I surprised myself when I retorted. I said angrily, 'If I can say McLaughlin, you can say Fawzia.'

Mrs Van Dael insisted on inviting me to her room for chats in the evenings and platefuls of rhubarb with custard. I hated the rhubarb but could not find a decisive way of saying no. She would tell me that she was worried about my soul because I was not Catholic. She told me stories about Mrs Mullin who did not keep the Friday fast, and pretended that a cup of hot Bovril was allowed until Father Cassidy told her in front of the congregation that she might as well have mutton chops for lunch and pretend she was fasting. One evening she told me that whereas she liked me, she detested Colonel Nasser because he nationalized 'our' Suez Canal. I turned towards her and said, 'It could have never been "your" Canal as it is on Egyptian soil, dug by Egyptian hands.' Before she could recover, I pushed the rhubarb away and said, 'Thank you but I do not really like this.'

I do not recall how I came to do posters for Trinity Players. I was very impressed with anyone who had the courage to act. I met Rickie at a function there, a Welsh rugby player with a friendly manner and a ready smile. When he said, 'Hello, Fawzia', my name sounded normal and easy. My feeling that I could be perceived as alien melted away. We had coffee and talked about

Lawrence, Frieda, Italy and Wales, and a little bit about Egypt too. One day he held both my hands in his and said passionately, 'My God, you are so beautiful.' This declaration was sealed with a kiss, which I thought meant we were going steady. No question of infidelity entered my mind. I was Rickie's girl and his good teeth, blonde hair and six-foot figure made me feel beautiful indeed. One weekend he told me he was going up to Belfast to play a match, and would call me from there. On Saturday night, I decided to see a performance in College. As the lights went up for an interval, there he was, my Rickie, with another girl. He was more embarrassed than I was stung by the betrayal. He introduced me to her then I went back to my seat, and made sure to exit before the end. My heartbreak got the better of me in my landlady's kitchen. I spilled the beans and she listened carefully. She shoved a cup of tea in my direction and asked me if Rickie was Irish. I said he was Welsh. That seemed to explain the situation sufficiently. She shook her head and asked: 'Protestant?' I said, 'Yes.' She said knowingly, 'Of course. Very deceitful, powerful in prayer, but awful liars.' When Rickie asked me out again, I said a definite no and he never asked for an explanation.

The Trinity Ball was the social event of the year. If you were not asked to the Ball, you missed a lot of anticipation and excitement. Trinity girls held special appeal to boys from the Royal College of Surgeons in St Stephen's Green. Mingling and pairing happened at Rice's pub in South King Street. I did not drink. But I did not want to miss the fun. I went to Rice's and had ginger ale. It was there that a very handsome Norwegian student whose name I have forgotten asked me if I had a partner for the Ball. I said I did not. He asked me if I would have a coffee the following day. We had coffee and walked around St Stephen's Green. How could I ever forget the cherry blossom and my excitement when he asked if I could go to the Ball with him?

I have always been practical, and able to rise to any occasion. There were only ten days left. I decided there and then to wear a white lace evening dress I had brought with me from Egypt. I did look good that evening. We met up with friends at Jurys Hotel, and then at Rice's for a drink. He asked me what I would like and I said ginger ale. He smiled sweetly and said, 'Try some brandy with it – it's very nice.' Too shy to refuse, and too anxious, I said OK. I remember the sensation well; two drinks and we were ready for the Ball. What I was not ready for was the feeling that I could not walk steadily. Two brandies had gone straight to my head. The dancing was great. He did not talk to me much. Then he asked me in a matter-of-fact way whether I would like to go back to his flat to make love. A sense of panic came over me. I felt cold and quite miserable. He had offended my romantic sense. So I did not hesitate when I said no. From then on, he decided to play the field with a new set of tactics. He decided to ignore me. I watched him dance with other girls. I sat out a few dances then went for breakfast with a group of friends before returning to my digs.

There was a first time for many new things in these first two years at Trinity. My initial encounter with pop culture happened in the cinema. Beatlemania was rife. I remember going to see *A Hard Day's Night* on my own. I was puzzled by scenes of hysterical girl fans, screaming, shouting and crying. I just had to ask why they were screaming. Pop music had not been part of my cultural experience. A woman sitting next to me at the cinema was equally puzzled by my question. She shrugged her shoulders and said, 'They just do.' I could never see myself throwing my underwear at a pop star. However, the Beatles came to play a decisive role in my musical taste. I still feel enthralled each time I hear 'I Want to Hold your Hand' and *Abbey Road* is still my favourite album.

Another memorable new experience was a harpsichord concert at College. I heard Bach for the first time and entered into a lifelong passion for baroque music, and for Bach especially. My first opera was Gilbert and Sullivan's *The Mikado* at the Gaiety Theatre in South King Street. I saw *The Mikado* with Peter Travis, who came from Pittsburgh to read Anglo-Irish literature for a year. I got my photograph printed in the *Evening Press* that day. In those days people dressed up for the theatre. I often think that it was the red rose in my dark hair that did it. It was the first time my name and image graced a newspaper. When I became a journalist, I would see my photograph with my printed work and reflect on that *Evening Press* photo when my future was still a mystery and a photograph in a newspaper was a singularly glamorous event, so much so that I sent a cutting to my parents.

Looking back, I feel that Trinity was a microcosm, a world that was made to measure, which allowed us to live a privileged life. You could stay in, protected by a sense of privilege in the face of an outside world, which secretly admired this privilege, but openly resented it and considered it a world apart. I often heard ordinary people describing TCD as a university for foreign and British students. Nevertheless, there was a whole world outside, rich and enticing: plays at the Abbey; songs, folkloric and patriotic; Irish music and dancing; Irish humour. A walk around Grafton Street, coffee and buns at Bewley's and a lustful glance at clothes in Brown Thomas's, or even a trip to Moore Street in search of Molly Malone was always an enjoyable activity in the fair city.

My intimate knowledge of Dublin really began when Chris and I became close friends. Chris is an Irish Catholic who was then a closet homosexual. When this boy from County Leitrim entrusted me with his secret I could not quite understand why he was so upset about who he really was. It made us closer because from that day on there were no barriers, or expectations. We were mates. We walked and talked endlessly. He has a rare artistic gift, a way with words, a penchant for music and architecture. He made me see how beautiful Georgian Dublin is. He also opened my eyes to Irish poetry, and to Irish social norms, manners, aspirations, values and inhibitions, with bits of Irish history thrown in. I remember hearing all about Annie in St Stephen's Green. There is a plaque telling her story. She was deported for stealing a length of cloth. He also told me the story of the potato famine, which made me truly sad and angry. A few days later, I threw my anger at a fellow English student as if he were responsible for his country's colonial past. He simply said that his ancestors suffered similar fates at the hands of the feudal lords who dispossessed the Irish.

Irish girls who knew me secretly hated me because they thought I was grabbing the attention of an Irish boy who was rightfully theirs. When I met Chris' mother, she did not smile. We both laughed a lot when he told me that his mother called me 'that heathen woman' behind my back. It is significant that Chris and I were good dance partners because we had a similar rhythm and because our dancing was free from sexual tension. This friendship has lasted and prospered over the years.

I define myself as a person who always knew what she did not want, and who was slow to discover what she did. Years went by before I decided that I did not want to be an academic for the rest of my life. The stress of academia pushed two of my friends over the edge. One committed suicide, the other displayed symptoms of schizophrenia before getting the coveted Ph.D. under his belt. Most of my friends had left and I was still at sea. I had to leave when a job offer in London presented itself.

When I left, I cried all the way to London. I shared a flat for six months in South Kensington with Andrew and Rosemary Gibb, my Trinity friends, their two children, Tammy and Jason, and their dog Emma. Rosemary and I shared the friendship of opposites. She was notorious for breaking every rule. She threw herself into the Liffey once to rescue a drowning dog. She seldom wore shoes. When she caught me looking at her bare feet she just guffawed. She drank and smoked, and befriended bohemians. Perhaps the biggest discovery about Rosemary was made at the Mill House, her parents' residence on the outskirts of Dublin. I was invited to tea. We had tea from a silver service. Her mother had permed hair and a genteel accent. That day I realized that the girl from the castle was a rebel.

When we hit the flat in London, she dispensed with furniture, painted psychedelic images on the walls and made do with a mattress and some cushions on the floor of her bedroom. I favoured a neat interior, which both Emma the dog, and Tammy the toddler invaded regularly while Rosemary was up in the garret finishing her literary thesis.

London opened its arms and doors to me. I carved out a successful career in Arab journalism, built up a reputation as a columnist, married and had a daughter.

I did not return to Dublin for many years lest Dublin should receive me as a stranger. Twenty-five years on, I went back as an invited guest on a radio show. My work done, I decided to visit Trinity. When I walked in, I realized that the buildings had been renovated. The whole place looked glorious. I went down the steps to the Buttery to be greeted by curious looks from 18-year-old undergraduates. I beat a quick retreat. The old Reading Room had become part of a new library bustling with young students, mostly Irish. I went to the English Department, now housed in a new building, and to the office of Brendan Kennelly, now the Department head. I asked to see him and his secretary looked me up and down wondering what a foreign, middle-aged, overweight woman wanted with the Department head. I gave her one of my business cards and waited. The door opened and Brendan came out to greet me with open arms. He had not forgotten me. He asked me what I had been doing. I had become a published author, a journalist, a wife and a mother. I had visited India, covered the Earth Summit in Brazil, toured in America, and travelled to the Gulf of Oman. I paused. Then I asked him about himself. He told me that his daughter was getting married. Then he paused too, and said, 'And here I am. I am just here.' Many years had passed since he gave me as a gift an inscribed copy of *My Dark Fathers*.

In Grafton Street Marks and Spencer had replaced Brown Thomas. Switzer's had disappeared. Bewley's was still in place. There was a new confidence, and a new energy in the city. Dublin had evolved into a European metropolis. A passer-by in Wicklow Street asked me how to get to O'Connell Street. I pointed him in the right direction enthusiastically and my feeling that Dublin was still my fair city renewed itself. And the stone buildings regained their lustre.

Fawzia Salama (TCD 1963–70; English M.Litt.) has worked in Arab journalism for thirty years as a writer, commentator and magazine editor. She is well known to television audiences as a presenter and commentator on social issues, especially those concerning Arab women. Her publications include a novel, **Al Firash Al abiadh** ('White Linen', 2008), two collections of short stories, **Al Maraa Al Okhra** ('The Other Woman', 1986); **Sharia Wahdan** ('Wahdan Street', 1991); and **Girls and their Problems** (three volumes of correspondence with young readers, 1985–1990–1995).

SLEEPWALKING THROUGH THE SIXTIES

Nicholas Grene

'**WHAT DO YOU MEAN**, you didn't do drugs?', my children ask me in outraged amazement. 'You were a student in the Sixties and you didn't do drugs, you didn't demonstrate, you didn't even burn your draft card?' (I did have a draft card that I could have burned.) 'So what *did* you do?' It's a fair question. What did I do as a student of English language and literature at Trinity through the years of my inadequately misspent youth from 1965 to 1969, and what sort of place was Trinity in which to do whatever it was I did?

My position was a bit unusual. The son of an Irish father and American mother, born in the US but having grown up almost entirely in Ireland, I found myself at seventeen coming up to Trinity the sole possessor of a farm, a car and rooms in College. It wasn't quite as opulent as it sounds. Where other people leave home to go to university, my family had left me at home alone; my parents had parted several years before, my mother went back to America that year to a university professorship in California, and my sister – a student generation ahead of me at Trinity – was also off to the US to do graduate work. So there I was in the farmhouse in Ballinaclash, County Wicklow, on my own.

The rooms in College came by virtue of an Entrance Scholarship: I must have been among the last group of students whom Trinity managed to squeeze in on this basis. Mrs Crawford in Accommodation at first laughed at the idea that I could be accommodated as an Entrance Scholar. It was only when I went in to register the digs I had found out in Rathmines that she casually mentioned that a College room had come vacant and I could have it. It was always grander to call them 'rooms': 'they' were in fact a bed-sit in the GMB, tiny kitchenette, bed, built-in gas-fire, desk and chair, with toilet down the hall. But I certainly wasn't complaining. Especially not with the magnificent Iveagh bathhouse right across from the door of No. 30, the luxury of longer baths, more steamingly hot water than anyone could possibly imagine. '*Has balneas* ...', the Latin inscription commemorating their donation by the 'Comes de Iveagh', along with one of those sumptuous 1930s baths, remain to this day secreted behind a door in the Gents in the Staff Common Room.

Whatever the delights of a cold and rat-ridden farmhouse in Wicklow, a respectable black Hillman saloon, the room(s) did wonders for my social life. The very first day of lectures I could casually invite the group of interesting-looking English girls up to my rooms – definitely plural there – for coffee. And as the term went on I acquired more or less permanent lodgers. Friends who had been ejected by their landladies from their digs in Clontarf promptly at 8.30 would show up at my door and settle down for the day. Sometimes some of us would wander down to a lecture – nothing so inhumane as a nine o'clock was scheduled by the English Department – but there was always someone left on duty to keep the kettle boiling for the next round of coffee. By Christmas I had a group of mates: some people I had known from school in Belfast but mostly fellow students I had encountered one way or another and who accreted gradually into a gang.

I came to Trinity with pejudices inherited from my sister Ruth (Rufus in the family because of her red hair) and with a few precious introductions from her as well. When still at school I had spent one of the most amazing afternoons of my then 16-year-old life in the back bar of Jammet's through the holy hour in the company of my sister and her friends. Numbered among them were Derek Mahon, Brendan Kennelly and Seamus Heaney: it was in the aftermath of the wedding of Michael and Edna Longley. I was agog. Even then I knew I had landed among the Olympians.

The prejudices had to do with what Rufus referred to as chasps and chas-pettes: 'chasps' because some drunken English student had been overheard braying to his cronies, 'Come on you chasps'; 'chaspettes' as their female coun-terparts. Trinity in Rufus' time (1961–5) was still dominated by English students. On her first day in Trinity Hall her room-mate woke up and asked, 'I say, I've been meaning to find out, is Dublin in Southern Ireland or Northern Ireland?' With their public-school accents, their superior sophistication, the resented belief that they came to Trinity for purely snobbish reasons as Oxbridge rejects, they were envied and disliked by Irish students in about equal parts. Rufus, though her schooling had been entirely in the Republic, hung out with the clever, duffel-coated students from Northern Irish grammar schools, an alternative milieu antagonistic to the chasps and chaspettes.

By my time, it felt different somehow. The chasps were perhaps less prom-inent or they didn't come my way. I ended up sharing rooms with a friend who had been to Haileybury, subsequently best man at my wedding. But then no one would have called soft-spoken Mike Godby, already passionately inter-ested in art history, a chasp. Being English was not synonymous with being a chasp. Some of Rufus' best friends had been English too: Nina Gilliam, Celia Whitehead, Mike de Larrabeiti. It wasn't where you came from but how you behaved that classified you.

I spent a good deal of my JF year in Players Theatre, that dark little space in No. 3 out of which one emerged occasionally into the sunlight dazed and blinking. I auditioned for anything and everything. I carried spears in a play about Gordon of Khartoum. I came on in a number of now forgotten minor roles in Buchner's *Woyzeck*. But there were beginning to be Irish parts in Irish plays also. At just eighteen I got to play old Dan Burke in Synge's *The Shadow of the Glen*, rising from his pretend death under the sheet, scattering clouds of talcum powder from his hair. I recited poems in a fiftieth-anniversary commemorative show on Easter 1916. And over the Easter vacation, a group of us took over Players Theatre to stage a play called *The O'Neill*, written by a mature student of English, Brian Trevaskis.

Mine was no glorious part. I played the young O'Donnell, only there to be a sidekick of Hugh O'Neill in the first act, and to die of a fever in a white nightshirt early in the second. But it was my only experience of a theatrical run, playing a part six nights a week for two weeks. And we had our fifteen minutes of fame when Brian Trevaskis appeared on *The Late Late Show* and called the Bishop of Galway a cretin. The occasion for this abusive remark was the completion of Galway Cathedral for which Bishop Browne had raised substantial funds from his congregation. It caused a brief stir and brought in a few more curious punters to see *The O'Neill.* What was perhaps more signifi-cant was that it didn't raise more of a rumpus. There were no repercussions for Brian or for College. Maybe mid-Sixties Catholic Ireland felt able to ignore a silly and boorish jibe from a Trinity student, or maybe things were shifting away from the more conservative Fifties.

By the standards of the time I was a student nerd, anxiously worrying about essays and essay deadlines, working my way conscientiously through prescribed reading lists. This was still the era of September exams, when it was considered bad form to be seen in the Library during term-time, when there was macho competitiveness on how late one could leave revision at the end of the summer; the really cool customers showed up just ten days ahead of the start of the examinations declaring that they hadn't yet opened a book. I recall one of my fellow students, later to make a spectacularly successful career in publishing, muttering as we went into the Exam Hall, 'If Keats and *King Lear* don't come up, I'm done for.' They did and he wasn't. In this atmosphere, I had the socially shaming consciousness of having spent all July and August slogging through the Romantic poets one by one.

Yet God knows I wasn't a diligent or attentive student by comparison with those I teach in Trinity today. I treated lectures and lecturers with a derisive nonchalance that makes me blush in retrospect. The English Department in my time had some excellent staff but the best of them never seemed to stay long. Chris Salvessen, Geoffrey Thurley, Eamon Carrigan (who converted a whole student generation to *Beowulf* and Anglo-Saxon poetry), all came and went; Eavan Boland stayed just a year before leaving to become a full-time writer. The biggest blow of all was the departure of Philip Edwards for another Chair in England. The merry-go-round of academic life eventually brought him to the King Alfred professorship of English literature in Liverpool in 1974 where I was teaching in my first university post, and he was to become a good friend; but his leaving Trinity in 1966 created an unhappy interregnum in which we felt no one was left but old buffers. There was, of course, Brendan Kennelly, who continued to enliven our lives, but it wasn't until my last year in College, with the appointment of Terence Brown and David Norris, that we had the sense of a changed atmosphere. These were lecturers who were almost our contemporaries, lecturing with a feeling of passionate engagement, even if in the case of Norris on D.H. Lawrence it took the form of an undisguised loathing.

The Russian Department, if you could call it that, was a different matter. Russian was not then available as an honours subject, only as part of General Studies. You could, though, take it as a 'voluntary subsidiary' subject, which is what I did with some grandiose notions of reading *War and Peace* in the original. (I was never to get further than a laborious plough through *The Cossacks*, one of Tolstoy's shorter novels: a multi-volume range of collected works in Russian sit on my shelves awaiting my retirement, or another life.) In the generation before me, it had been mandatory for medical students to take a subsidiary arts course, and many had opted for Russian. Not for long. Winifred McBride, in her sharp Scottish way, soon disabused them of the idea that Russian would be a lark and they fled to easier options elsewhere. In the class in which I began in 1965, there were just three students. And by the second year I was a class all on my own. At that stage, Winifred was the Russian Department, just as I was the SF year, though she had some help from Miss McMakin as a part-timer who, rumour had it, was an old-style Communist who had lived in Russia through the 1930s. And there was Count Tolstoy who came in to give Russian conversation classes. These classes were a doddle. All you had to do was ask the Count a question about his ancestors and a full hour's worth of anecdotes about 'moi pradedi' would ensue without you needing to think up a single further Russian sentence. Mind you, among those 'pradedi', the author of *War and Peace* was not a particularly significant figure – one of the less important members of the cadet branch of the Tolstoys.

What a change with the arrival of Julian Arkadych Kamensky. He was a passportless individual who had washed up in Ireland as part of some UN scheme for the relocation of stateless persons. An expatriate Russian who had lived in China for many years, he was imprisoned for four years in the wake of 1948, and therefore stripped of his Soviet citizenship presumably on the grounds that he had proved himself an enemy of the Revolution. He was an expatriate

Russian, but not in the Count Tolstoy style of expatriates: because the terrible truth emerged that he had fought with the Red Army in the Civil War, and had been employed by the Soviet government in Harbin before moving to China in the 1920s. (I once asked him why he had joined the Red Army, because he did not strike one as a man of strong political convictions. There was a simple answer – the whole regiment in which he had served through the First World War had gone over to the Reds: that was what their commander decided.) Anyway, his past hung like a bad smell about him in 'The Haven', the home for expatriate Russians off the Drumcondra Road where he lived, otherwise peopled by distressed ex-aristocratic emigrés who had lost everything in 1917.

There was nothing else that smelled bad about Julian Arkadych. A short, stout dapper man with a well-clipped moustache and a remaining circlet of white hair about his bald head, he particularly liked expensive perfumes and aftershaves. A businessman by training and inclination, he didn't have much real interest in literature or culture. When hired by the Abbey to act as interpreter for Mme Knebel from the Moscow Art Theatre to direct Siobhán McKenna and Cyril Cusack in *The Cherry Orchard*, he would summarize the director's elaborate notes to the actors succinctly: 'I just tell Siobhán to move to the left.' Julian Arkadych and I would sit puzzling over a translation exercise in which I was required to render P.G. Wodehouse into Russian, each of us with our restricted linguistic knowledge on one side of the exchange almost equally baffled: 'But, Nick, what are these eggs, beans and crumpets?' Whatever amount of Russian I learned from him, to be with him was to feel in contact with all the history he had lived through. After I had graduated and got married, he used to come to visit us in Clash. My wife Eleanor one night showed him some fire irons she had inherited made from WWI bayonets. 'Would you recognize that?' she asked Julian, handing him the poker. 'Oh yes,' said Julian, without a second's hesitation. 'That's the bayonet-head that was used in the Austrian army. In the Eastern Front I was often on the wrong end of one of those.' It made you feel differently about poking the fire.

My Russian was never up to much; I struggled through the four years, at one point having to repeat the SF exams (which I had failed) at the same time as taking the JS exams. But I was the more grateful to Winifred for having allowed me to continue, giving me so much one-to-one teaching time. They were classes unlike any others, unimaginably unlike anything that could take place now. We would sit in her office in No. 38, companionably smoking together. I remember her once stopping me as I was about to walk off with her matches: 'Nick, you have already stolen three boxes of matches and four biros from me this term: now will you give those over?' What should have been my Russian oral in 1968 was derailed by our shared shock at the news that had just come in of the assassination of Robert Kennedy. Neither of us felt inclined to make this the subject of stilted set phrases in Russian.

These *were* the Sixties. I may not have taken drugs but I did hear about them, for the first time, appropriately enough, in Greenwich Village in 1965. I was in New York for my sister's wedding and was having lunch in a Chinese restaurant with a girl I had met at a party: this for me at eighteen was going it some. She kept talking about LSD and the wonderful colours it enabled you to see, and I kept wondering why pounds, shillings and pence, beneficent though they no doubt were, should provoke hallucinations. Nearer home, in my later College years there were the Internationalists, devout followers of Mao, denouncing the running dogs of the Tsarist Board from the Dining-Hall steps.

Of more immediate moment in terms of changing times, was the announcement of the merger. I was washing up in a London youth hostel when I was told casually by a fellow washer-upper that the two Dublin universities were going to be merged. I thought he had to have got it wrong. After all, I was a student at Trinity and I should know. But, no, during the few days I had been over in England, unheralded, Donogh O'Malley, the Minister of Education had decreed that UCD and TCD should become one. Great discussions and debates were to follow. I can remember sitting in a packed and hostile Exam Hall to listen to Brian Lenihan defend the merger; he had succeeded O'Malley in Education when O'Malley died of a heart attack.

I can remember attending a Scholars' Committee solemnly pondering the issue. The Foundation Scholars, as a formal part of the body corporate of the College, took their responsibilities seriously. Most of us were pompous self-important twits, puffing out our little Scholars' chests; it was already apparent that this was not true of the committee chair, one Mary Bourke, later Robinson – she was to marry Nick Robinson whom I had known as a fellow performer in the Players 1916 show. One of the great heroes of the merger debate was my tutor R.B.D. French. A speech he made to The Hist defending the integrity of Trinity is often thought to have turned the tide against the merger, making it clear that the plan *could* be opposed; we didn't just have to lie down under the government plans. Was it The Hist or was it The Phil? I cannot be sure because I wasn't there; I wasn't a member of either society. After my stage-struck first year in Players, I became a non-joiner, living my split life between College in the week and the farm at the weekends, absorbed in my own doings.

How can you tell what is symptomatic or historically important about what you experience as a self-absorbed late teenager? I sleepwalked my way through four years of College, dimly aware if at all of what was going on around me in any wider world. I was literally given to sleepwalking at the time. I remember vividly one night waking up in the moonlight of Front Square with my hand on the door handle of David Thornley's car. I have no idea whether I intended to go joyriding, only the disorientating sensation of coming to consciousness with the cold metal making contact with my hand, my bare feet on the cobbles.

From Terence Brown's *Ireland: A Social and Cultural History* I belatedly learned something of Thornley's significance as a political thinker in the Ireland of the time. All I recall was a short, squat frog-faced man and the glamour of the red two-seater sports car parked by the Campanile that I somnambulistically tried to break into. Through my father's connection with Saul Bellow, a colleague at the University of Chicago and friend of John Berryman, I had occasion to meet the poet with my father in Mooney's on D'Olier St, and to witness their confabulation over a doctoral dissertation on Yeats. The meeting was to be of some interest when I recounted it many years later to my Trinity colleague Philip Coleman, a specialist on Berryman's poetry. To me at the time, he was just another embarrassing loud-mouthed drunk in a pub. Because of his friendship with my sister, I had some contacts with Derek Mahon, and gave up my rooms to him one afternoon so he could have an uninterrupted encounter with Eavan Boland. Steve Enniss, Special Collections Director at Emory University where Mahon's papers are deposited, researching his biography, interviewed me about my memories of Derek. But he already knew everything I could possibly tell him and much more, down to date, time and place.

What did I do in Trinity in the Sixties? I don't know, I don't remember; I was only there.

Nicholas Grene (TCD 1965–9; English) took his Ph.D. from Cambridge and taught at the University of Liverpool before returning to Trinity in 1979 where he is now Professor of English Literature. His main interest is in modern Irish drama and in Shakespeare. He is married to Eleanor Lenox-Conyngham (TCD English and French 1964–1968); they live in Wicklow and have four children.

Week of Trinity Ball, summer 1964. Right foreground: Heather Lukes (in hat); to her right: Anthony Weale; Petra Lewis, née Freston (wife of Jeremy Lewis), in striped dress.

A Day at the Races, summer 1964. Photographs courtesy of Michael de Larrabeiti.

A TRINITY TALE 1965–1969

turlough johnston

I **WAS LIVING** in a London Transport hostel just outside Watford when I received the news that I had been accepted by Trinity to read Ancient and Modern Literature, Latin and English. The hostel looked like a collection of prefabricated huts left over from the Second World War and of the sixty or so London Transport staff living there, fifty-nine were Irish. The sixtieth was George, an English bus conductor who had had a nervous breakdown when irate housewives in Rickmansworth attacked him because his bus was late. It was a rainy Saturday lunchtime and the bus in front had been taken off the route. I had been living in the hostel and working as a bus conductor, trying to save enough money to go back to Ireland and Trinity. The following September, I had enough to see me through one year, so I packed my cardboard case and made my way to Euston to catch the boat-train.

In 1965, Trinity was a small university, with a few thousand students. The majority seemed to be English, Anglo-Irish with county accents, or Northern Irish speaking from the back of the mouth, sharp and hard. I knew that I was one of the few Catholics there and one of the very few Irish Catholics. I had dutifully applied to Archbishop McQuaid for permission to attend this outpost of the British Empire and a curate from Westland Row had called to our flat to instruct me on the dangers awaiting my faith. I promised to join the Laurentian

Society, which apparently had the Archbishop's approval, and to stay away from the Communist Party, which did not. I later met the entire Communist Party late one afternoon as he supported himself against the bar in the Buttery. It would be 1970 before the Archbishop lifted the ban and the floodgates opened.

The Laurentian Society, named after St Laurence O'Toole, held weekly meetings, debates, and social evenings. It was populated by some earnest, badly dressed people, impressed by their own audacity in defying the Archbishop, and by English Catholics, mainly upper-middle class, appalled at finding the rest of us to be earnest, badly dressed people. By the end of Hilary term, I was avoiding as many Laurentians as I could.

Memory is unreliable. My first day's lectures were, I think, quite traumatic. The Latin lecturer was a woman whose name I forget. Most of the people in the class were Northern Irish and were dourly headed for the church. Men who seemed to have surnames for Christian names. Two earnest Englishmen and I formed a minority. The Latin sounded hard in my ears, attuned as they were to the soft Latin that I had learned when I was an altar boy. It was glaringly obvious to them that the class had been infiltrated. Maybe their curate at home had warned about the likes of me luring them to apostasy? Better the Communist Society than …

The light in the lecture hall for English lectures was bright by comparison, and the English lecturer threw a piece of chalk from one hand to the other as he spoke about Wordsworth. There were many more students there and most of them were girls. Girls of wondrous aspect. Confident, bouncy, with bright, English public-school accents and skirts that seemed amazingly short then but would become even shorter as the decade aged. Quieter Northern Irish girls, who came in groups, had more decorous hemlines to begin with.

The afternoon session was a tutorial in the lecturer's rooms in the Rubrics. Eight students assembled there and sat on well-worn couches and armchairs, while the tutor explained what was expected of us. Two English girls, two Northern Irish, the two Englishmen from Classics, a Northern Irishman who was not a Classicist (I looked at him curiously), an American, and myself. The tutor was curious to know what schools we had attended. Public school, public school, public school, grammar school, grammar school, grammar school, high school, St Munchin's College.

'I beg your pardon?'

'St Munchin's College. The diocesan school in Limerick.'

'Ah. Mr ehm Johnston?'

'Yes.'

'I see.'

Essay assignments were agreed upon and one of the public schools bravely agreed to be the first. We clustered around her afterwards, gratefully impressed by her bravery, while she seemed to have breathing difficulties at the thought of what she had done. The non-Classicist Northerner looked on a trifle sceptically, a look I came to know as a hallmark of those from north of the Border. The essay was, of course, quite perfect.

A month into Michaelmas term, a month of stifling Latin lectures and translations, a month of mind-opening lectures on the novel, on poetry, on plays. One lecturer spoke on *portray*, and I thought I had come to a class on art, until it dawned on me that he was talking about poetry. I understood that I was not cut out for a world where Caesar was pronounced Kaysar. A quiet and understanding tutor arranged for me to transfer to English Language and Literature. Anglo-Saxon was at least a younger language and everyone was struggling equally with Beowulf's word-hoard under the enthusiastic beam of the Anglo-Saxon lecturer. The years at Trinity were going to open my eyes to literature and to the world.

The question of finance was always in the air, and my quiet tutor found some bursaries that, having fallen into disuse, were awarded to me. Free Commons for four years made sure I would never go hungry, and I was soon on good terms with a number of Scholars who also had the same privilege; they must have wondered when I had taken Schol. Those living in rooms also ate in Commons and the Dining Hall would always be filled with voices and the clatter of knife on plate. The High Table at the head of the Dining Hall, where the teaching staff sat, looked out over the sea of gown-clad male students. Women students were not allowed in Commons.

The Dining Hall on Saturdays and Sundays and in the holidays was comparatively empty. Those left would gather at one table below the High Table. I became good friends with a scholar from Kenya, a man who claimed to have finally understood Milton after drinking half a bottle of brandy when reading *Paradise Lost* under the table in his rooms. Try as I might with a bottle of Preston's whiskey under my mother's dining table, I never reached his level of clarity with the blind poet. The Kenyan scholar showed a somewhat surprising interest in horse racing and we began to spend our Saturday afternoons at the wonderfully named Kilmartin's Turf Accountants near Side Gate. A 'one shilling each way' that gave a place or a win would have us waiting outside Mulligans for the end of holy hour. 'Yous two again,' Con the barman would grunt as he opened the door.

Dublin in the 1960s saw the rise of the ballad-singing pub. O'Donoghues on Merrion Row was maybe the first of them, and that was where the Dubliners had started. I soon needed another source of income and managed to get a job as a barman in the Parnell House on Parnell Street, an amazing ballad-pub where over a hundred drinkers would gather to listen to Dubliner lookalikes. Like a lot of pubs in Dublin, this was owned by a Cavan family, six brothers and a sister. They needed extra staff to help them out on the weekends, and in the end I spent about three years part-timing there. I could soon pour a Perfect Pint and even today believe that the pouring of the PP is an art not to be scorned, a belief that has got me into trouble in pubs all over the world, where slovenly pint-pouring and a disrespect for settling time has led me into heated altercations with couldn't-care-less bar staff.

My time at the Parnell House resulted not only in the aforesaid ability to pour the PP but also in the inability to forget any of the long and sometimes tedious ballads that were sung there nightly: 'Bold Robert Emmet', 'The Waxies' Dargle', 'Little Ball of Yarn', 'Maids When You're Young', 'Preab san ól'.

Apart from the bar trade, I learned quite a bit about sheep farming. In the first weeks of Junior Fresh year I got to know a man who was so much at home with English literature that his first-term essay came back with the simple comment, 'Yes.' Although he took it seriously, his scholarship lay lightly on his shoulders, and it was always clear to us others that this was the Future Professor. He had a fascinating background that had resulted in, among other things, a small farm in Wicklow that he would visit at weekends. When I could get away from the Parnell House, I would accompany him into the Wicklow hills in his ancient Hillman. It was a magical place for a city boy, the farmhouse kitchen with its huge open fireplace, the rooms filled with books from floor to ceiling, the hilly fields with their sheep, the awesome ram called Sambo. I spent most of the time in wellingtons, counting sheep, dipping sheep, herding sheep to the market. In the evenings we would read or sit playing cards with a good neighbour whose stories filled the night, and empty the bottle of Redbreast.

I found studying at home difficult so I did most of my reading in the 1937 Reading Room. Well, frankly, I found studying difficult (hence my results) but reading a delight (hence my lifelong love of books). Evenings in the Reading Room were wonderful, the green glass lampshades shedding a warm light over the long desks. As closing time drew near, the word would pass around that we would be meeting in the College Mooney. I would check my pocket carefully to ensure that I had the price of a round. If the necessary was not available, the non-Latinist would insist on my coming along, penniless or no. So out through Side Gate, across the road, and up the stairs to the lounge, where, although the pint was a penny more expensive, we had Ted to look after us – he had come to regard us as 'his students'. Clad in a green jacket and dicky bow, he would carry over our pints with the air of a priest approaching the altar. Some evenings, a man would come in selling freshly cooked Dublin Bay prawns. A snack fit for a king: prawns and a pint. The College Mooney was our local of choice for the first year or so, before we discovered Mulligans, where Con and Tommy ruled with a firm hand.

In our third year, Junior Soph Year, the non-Classicist moved into rooms in Botany Bay and these soon became a focal point for all those who lived outside College. By this time, we were a diverse group: a medic from London, permanently dazed by long hours of study and early-morning lectures; another Englishman, clever but quiet; the Future Prof; several Northern Irishmen, some more sophisticated than others; a Mod. Lang. man from Greystones (the only other Catholic in the group). Still startled at being in the Republic, especially as the Civil Rights movement began to grow in the North, some of the Northern Irish seemed a little ill at ease. But all of them gathered regularly in the rooms in Botany Bay, and we would frequently wake the non-Classicist up at midday, having attended the first lectures. He had lost any belief in the efficacy of attending lectures, if indeed he ever had any, and would spend his waking day sprawled on his couch with his twelve-string guitar, picking out the latest Bob Dylan song and hatching plans for drinking expeditions to musical pubs such as Slatterys of Capel Street and the Abbey Tavern in Howth. He was the instigator of the Grafton Street Crawl, a frightful drinking expedition that took place after the moderatorship exams in September of 1968 and 1969.

The exact numbers who made up the party on each occasion have been lost in the years, although many more claim to have been there than were actually there, just as 30,000 Irishmen saw Munster defeat the All Blacks in the 12,000-capacity Thomond Park rugby ground in 1978.

The crawl began off the top of Grafton Street and took in one public house on each side of the road on all the streets that crossed Grafton Street as we moved south in a slowly disintegrating group. We started in Rice's of South King Street and should rightly have ended in O'Neills of Suffolk Street, but a dispensation was granted to the Palace Bar and to Mulligans, these being the only places considered to provide a truly respectable pint. Our palates had apparently been refined by three years of drinking the pint of plain. An extension that was discussed at one stage of the first evening was to continue down Pearse Street, turn right up Westland Row, and finish in the Lincoln on Lincoln Place, close to Back Gate. That was before we realized that no crawlers would still stand after Mulligans, if indeed any of us ever got that far.

Women were still not allowed to live in rooms within the walls and they had to respect the midnight curfew. Young love often forgot the passage of time and girls who overstayed the allotted hour had to ask to be let through Front Gate. They then had to face embarrassing lectures from the Junior Dean or his assistants and were also heavily fined. One night after midnight I was startled to meet one of the most attractive girls in my year in New Square. 'You have to help me get out of here!' she hissed at me in her public-school accent, converting me into a willing accessory on the spot. The only way out was over the railings by the cricket pavilion. The wall on which the railings stand is high, as are the railings themselves. Athletically hoisting herself onto my shoulders while steadying herself on the wall, she stood up with one foot on each shoulder before hopping onto the wall.

'Were you looking up my skirt?'

'Ahm, yes, actually.'

'I thought you were. Well done.' With that, she climbed up the railings like a monkey and dropped off into Nassau Street and vanished into the night. I never did find out in whose rooms she had left her underwear. Some time in the early 1970s, women were allowed to reside in rooms.

All our drinking was not necessarily of the alcoholic sort. Afternoon breaks were often taken in Bewley's on Grafton Street. Those were the days before self-service, and our table was more often than not served by Tattens, a very capable and good-hearted waitress with a rather grand accent. She always wore the traditional black dress and white apron, heavy makeup, and her blonde hair tightly combed. Tattens, too, came to look upon us as 'her students' and would allow us to while away the hours as we nursed our tea or coffee, eagerly talking College gossip, literature, the student politics of 1968, and anything else that needed to be aired by our loquacious tongues and voracious minds.

Iced coffee became my favourite drink at Bewley's but when I brought my daughter there some years ago I found that the iced coffee I had spoken so lyrically about was not served any more. But Tattens, as smiling and gracious as ever, was now maître d' and stood at the inner entrance to the café, welcoming me as if I had never been away. Now Bewley's as we knew it is gone. About a year ago, I saw Tattens' obituary in *The Irish Times*.

Many lasting friendships were forged in those four years, which finished before I had quite understood what I was experiencing. I have often felt since that I would like to redo the whole four years, knowing what I now know. Although I had never got further than a factory in England during the summers, my friends would come back with tales of sleeping on beaches in Greece, taking the Greyhound bus in the United States, driving old Morris Minors around Spain, running out of money in Turkey. The world was opening.

Turlough Johnston (TCD 1965–9; English) worked in advertising and in publishing until 1971, when he moved to Sweden, where he was an editor before starting his own publishing company in 1974. He still works in the book business but on the printing side, and lives most of the year in the south of Spain. He is still married to the reason he moved to Sweden, Eleonore, with whom he has three children.

TRIBALISM, 1967

roy foster

IN 1967 Trinity's relation to its immediate surroundings was still faintly exotic. My first lecture from Professor Otway-Ruthven that October was interrupted by the arrival, a careful ten minutes late, of two girls, one red-haired, one honey-blonde, both in purple miniskirts, purple feather boas, floppy hats, and heavy eye-liner; both English, both called Sally. It wasn't exactly the light of evening, Lissadell, but it was refreshingly different from Waterford. Professor Otway-Ruthven looked less impressed than I was.

Trinity, as I would find, was divided into tribes. Looking back I can distinguish Posh English, Boho English, Local Intellectuals, Politicos, and Clever Country. The Posh English bred a small subset of Irish Sloane Rangers (though that nomenclature was yet to come). Northerners tended to make up tribes of their own, divided between those who had long hair, and those came into the Buttery carrying motorbike helmets protectively in front of them. Some managed to slide out of either rank and adopt a local tribe. The gap between arts people and scientists yawned like a chasm: the latter were seen, rather unfairly, as people who slipped in and out of the Lincoln Place Gate wearing anoraks. Mathematicians and Engineers, as in all academic communities, were a law unto themselves. The trouble with tribalism was that you went through four years never meeting people with whom – you might discover in afterlife –

you had a good deal in common. One of my best friends nowadays turned out to be an exact Trinity contemporary whom I never encountered at the time.

Girls like the Sallies tended to live first in Trinity Hall, then in flats around Dublin 4, before it had become 'Dublin 4'. My own domestic progress took me from chilly digs in Glasnevin, with a vaguely psychotic landlady who locked everything up, on a zigzag odyssey south, never quite reaching Dublin 4. There was a bed-sitter in Great Denmark Street off Mountjoy Square, owned by one of the area's many madams, a flat above The Old Stand pub in Wicklow Street, where everyone I knew seemed to have lived, and eventually a rambling place perched high up in the beautiful Corn Exchange Building on Burgh Quay, where Daniel O'Connell had held Repeal meetings. Here, our landlord was the louche tenor Josef Locke. Other tenants included a straggle of sad-faced ladies of a certain age whom he called on late at night, leaving his yellow Jaguar E-Type run rakishly up on the pavement outside. Once I found him asleep in it when I was leaving for a morning lecture, an imposing figure in his loud check jacket, canary waistcoat and silk cravat.

From 1969, a Foundation Scholarship brought me free Commons with all the stale stout I could drink, a stipend, and rooms in College – rescuing me from flat life, which I rather regretted. The atmosphere, if not monastic, tended to the boys' boarding school; women could not live in College and were supposed to leave the precincts by midnight. Worldy-wise skips with an eye to a bribe for an overnight guest knew different. 'Five shillings for a boy, ten shillings for a girl.' But from my eyrie at the top of No. 3 I could see everyone who came in and out of Front Gate, and watch the Internationalists selling Chairman Mao's Little Red Book, famously torn up in a ritual protest by someone called David Naisby-Smith (Posh English, he wore a cravat too), and observe the progress of Local Intellectual Ros Mitchell's sit-down strike or hear another Maoist protester, David Vipond, intoning 'Junior Dean, Explain Your Actions!' No. 3 had other advantages too. When Trinity received a regal visit from Senator Ted Kennedy, hastily substituted for his assassinated brother Bobby and trying to salvage his reputation post-Chappaquiddick, it was felt to be worth a protest. Both speakers of my stereo were directed out the window and as he entered College the words of *Private Eye*'s latest Christmas record were played at surprisingly effective max volume into Front Square: '*Poor Cold*

Ted! He took a wrong turning on his way to the beach and landed up to his neck in trouble! You can't expect a man to drink, drive and make up a good story afterwards!' Faces turned up to my window as to the Pope on Sundays at noon in St Peter's. But the spell was broken by the sound of thundering feet on the stairs, my door was kicked open, and Special Branch detail who had been positioned on the roof above stormed into the room. They probably expected to find Sirhan Sirhan. I suppose I was lucky not to be shot.

Memories of living in College are less vivid than the life outside its walls, and scholarly life is something of a blur – though I liked the dim oasis of the Lecky Library, still in the Museum Building, its mahogany and wrought iron glowing in the light of green-shaded lamps. By contrast the brand-new Library smelt strangely of rubberized flooring and newly varnished wood, and you spent most of your time looking for a space to sit down. When I was eligible for the National Library I preferred it, and still do. Teaching was oddly formal. Professor Otway-Ruthven remained as discouraging as at the first lecture, perhaps because I became rapidly committed to the Other Side, in the shape of her *bête noire*, Theo Moody, whose Home Rule Special Subject set the tenor of my future professional life. Professor Moody was first glimpsed as an alarming reincarnation of Ludwig van Beethoven as he crossed New Square with his long hair lifting in the breeze. He would in time become a great mentor and friend, but that seemed an unlikely prospect at this stage of my College life. There seemed to be few interactions with local academic gods. One exception was the great botanist David Webb, who wore long crinkly grey hair and a smart outfit of denim jeans and bomber jacket set off by a jaunty red scarf. Members of various tribes were invited to luncheons in his beautiful rooms and summer parties in the Botanic Gardens, to eat intimidatingly delicious food, meet interesting and often rather grand people from outside the walls, and be barked at by one's irascible host for saying something ill-thought-out or stupid. It was another kind of education.

Though I was no longer living nomadically in Dublin's flatland, the city was still at the door, and the countryside seductively near. Suburban sprawl was comparatively contained; as long as you had A Friend With A Car it took no time at all to drive up to Feather Bed or the Sally Gap on a warm evening, or down to Brittas Bay (where one of the Sallies rented a converted boathouse for one happy summer), or out to the Stawberry Beds on the river near Chapelizod, where you lay in the lush grass by the weir and took it in turns to bring large bottles of stout from the Wren's Nest. Pubs featured large, eating out did not. Rich students may have gone to Snaffles, the Soup Bowl or Elephants; for the rest of us there was only the Universal Chinese Restaurant, which lived up to its name, or Gaj's, where politicos conspired in an upstairs room on Baggot Street over comfort food. I once brought an exquisite and food-faddy friend there, who after an appalled perusal of the menu enquired faintly, 'Is all your food deep-fried?' 'Yes, ma'am,' the waitress proudly reassured her, '*everything* is deep-fried.'

But there were other, cheaper, pleasures. The city itself was invitingly intimate, curiously uncrowded, with surviving pockets of atmospheric urban decay that suggested the Dublin of Sean O'Casey or *The Ginger Man.* (Years later, a contemporary from those years found himself drunkenly telling a small bearded American in a tweed suit, whom he encountered at a party, about what Dublin used to be like in the Sixties; it turned out he was imparting this information to J.P. Donleavy.) On an early Saturday afternoon, when pubs shut for the holy hour, a curious tranquillity spread through the streets, as people gathered their resources for the night. Where to meet? Several tribes intersected in Toner's pub, run by the impeccably formal Mr Toner, with a large and bulbous growth in the middle of his forehead: his imperturbable reserve never cracked, not even when an art college toper remarked, 'Jaysus Mr Toner, you look very like a Cyclops.' Mr Toner was abetted by his diminutive sidekick Charlie, and upstairs there was Miss Toner and a large off-white dog, surreally encountered by women in search of a lavatory. For more sophisticated entertainment there were impromptu performances at the International Bar, where Elgie Gillespie (Boho English) read Sylvia Plath and Chris Meehan (Clever Country) sang Bessie Smith. And late at night, when everything closed, there were still places like the Manhattan Café at Kelly's Corner, with its legendary jukebox and a raffish clientele who included elderly queens, ladies of the night, broken-down jockeys – and students, of course.

Nor were they all from Trinity. In those days UCD was still in Earlsfort Terrace, though in the process of moving to the windswept wastelands of Belfield. The UCD pub O'Dwyers on Leeson Street was an alternative focus to Toner's, DramSoc (featuring the soon-to-be-famous Sheridan brothers) seemed more avant-garde than Trinity Players, the L&H more grown-up than The Hist, and Iveagh Gardens behind the university was another of those hidden corners of Dublin where long afternoons could be eliminated in a smoky haze. When UCD moved to the suburbs, the chances of interaction diminished. But I was already going out with someone from the Terrace, meeting under the Clock or on the bridge in Stephen's Green, the halfway point between the two universities. Some UCD departments hung on in central Dublin. The School of Architecture was the last to go; it eventually moved out in 1981. By then we were married, living in London, and Dublin was changing beyond recognition. But we happened to be back in town when the architects, finally forced to abandon the old building, organized the 'Terrace Wake'. Electric power had been cut off, but the Aula Maxima was lit by candles and generators had been brought in to amplify the roaring rock bands. Drinking and dancing continued into the small hours, and faces from the 1960s swam up and disappeared again in the gloom. We left at about two in the morning and as always, there were no taxis. So we went to the Manhattan, and it was just the same as ever.

That was 1981. Now it is more than forty years since I sat watching the two Sallies totter up the steep rake of that Museum Building lecture room. I don't suppose anyone goes to lectures there any more; the centre of gravity has shifted to an Arts Block that makes the 'new' Library look minuscule; Trinity, like Dublin, is bigger, sharper, glitzier, and the tribes of my youth are extinct, replaced by new denominations. When I go back it is often in some semi-official role, and I am doubly disorientated: both because my accommodation is improbably luxurious (where are the communal baths behind the Buttery?) and because the parameters of the domestic geography have shifted. No. 40 has been turned into guest rooms. Sometimes I find my bedroom is where Theo Moody used to hold his Rankean seminars ('Not the first time you've fallen asleep in *that* room,' someone remarked), or in the office overlooking the rugby pitch where Jim Lydon subjected us to terrifying interrogations over medieval essays. On one recent occasion we were accommodated in the Rubrics, and I slowly realized I was sleeping in David Webb's sitting-room, surrounded by his pictures, which had been left to the College. It is all rather like the last volume of those novel sequences about searching for lost time, or dancing to its music:

the people have changed, the landscape shifted, yet the dance goes on. But for Trinity, a curiously self-renewing place with a brusquely realistic approach to the past, it is just another chapter.

Roy Foster (TCD 1967–71; History) was a postgraduate from 1971 to 1974. He is now Carroll Professor of Irish History at the University of Oxford and the author of several books, including **Modern Ireland 1600–1972** (1990), the two-volume authorized biography of W.B. Yeats (1997–2003), and most recently **Luck & the Irish: A Brief History of Change from 1970** (2008). He received an honorary doctorate in litteris from Trinity in 2003.

ANGELA OF THE BUTTERY

ray lynott

HER NAME was Angela Thorpe.

How do I remember the full name so easily when these days I often find myself walking down the street juggling syllables in an effort to reassemble the name of an approaching neighbour? It seems ANGELA THORPE is monumentally inscribed. So, how is this and why?

Because she is part of me, or because she became part of me at a time in my life 'before the wax hardened' (to borrow the title of a friend's autobiography)?

Yes, maybe. But I think there is more – that is not to do with me at all, but with the woman herself. Angela was a 'self', an integrated being, somebody who within her own limitations was full to the brim of selfness, who, without ever going beyond first-level education, had achieved the ideal written above Plato's Academy – 'Know Thyself'. And I don't mean by 'selfness' that she was selfish, quite the contrary. She lived her life for others, for us – and maybe a little 'through' us – the students of TCD in the years between about 1965 and the early 1980s.

She came to the College after her mother died, she told me once: so she wasn't young in 1965. For many years after her father the breadwinner died, she and her mother ran a little shop in Drumcondra – in one of those terraced, red-brick, two-up, two-down, northside houses, which had its downstairs front window 'gunthered bigger'* to throw light into a tiny front room where a wooden bench acting as counter along the narrow back wall allowed the neighbours to be served with 'essentials' – milk, bread, tea, sugar, quarter-pounds of butter, and on weekdays Mr de Valera's *Irish Press*. When her mother died she didn't want to live on her own over a shop with its bigger front window, for fear of 'the worst', she said, with a meaningful shake of the head. So she got the guntherer in again, had the window boarded up, and felt safer. But she knew her life had changed. Now she would have to go out and earn a living somewhere else. The 1960s were not prosperous times.

'Trinity took me in' was the way she'd describe what happened. Angela always spoke of College as if it was a person – tall, male, broad-shouldered, a benefactor in silk-swishing cloak who suddenly swooped down, rescued and enveloped her in her hour of need. And of course something vaguely of a kind but much less romantic, less dramatic, may have happened. I'm inclined to think that a benevolent network rescued Angela. Her name was Thorpe. I think she may have been one of that small but significant group of Dubliners that is often ignored in sociological studies of our city – the working-class Dublin Protestant (if one can use a questionable epithet more relevant to the 1960s and before). Certainly, there was a population of porters, skips and attendants in College then, whose tradition was of the Church of Ireland and (can it be said?) Unionism. But be all that as may be, Angela Thorpe in middle age was welcomed into Trinity College and given the job of cleaner and trolley-lady in the Buttery.

One began to notice her, especially at hectic lunchtimes. Of less than medium height, tottering slightly in broad Minnie-Mouse 'heels', depending on her trolley to get her between busy tables. Full in figure rather than buxom, wrapped tightly in a blue house-coat, she would lean over our student heads making no apology for interrupting the most heated discussion as she went about her job, head erect: it was the head more than anything else one noticed. Luxuriant hair, steel-grey as wire wool, bunched to the back where it was

* 'gunther' (gunter/gundher): variously pronounced Dublin word applied to a cheap, hastily completed masonry, carpentry, plumbing or electrical job, which may or may not be adequate, but is certainly not elegant or fully satisfactory. A 'guntherer' is somebody known for such work.

caught in a bejewelled clasp; or at the front allowed to topple jauntily down over the forehead and the made-up face. The small greyish-blue eyes twinkled whenever they were met. Plump powdered cheeks swelled to a smile, tiny lip-sticked mouth opening ever so slightly – bright-red Clara-Bowe lips parting just enough – to allow out a ladylike 'helloo'. Few objected to this amazing apparition hovering over the table while a strong thrusting arm parted our ranks and asserted, like Moses, the right to a clean sweep. The twinkling eyes and gleaming puckered lips with their breathily ushered 'helloo' were enough.

And I think, even today, if Cupid's-bow lips are evoked among Trinitarians, Angela Thorpe may hover like Alice's Cheshire cat.

Maybe I got to know her more than most, because I have a gossipy side, which I must admit I sometimes like to indulge. I love stories, personal stories; and I found that in time Angela was becoming a wonderful repository of same. People had begun to confide in her, trust her middle-aged motherliness. Maybe in the old Greek arrangement of things she would have been a kind of nurse-become-message-bearer, or small-accounts records-keeper – a Klotho or a Lachesis (spinning and measuring, well before the final length of lifethread is cut by their more severe sister). One went to her to find out if somebody was in College that day, or where they had gone if they were away. And the extension of this information service was that Angela began to know not just movements of people, but also whys and wherefores of movements and ultimately all that was going on in their/our lives: people, names, facts, fictions, addresses, and often even – if necessary – some important pieces of family background. And, like all good storytellers, if she didn't know what one asked she was willing to guess, because she was a bit of a psychologist too, as storymakers must needs be.

But what of her own story?

By gossips' agreement, I began to piece that together slowly if unsurely. Or I found out some of it by direct question.

'Did you never think of getting married, Angela?'

'Never.' Pause. The red lips puckered more than usual. Impishness in the glistening eyes.

'Never?'

'Well, almost never. We had a lodger once, after Daddy died, before Mammy decided on the shop. We gave him the front room. Now *he* was a nice man, a real gentleman. Mammy liked him too.'

Out of the blue! I hadn't expected a straightforward statement of so much fact. Mammy liked him *too*!

The not-too-clean evil-smelling J-Cloth is going over the table for the second time, small, full, blue-smocked body bent over, plump face toward the work, wire wool dancing on the head. I wished I could see the expression, but the face is somehow held down, as if once more she is privately seeing 'the nice gentleman' that both she and Mammy liked and the vision is not for further sharing.

We're alone. I'm nursing a mug of Nescafé at the other side of the table. It's afternoon, and I have already decided enough is enough, no more exam work, for the second day in a row. I'm desperate to find ways of overriding guilt. And here is Angela, coming clean … or about to … maybe …

'Was he now?' I have to be careful, I know that. No overeager curiosity.

'When he left, I decided that was it. That was that.'

'He left?' I couldn't conceal surprise. 'Why?'

Wrong question. I had intruded. The blue-smocked body with wool-crowned head was suddenly erect, face turned to me, eyes widened in dismissal.

'Now, aren't you the right wee nosy parker, you are. All agog to hear everything. And is it news or a long chat you want, is it?' She had copped me!

Before I could retract or react, chariot and message-bearer were turning; gone! I could only watch the bejewelled clasp quivering in its grey mesh, atop the upright, proud little figure pushing its way haughtily into the wash-up scullery, faster than I had ever seen Angela move before, not a totter in the Minnie-Mouse shoes. I knew I had blown it, but I didn't know whether I had given mortal offence or not. The face was kept in the other direction all the way.

But, of course I hadn't. Angela wasn't like that.

However I was never to know the full story of the vanished lodger. The most I learned subsequently of romantic entanglement or the lack of it in Angela's life was that nothing would ever be yielded, nothing allowed until 'the little gold band' was put 'on that finger'… the softest, plumpest, little pink left-hand finger you could imagine, bare, held out for one's inspection.

But the fuller truth is that Angela wasn't prudish. She could hardly have been, guardian as she was of our inner and outer lives. One could ask her about alternatives.

'What about just living with a fellow, Angela? You have your own house, how about taking in a nice fellow from your own area, or one of the lads from here, one of the porters?'

'What would I be doing that for? Either the gold band goes on this finger or nothing.'

'Come on! Do you want to die lonely, and wondering?'

'What are you talking about? I'm not lonely. Haven't I me nice job here, don't I meet all of yous and hear enough about your wild outrageous goings-on? And then when I get home I have peace, nothing nor anybody to bother me. What would I want anything else for? I can go to bed in me pinks and me blues and wake up the same way in the morning, and not have some aul' fella pulling and dragging at me half the night and him maybe dead drunk and reeking from it. No thank you!'

Respectability? Angela would have put a value on doing the right thing, keeping 'her end' up, she might have called it, maintaining 'the fitness of things' the way her Mammy and her Daddy would have taught her to do.

I once met her outside Trinity, at the opera of all places. I was taking my sister to the gods in the Gaiety during what was then the Dublin Grand Opera Society season, and at the interval who should hail me but Angela. I could see she was glad we were meeting in such a place on such an occasion, and she told my sister she always went one night in every opera season, as much as anything else because she and the Mammy always did it, always queued, got their tickets well in advance, and came to the gods. Indeed she remembered the first time she ever came to opera in the Gaiety, and she should tell us about it because things were so different then. That night there was lots of applause for a young singer after she sang her first piece; and of course she, Angela, joined in applauding enthusiastically. But then, an old gruff fellow beside her, hands firmly clasped together on his lap grunted crossly, 'Stop that, will ye! If you clap her like that, how'll she'll ever learn?' We were told the punchline with head thrown back, diva taking a high note, grey hair in shock waves, small body convulsed in laughter. And then after a ladylike cough we were told that tonight she was doing what 'poor Mammy' would have wanted – she was here again with her 'friend'. At that moment two rows down a lady of similar age, similarly done up in Sunday best, and smelling I'm sure of the same powerful perfume, was waving back to us, appreciating Angela consorting with some 'Trinity' friends.

That may have been the last time I saw dear Angela Thorpe. Or did I meet her once more outside the College gates, long after I had left? She was going home. She always left by Front Gate, smart, tight-belted, camel-hair coat replacing blue smock, silk paisley headscarf high above the grey hair and tied generously at the chin, framing freshly powdered face and newly gleaming Cupid's-bow.

'Helloo, Ray.'

'Hello, Angela.'

Small talk: neither of us married yet. Laughter …

'Cheerio, Ray.'

'Cheerio, Angela.'

Years passed. Maybe it was the early Nineties or later, when and one day I decided to have a stroll through College. The Buttery had been completely revamped by then. I didn't expect to find Angela there, nor was she. But as I was leaving Front Square I went to the porters' office and asked if anything was known of her.

'Angela, ah yeah … she retired years ago. But she's still here.'

'Still here?'

'Yeah, over beyond College Park in the Department of Anatomy. She's in jars over there, or she was. When she died she left her body to science ye know, to the College.'

Indeed, what else should I have expected!

In this moment as I write – or in the minutes it takes somebody else who knew you to be reminded – the gold band of memory encircles you, Angela Thorpe, and keeps you resplendent for all of us in your pinks and in your blues.

Ray Lynott (TCD 1967–72; H.Dip. in Ed.; M.Litt.) had a collection of short stories **A Year in the Country** published by Irish Writers' Co-op in 1978. He worked for twenty-seven years in RTÉ as an announcer and radio producer, and now in retirement has once again taken up writing as a pensioner's hobby.

MAIDEN SPEAKER

donnell deeny

FRONT SQUARE. The beauty of it. I still remember the heart-expanding joy of first crossing it in the week of registration, never having been in Trinity before. The sense that one had made the right decision. I swiftly abandoned my brother's idea that I should follow him, and Oscar Wilde, to Magdalen College, Oxford. Front Square, perhaps the finest man-made space in Ireland and one of the most beautiful squares in Europe, lay relatively unknown behind the closed gates of the College. The old Library lay at one corner containing the Long Room, where the Book of Kells was displayed. American tourists who asked for 'Kelly's Book' were directed to the bath-house.

At right angles to the Library was the last remnant of the Williamite college, the Rubrics. I went several times for drinks there with that lively legend, R.B. McDowell. The drink was never the same. Good claret one night, cider another. Was it there I first tasted the soft and golden fire of ancient whiskey? If I got five words in edgeways in the course of the evening that was all. But I did get a one-man tutorial in Anglo-Irish social and political history. It occurs to me, only now, that I never invited him back to our rooms but I rather think we did not keep any drink there. I hope he, who has written so much and so well, will accept a belated apology.

On the north side of the square was the Graduates' Memorial Building, which housed, inter alia, the Conversation Room of the College Historical Society. It was on the first floor, with windows on three sides, a true piano nobile, and can be seen as Michael Caine's study in the film *Educating Rita*. I remember sitting in an armchair when a sturdy Anglo-Irishman plumped down opposite me. We exchanged greetings.

'You know the Hist Bi-centenary Ball? I asked that very pretty girl, Jenny X, would she go to it with me.'

'What did she say?'

'"No, but when is it?"'

Oh what a cruel line, with its implication that she would keep the date in mind for some more appealing suitor. But I confess that as soon as I decently could I slipped out of the Conversation Room, sought her out and asked her myself. She said yes!

Next to the Conversation Room was the mid-eighteenth-century Dining Hall, austerely classical, with its broad terrace and steps, where, in 1969, Patrick Boyd-Maunsell staged the *Agamemnon* by Aeschylus in the poetic but scholarly translation by Louis MacNeice. True to the Greek tradition of plays being entered in competition at a festival, there was only one performance, albeit preceded by a dress rehearsal. A thousand people sat in rows of seats on the cobbles of Front Square facing the open-air performance. Nothing ruffled the concentration on the play. If any hoi polloi by chance did pass, they kept their comments behind the hedge of their teeth. King Agamemnon crossed Front Square to triumphant music from the rooftops of the Examination Hall and strode between the rows of seats to the head of the steps where Queen Clytemnestra awaited him. He flung out his arm in greeting – and forgot his lines. But Sorcha Cusack, a quintessential professional even then, prompted him until he returned safely to the stirring text of the great play and led on to its bloody and successful conclusion.

> And who above this god-like hero's grave
> Pouring praises and tears
> Will grieve with a genuine heart?

When Paul McGuinness and I went up at the end of the 1960s there was still a good deal of the never-never land that Trinity in that decade embodied:

the sunlit idyll that moved Roy Jenkins to say that Trinity then made Oxbridge seem red-brick. A bell in the early evening would summon those resident in College to Commons and they would attend wearing gowns, as one was required to do also for lectures.

Matt Russell, who refused me credit for wearing a coat over my gown one winter evening, gave a nine o'clock lecture on Saturday mornings. After it, Jenny Thomas, Tony Aston and half the class would repair to the Fellows' Garden. There was no Arts Block there in those days but a delightful miniature Greek Temple, inside of which there was a box of croquet mallets for general use. We would play croquet for the rest of the morning, the lawn framed by the back of the Provost's House and the excellent new library. I spent many soothing hours there reading widely.

A party in The Hist was called 'a blind' but one in the Boat Club was 'a thrash' – not that I was ever a member of the Boat Club. One learnt at Freshers' parties that if one was going to drink very cheap wine it was safer to drink red than white – less likely to make one violently ill. The College numbers, of course, were infinitely smaller then, and when the pubs closed one might end up almost anywhere. I found myself in a small house beside Merrion Gates one night with the outgoing president of the SCR, bearded, balding, who put a revolver to my temple and threatened to shoot. His clever girlfriend gently guided him away. I sometimes wonder whether the gun was loaded.

A very different figure in the College was Professor Bedell Stanford with his resplendent quiff. I fear he was less famous to some undergraduates for his great classical scholarship than because you could shake his mother's dead hand in the crypt of St Michan's if you paid the sexton sixpence.

Undergraduates have this in common with men in their sixties and seventies. There is a lot of variable ageing despite chronological parity. I remember standing outside a lecture room in the Museum Building. A quiet Campbellian in a slightly excited voice said to Paolo Tullio and me that he had read that having sexual intercourse used up as much energy as running a mile. What did Paolo think?

'Don't know. Never run a mile,' said Paolo. Small and dapper, Downside, the only son of an Italian with a chain of cafés, Paolo had an air then of quiet, self-sufficient sophistication. His conversation was a delight and his comfortable home in Booterstown a change from my digs.

My digs, too, were part of an older world. I was one of two guests in a charming little house right on the River Dodder in Donnybrook. There was a coal fire in my study-bedroom. The landlady brought a cooked breakfast to me in bed every morning! Her only requirement was that Hans, who worked for Cement Roadstone, and I would be home for a substantial three-course meal at six o'clock every evening. I fear Hans was more punctual in his habits than I.

The following year I came up late for some reason and no accommodation was available. For the first term I lived in Hatch Place. For five nights a week I slept in the bed of a beautiful young schoolteacher. Sadly she was not in the bed at the time but with her photographer lover. In a splendidly dutiful, perhaps Irish, way, he would go home to his widowed mother on Thursdays and Sundays and the beautiful girl would return to her bed in 3 Hatch Place. On those nights I slept on a camp bed in the house next door, No. 2, which was occupied by my sister and three other industrious and virtuous students of University College, Dublin. For some reason in that term I seemed to stay out terribly late. Debates and political meetings would be succeeded by the public house and a curious place that Paul had discovered, called the Manhattan, where late-night nourishment could be had. I would lie in late in the morning. One Monday morning I woke up on my camp bed and established the time and decided that while I would like some more sleep I would have it in the bed next door that by then ought to have been vacated by the beautiful young schoolteacher. I pulled on a dressing-gown, shuffled out the door of No. 2 and next door to No. 3 and put a key in the door. I then heard a curious noise. It sounded like applause but I could not think why. I turned around and just across the lane there was a building under construction. On the recently erected scaffolding there were a number of workmen who were indeed very handsomely applauding me. I stood there completely puzzled for a moment. I then realized they had been observing my movements over the previous weeks. They had seen the industrious young ladies leaving No. 2 Hatch Place to go to their lectures and had surmised that having done my duty in No. 2 Hatch Place I was now moving into No. 3, where the ladies lay rather later in bed, to attend to my responsibilities there. Unfortunately, this was a complete fantasy on their part but I bowed to them in an appreciative fashion and entered No. 3.

At the end of the Sixties Trinity was on the cusp. The historic decision in 1970 to lift the general ban on Catholics attending, combined with the receipt of larger sums of money from the Irish government, led inevitably to the University not only growing but granting its places to the affable bourgeoisie of the south of Ireland in preference to solid Ulsterman like myself and flamboyant Etonians. Regrettably Northerners are now reduced to a small percentage of the University. Nor was it, even at the end of the Sixties, all garden parties and croquet. The Civil Rights movement was starting in Northern Ireland. Paul McGuiness and I thought it our duty to attend a demonstration in Armagh but we did not have a car and Armagh was not on the railway line. We decided to hitch from Swords. No one would give us a lift. This may have been because of our long hair or possibly because we were both wearing military coats: drivers may have suspected us of being a paramilitary unit on our way to the Border. The coats belonged to our fathers. Paul's was of the RAF and mine was of the Irish army; a wonderfully full-skirted greatcoat suitable for wearing on a horse, which, if it had not been green, would have looked at home in *Dr Zhivago*. We did not make it to Armagh but I did manage the march to Burntollet, which took place during the vacation.

There was a great housing agitation in Dublin at the time. In support of it we went to spend the night, a rather rough one, in a Georgian tenement in Mountjoy Square to prevent the bailiffs from breaking in and evicting a woman and her children. That was a happy coincidence, preventing hardship and saving Georgian Dublin in one go. One turned out, of course, for anti-apartheid demonstrations, conveniently located a few yards from the College on O'Connell Bridge. One did not often cross that bridge to the north side but Shane Ross lured me there one day to demonstrate his superior skill at table football, which he had learnt when he was meant to be learning French at Besançon. Easons on O'Connell Street had a big basement full of second-hand and remaindered books where I picked up Patrick Kavanagh's *Collected Pruse* for a few shillings. The first stone, I suppose, in the cairn of my collection.

Poetry itself no longer had the high profile it had enjoyed earlier in the decade. Longley and Mahon were gone, although I once heard the latter, slim, slight, stubbled and saturnine, read his poetry in a ghastly room at the back of the College. A little later Brendan Kennelly lived across the hall in No. 9, but I do not remember him ever giving a reading in College. When, again a little later, I took over *TCD Miscellany*, I introduced a section on poetry and verse, which attracted a blizzard of submissions. I had the pleasure of publishing the distinguished poet-publisher, Peter Fallon, of Gallery Press fame.

One of the marvellous things about Trinity then and now is its location in the middle of a capital city. All sorts of entertainment were available. I recall Joe Revington rushing into the Buttery one evening and handing out delegate cards for the Fine Gael Conference, which was then taking place in the Mansion House close by. The fact that none of us were members of Fine Gael and that I was myself a member of the Irish Labour Party in no way delayed us downing our pints and hurrying off to cast our votes for Garret Fitzgerald in some internal party election.

I have never told, in print at least, the story of Shane Ross, now father of the Irish Senate, confiding in me his intense appreciation of a young lady who lived close to him on Upper Leeson Street. What should he do next to get to know her?

'What about a date?' I said.

'A date? But it might seem a little forward to invite her out to dinner?'

'You could take her to the theatre.'

'Are there any theatres in Dublin?'

Shane had been to Rugby and insisted on referring to London as *town*. I said there was a well-known one called the Abbey. It was there I met the lovely Ruth Buchanan a week or so later on her first date with Shane.

And then there was Sebastian. I rather think his real name was Michael Greene but that could be wrong. He directed me in J.P. Donleavey's *Fairy Tales of New York* in the Players Theatre. He evoked some envy in my teenage heart. One would see him every night in The Old Stand with a different very pretty girl. He also had a Gladstone bag, which contained his few belongings, chiefly some purple ladies' sweaters, from Arnotts, I was informed. Thanks to his powers of attraction and the absurdly short terms at Trinity he never actually bothered to waste money on accommodation while up, but stayed in the beds, or if necessary, on the sofas, of various admirers for the seven weeks he attended, thus no doubt releasing income for other more important things.

The Hist, with its long-established claim to being the oldest university debating society in the world, at least a half-century older than the Oxford Union, originated in the Historical Club, founded by Edmund Burke as an undergraduate in 1753. When I was speaking at a conference in the University of Pisa in 2006 to celebrate the great but largely forgotten Trinity novelist Charles Lever, Professor Mario Currelli was good enough to confirm that no similar student body of that antiquity existed in Italian universities, which reinforced that claim to primacy. Conor Cruise O'Brien was president of the Society for many years but earlier on had been less part of its establishment. The obituary of him in *The Times* of 20 December 2008 points out that he was defeated for the office of Auditor, as the student head is called, a title coined by Burke. In fact I had an impression when I looked at the records of the Society many years ago that those defeated for the Auditorship tend to be more distinguished than those elected. A year or two later Richard Clarke, then Records Secretary, now Bishop of Meath, urged me to run for the Auditorship as the candidate of 'the Left' because he thought I might win and he would not. This was an excellent example of Christian forbearance as I was a mere Freshman member of committee. My opponent was Nicholas Simon Fitzgerald Browne, a fine, tall, blonde, smartly turned out product of King's School, Canterbury. He was keen to project an aristocratic air although his claimed relationship to the Marquis of Sligo was never quite established. He had the wholehearted support of a wide range of rather conservative-minded students in the University – but not all. His fellow white African, Rupert Pennant-Rea, later Deputy Governor of the Bank of England, walked into The Hist Committee Room and filled in his ballot paper in favour of myself, in public, so as to allow his views to be known. Nick and two friends, who ought to have known better, sought to take advantage of the rather antique election process in The Hist. There was a ballot box, which was in the charge of one of the Officers. It would sit in the Conversation Room all week and ballots could be placed within it if they had been properly obtained from another Officer of the Society. The ballot box was then carried to the Porter's Lodge for safekeeping each night. These friends of Nick Browne, as he later described in *TCD Miscellany*, bluffed their way into the Porter's Lodge, removed the ballot box and opened it. They altered seventeen of the number

1s for myself to 2 and put the 1 opposite Nick's name and presumed that would make him safe. Fortunately for me Nick was not a very good debater and it was after all a debating society. Furthermore, my voters, most of them gathered for me by Ted Smith and Derek Moran, tended to vote later in the week than Nick's and I managed to get home with a comfortable majority.

IN THE 1960s The Hist was for men only, and I declined to speak in such a Society. I missed the famous row in which Conor Cruise O'Brien, chairing a meeting of the Society, co-operated with the opponents of the all-male society and embarrassed the then-Auditor, David Ford. Expulsions and resignations followed, but a few weeks later we were there to vote successfully for the admission of women. Two weeks later I made a maiden speech, which was kindly received and a little after that I was elected to the Committee.

The great curse of oratory as an art form is its ephemeral nature. No matter how strong an impression a speech makes upon you at the time, it is almost impossible to convey that later in print. The quality of speaking in The Hist at the end of the Sixties and early Seventies was extremely high, although one would not guess that from the well-produced but partial *The Hist and Edmund Burke's Club* (1997). Ernie Bates, a little older than us, who spoke in his scholar's flowing gown, a once and, for all I know, present Republican, struck a dramatic note. Greg Murphy, later a silk, now sadly deceased, whose socialism did not inhibit him in any way from wearing shirts by Turnbull & Asser and pinstripe suits, which contrasted effectively with his red bushy beard, had a rich voice and richer vocabulary. Jim Hamilton (now Irish DPP), Alex Martin and Declan Kiberd (now Professor) were three more very able debaters in different styles.

The Hist was something of a paradox. The Private Business with its detailed rules had clearly been something evolved by law students in the past and was an excellent preparation for the cut and thrust of motions, courts and trials. But in fact in my time law students rarely participated, preferring the gentler ambience of the DU Law Society. But the standing of the Society and of Trinity was manifested when the Bicentenary of The Hist, calculated from its refounding in 1770, was held in 1970, the last year of the decade. There was a marvellous lecture by R.B. McDowell and a national debate of prominent figures including Erskine Childers, Gerry Fitt and John Hume, in which I was lucky enough to speak, as the only undergraduate to participate in the week's events. Charlie Haughey opened an exhibition in the National Gallery. There was an international debate, chaired by the then-taoiseach, Jack Lynch. He seemed a more formidable figure than his successor, radiating authority without exertion. We heard spellbinding oratory from Michael Foot and stately eloquence from James Dillon, who was the son of the last leader of the Irish Parliamentary Party and had previously been leader of Fine Gael. Senator Eugene McCarthy, who had challenged for the democratic nomination for president, and Andreas Papandreou, then an exile, but later succeeding his father as prime minster of Greece, also spoke. And last, but by no means least, was an address from Senator Edward Kennedy, his first public appearance after the accident at Chappaquiddick in which a young female companion had died. It is worth recording how good he was.

I end these few thoughts with a question. Not, *Mais où sont les neiges d'antan?* although Villon's line must haunt all these pages, but where is the statue of Provost Usher that used to lie out on a plinth in the rain between the Dining Hall and the Chapel? I would doubt that it ever existed save in my imagination were it not that it figures in Derry Jeffares' delightful sketches of Trinity in the 1940s. Half-ruined by weathering and tucked away it seems to me to have epitomized not only the intimacy of Trinity but its rather relaxed attitude to its own antiquity. Where is it now?

Sir Donnell Deeny (TCD 1969–73; Legal Science) practised at the Bar of Northern Ireland, taking silk in 1989, until his appointment to the High Court in 2004. He is a Bencher of the Middle Temple and a member of the Inner Bar in the Republic of Ireland. He has also been High Sheriff of Belfast, Chairman of Opera Northern Ireland, Chairman of the Arts Council of Northern Ireland and founding Chairman of the Ireland Chair of Poetry. His two younger brothers, Arthur and Godfrey, his wife Alison and his eldest daughter Maeve followed him to Trinity.

CERTAIN GOOD

christopher jane corkery

IT WAS JULY, 1969. The weather was excellent, frequent sun, and, when it rained, the wetting was quick and gentle. My friends, all women I'd been at university with in the US (though we said 'girls' then), had flown back to Washington DC, where we lived, but I was staying longer in Ireland, to attend the Yeats Summer School in Sligo, then in its relative infancy.

I entered Front Gate just after the porter had opened the door that morning. I felt out of place, and shy, but I was in a hurry, too, soon to be taking a train to Sligo. But before I went west I wanted to see this place of which I'd heard so much. I thought my stop would be brief. Then I came out into the light of Front Square and was astonished at how ... pretty it was. Not beautiful, nor stately, though it surely can seem so and has to many, including me, but that morning it was delicate, and gentle, and friendly. Each blade of grass looked as if it had been polished; not a piece of trash lurked amongst the cobblestones; the statue of Lecky did not look a bit forbidding, just pleasant and even a bit dotty. The sun had just illuminated Regent House and was making its steady way around: now the Commons and Chapel on one side and the Provost's House and the Reading Room on the other were brightening. It was quiet and in the distance, down by the Rubrics, one young man walked slowly towards College Park. He had long hair.

I had reason to be shy. After all, I was a Yank, and though I'd grown up in Europe and in Mexico, this was my first trip to Ireland, land of all of my forebears, and my mother, who had introduced me to in Irish literature, had told me that Trinity was the country's pre-eminent university. But I was headed for Sligo, home of my first love, W.B. Yeats. Forty years later I wrote a villanelle whose first line – 'It was Yeats who took me. I was seventeen,' – really does go a long way to explain a fundamental attachment I had to Ireland, to poetry. It must have been my mother who pointed me, when I was a child, to 'The Lake Isle of Innisfree', and 'Down by the Salley Gardens'. Then a chilly professor at my college had introduced me to the Irish Renaissance. But it was W.B. I loved. He spoke to shells, he loved myths and fairy stories, he understood the importance of masks and the spirit and, as he grew and matured, heroism in all its forms. Art for him, as I saw it, was a form for heroes, and love a long form of loss. I was interested in Irish history, too, of course, descending from people who'd come over on the famine ships, But it was my instinct for poetry and my developing knowledge and writing of it that signalled me I'd better get to the source, quickly.

It was July, 1969. The US had put a man on the moon a few days earlier, but I was uninterested. Three days before that my neighbour in Washington DC had drowned. Her name was Mary Jo Kopechne and she and I, in the heady days before April and June of 1968 (heady for those young and willing to commit mayhem for political change), had had the same boss, Robert F. Kennedy. In the wake of Martin Luther King's and Bobby Kennedy's assassinations, of Nixon's election, and of Kopechne's death, the moon seemed irrelevant.

I never planned, of course, to do anything more than visit Ireland that summer. But when I saw Front Square something changed. I thought, quite clearly: I am coming back here to study, to live.

IT WAS JULY, 1969; just four months after Bernadette Devlin had won a seat in parliament. Even our battle-scarred, blood-soaked evening newscasts in the US announced it, even there we were interested in this young, determined, short-skirted fighter for the rights of the embattled Catholics in the North.

But we didn't notice long. Instead we kept looking at the 27 June issue of *Life* magazine that published this: photographs, names and ages of the men who had died the previous week in Vietnam. There were 242 of them. In one week. In that year, 1969, 11,616 US soldiers would die, along with thousands of Vietnamese. There were half a million US personnel in Vietnam then.

But I was in Dublin. I had no idea, as I walked around Front Square and saw my new life unfolding before me, that in two weeks I would be sitting in a pub in Sligo with poets and would-bes and hangers-on and we would not be carousing or spouting limpid lines at all, but watching on television, mouths agape, as the Bogside and its citizens were plundered, maimed and killed. I felt useless, ridiculous, and completely, irrationally enraged at the Irish who were in the pub with me and who seemed to believe they could do nothing. This conflict, not an hour distant, seemed so utterly local! It was so unlike Vietnam, I thought, so, it seemed, solvable.

The group in the pub broke up late that night in misery. But the next day I was back in a Sligo seminar on Yeats' drama. I also decided, from one day to the next, to fall in like. I thought it was love, but it was only attraction and with its source I managed to spend the next days and months in a state of intensity, thus pushing aside the world. When I came out of this illusion it was December 1969 and I sent my first application to Trinity.

How surprised I was then to receive a letter fairly soon, and to be denied entry to the incipient Anglo-Irish literature diploma programme at TCD! I had a BA from an excellent American college, but the letter I received from Trinity said I'd have to study a year before I was admitted. I was shocked! I had been accepted at UCD but wanted, of course, to be a member of the club that – at that moment – would not have me.

But back in July 1969, I somehow knew, already, that Brendan Kennelly, who was a star of the Yeats Summer School, was on the faculty at Trinity. I asked the porter that pristine July morning where Kennelly resided and though I did not track him down then I would meet him in a few days later in Sligo, tell him of my desire to come to Trinity (to which he undoubtedly said, 'Ah, that's grand') but that July day I did not find him. A little more than a year later I would follow him, mercilessly really, all around Trinity, until he acceded to my demand and let me in to the Anglo-Irish programme.

But that July I walked around Front Square several times in almost total solitude, then down past the Rubrics, whose stairways would come to intrigue me, whose pink-red colour I found impossibly attractive. I wanted, in the following years, to live there, in the Rubrics, and was astonished that this could not possibly be done: I was a woman!

I walked back toward the English Department, where I would come to know the quiet-voiced Miss Gwynne, and Terry Brown who directed, briefly, my M.Litt. thesis. Terry was kind and patient and wrote me encouraging notes when I'd gone back to the US, thinking I could finish my work there. I had run out of money and, back on my own US shores and away from Trinity's, and Ireland's, pull, I chose not to hear his encouragement and put an end to my work on one William Carleton.

I WOULD STUDY Anglo-Irish fiction, poetry and drama at Trinity and would do so in the buildings at the back of New Square. 'Words alone are certain good,' said Yeats, and at the time I thought so too. There I would meet and learn from and laugh with David Norris, who gave us his Joyce, with Kennelly who covered poetry and many another thing, and with Brown and Clissman who dealt in prose.

In July of 1969 I could not look up Kennelly's poems on the internet, but I could buy them and at the Summer School would acquire a copy of 'Dream of a Black Fox.' Little did I know that two years later I would sublet Brendan's and his then-wife Peggy O'Brien's house in Sandymount, with my fellow student Barbara Schmidt who finished our diploma programme, stayed on in Ireland, and lives there still.

Perhaps I could tell from Brendan's extraordinary voice in Sligo that summer that I'd sit in a little informal group on Friday afternoons in a class-room in the 'new' English building. A group of us read poems or recited, and once, for some reason lost in the mist, I turned Joyce's 'Ivy Day in the Committee Room' into a play, at Brendan's suggestion, so that we could act it. I also sang, at his instigation, and the group joined in. It was Yeats' 'Come Gather Round Me Parnellites' sung to the tune of 'The Wearing of the Green'.

But there was another subject Trinity gave me instruction in: the laby-rinthine categorizations and nuances of class the Anglo-Irish imposed on, or perceived in, social relations. I was astounded at the snobbery I saw and, perhaps, in some cases, imagined. I had come from the US where all was in

ferment and it would take me a long while to understand divisions and asso-
ciations at Trinity. I was to receive part of my education in the blasting away
of those same boundaries from the woman who would become one of my best
friends, until her death in 1997, Rosemary Gibson Gibb, and an education,
too, in friendship and hospitality and fun, from her stellar husband Andrew.
Rosie took me under her capacious (metaphorical here: she was, in reality,
tiny) wing. And oh, the nights and days I would enjoy with her in Swords at the
Mill House, in Naas at her parents' castle, and at TCD where she knew everyone
and I no one.

Was it Rosemary who introduced me to Tommy Murtagh, whom I knew
very briefly, but who told me about a book that would influence me for its tone
and style, a book having nothing to do with Ireland but with France, his arena?
It was Simone de Beauvoir's *Une Mort Très Douce* and I suspect it appealed to
me because it was by a woman, because it was personal, and because I was still
preparing myself – at twenty-three! – for adulthood. I read it in the dim and
peaceful corners of the 1937 Reading Room, a place forever associated in my
mind with scholarship and art and blissful quiet.

It was not there, though, but in the Graduates' Common Room, that I
would meet Elaine Oakley and Jean Tarbox. And somewhere in Front Square,
on a sunny day, I would meet Joan McAuley. Over time and continents, these
friendships have endured.

But this was July, 1969. I was determined to live a new life, one I thought
distant from strife! That dark night in the Sligo pub, 15 August, had not yet
happened. The extent of the Cambodian bombing was not yet known. The
architecture of Trinity and its peaceful acres – the stunning centrality of the
Campanile, the surrounding buildings that both asserted and questioned their
connection to it, the rose-coloured Rubrics, the profound contemplative green
of the grass – embodied order to me that day, and calm. Both of these I came
to know, along with passion, were prerequisites for poetry.

BUT THE TRINITY I came to in July of 1969 was no longer caught in amber
suspension, no matter what I imagined. The North had not fully imploded yet,
but that was coming. Vietnam would continue in a bloody roil for three more
years. The male control of all at Trinity would start to crack, the social classes

were already blending and blurring, creating wholly new identifications and divisions.

Reader, I came back. It was 2003. Our country was in another bloody, senseless war – this time one we had started – but my family and I were taking three weeks off. With my husband and sons I entered Front Square and watched as they looked and took in their breaths, and let them out, voicing their approval. It was July, in fact, and sunny, and bright. But it was also almost noon and the place was full of people from all countries – tourists, students, workers. It was noisy. My family, of course, knew of my time at Trinity, that I had studied there, that I still had a few friends from those days. But on that morning they were looking at only a place, albeit a pleasant one, but one of many they would see in Ireland.

I, however, was looking at my past, and gratefully. It was July, I was fifty-seven, and I showed my sons (Patrick and Eamonn) Lecky's statue. I told them who he was, told them he had become a senator in his later life, told them that David Norris, once my professor, was now a senator. Yeats too, I said, had been a senator. Then I told them that Yeats had received a degree from Trinity; it was an honorary one, though, since he had never studied there, and it came in 1922. He too was fifty-seven.

Christopher Jane Corkery (TCD 1970–2; postgraduate Diploma in Anglo-Irish Studies) is a poet and has taught for extended periods at both Harvard's Summer Writing Programme and at the College of the Holy Cross. Her book, **Blessing,** was published by Princeton University Press in 1985. Her work has appeared in magazines such as **The Atlantic Monthly** and **The Kenyon Review**, and is also included in the recently published **The Book of Irish American Poetry: From the Eighteenth Century to the Present** (2007).

THE STUDENTS ARE REVOLTING

John Stephenson

'THE SIXTIES'! There was no such thing. Dates don't lend themselves neatly to events. Nor do times change in handy decennia, except in lazy journalism, trite television and the reductive exigencies of popular culture. Even in those pop terms, 'The Sixties' began in 1963, with the ascent of the Beatles; and ended in 1969 at a Rolling Stones concert in Altamont. More likely they ended as late as 1975 with the fall of Saigon; or with the Sex Pistols in 1976, or even 1979 with the election of Margaret Thatcher.

Trinity has always been, or become, an expression of its times. So it moved with the times in the 1960s, but not precisely between 1960 and 1970. Rather, I reckon, there were three phases: pre-1964, 1964 to 1968, and post-1968. Although I wasn't a student during the 1960s, I was very much a part of Sixties Trinity as it had developed. Any student generation has an average lifespan of four years, shifting incrementally per annum. In 1966, College was still dominated by a pre-Dylan generation, but the times were a-changin', and in 1968, a hard rain began to fall on the Board of TCD.

When I entered College at the end of the decade, I joined a cycle of radical student activism that had taken flight only a few years before. I entered a Trinity in which Kate Cruise O'Brien and Mary Bourke (later President Robinson) had graduated as heroines. A schoolboy debater, I joined The Hist in Freshers' Week, along with many other boys and girls. I discovered that up to two years before, no females could even have attended the meetings of this great debating society.

In 1968, the women of Trinity finally defeated the male club rules that had dominated College and its student societies. This was long after Annette Jocelyn Otway-Ruthven had obtained a Chair in History and a place on the College Board. This formidable character must have been an inspiration to all women scholars in the preceding decades. But even the venerable 'Ott' had to wait until 1968 to become the first woman Fellow of Trinity College Dublin. So the gals had smashed the last bastions of the outward show of male supremacy in TCD. The curfew on women in College, and all other related prohibitions, were ended then. In my first term in the GMB, I was regaled with first-hand accounts of the night they burned Old Dixie down. The last battle of the Suffragettes had been won. The Women's Liberationists were yet to come. In my time in College, it was perfectly natural for women students to play as full a part in social, academic and executive functions as men. And in 1975, our era witnessed the election of Mary Harney as the first woman Auditor of the College Historical Society: a fruit of the late Sixties.

The 1960s in TCD were not, as popularly imagined, a decade of sex and drugs and rock 'n' roll. It was not defined in 1966 by Ian 'You Turn Me On' Whitcomb making it into the US singles charts, nor by Father Michael Cleary's wild 1968 claim that TCD was 'the seat of the drugs business in Ireland'. For most Trinity students in the 1960s, music was background, politics were uninteresting, drugs were a rarity and sex a mystery. Sexual discovery and fulfilment are natural to any generation of students, anywhere. But, sexually, Trinity undergrads of the time were a relatively innocent and pretentious lot. Kinsey may have impinged on the American campus, but most students here were still fumbling cluelessly in the dark.

There were hardly any 'swingers' anywhere in the 'Swinging Sixties'. The term *swinging* was just another hip adjective meaning 'groovy, cool, happening'. Sex only really got swinging in these parts in the 1970s, with the onset of the sexual liberation movements and the readier availability of contraceptives. Sex was not invented by either the Beatles or by Gay Byrne's *Late Late Show*. Sex was invented much earlier, by the Catholic bishops. What made Trinity irresistible to many Catholic-educated schoolkids in the late Sixties was the bishops' prohibition on entry, intended to protect our 'faith and morals'. But even those who hadn't already lost their faith had decided to reject clerical control of their lives; and couldn't wait to dump the repressive, hypocritical cant that prescribed 'our morals'. Yes, my fellow Catholic schoolboys were also attracted by Trinity's reputation as an international centre of academic excellence. But, whilst an NUI degree was no less valuable, we felt we were less likely to get laid there, freely and happily. Whatever about sex and drugs and rock 'n' roll, I believe that the Sixties in Trinity are better defined by the development of government policy, a radical student activism, and a related institutional liberalization.

In the 1960s, Trinity students took possession of their power to demonstrate serious concerns about their own rights, and the political wrongs in the world. By the end of the decade, they had the will and confidence to do this through direct, disruptive action, and to succeed. If this decade in Trinity is to be circumscribed by one event in 1960 linked to another in 1970, then it would surely be the contrast between student reaction to the Sharpeville Massacre at the start, and the Springbok rugby tour at the end. The first event caused barely a ripple in the hallowed Elizabethan halls, except perhaps one of applause amongst Empire Loyalists, and impotent dismay amongst Fabians and liberals. By contrast, the second event brought thousands onto Lansdowne Road in an anti-apartheid demonstration in which Trinity staff and students played a major role.

Trinity began to change fundamentally in the Sixties, but the full nature of this change only became apparent in the Seventies and after. Between 1954 and 1964, Trinity's student population had remained more or less static at about 3000. By 1974 it had increased to around 4500. It has since risen steadily to more than 15000, over 60 per cent of whom are women, and about 85 per cent are Irish nationals.

It is evident that TCD in 1964 was little different from 1954, bar a few 'Rocker' graduates and 'Mod' Freshmen. Until the Sixties got 'Swinging', Trinity was square, very square. Even Dev and Elvis hadn't shaken the walls of an institution steeped in archaic tradition, Protestant hegemony, an anti-nationalist ethos and a profound sense of 'clár eile' (another place). Up to the mid-Sixties, it remained proudly so. Indeed, 'Trinners' remained a 'place apart' in the Republic of Ireland well after pop and youth culture took hold amongst its undergraduates. The social rebels of the period from 1964 to 1968 were still predominantly Protestant and British, and somehow anachronistic and harmless. They took their cue as much from J.P. Donleavy's novels as from Carnaby Street, or their scratched LPs.

Their culture of thwarting College rules would later develop into confrontation, but its own subversion was ineffectual. This was a transitional phase, rather than a defining one. So the rigid prohibitions on women, casual dress and general student rights were bucked against, not fully opposed. Women were smuggled onto forbidden ground in escapades. They did not walk in, as of right. Parkas and reefer jackets replaced academic gowns off-campus. They were not worn to lectures, as of right. Students did not participate in University decision-making. They were told what to do by the College authorities. Throughout the 1960s, the Junior Dean was an authority figure, whose rule was law. The most that many transitional rebels of the mid-Sixties sought to do was dodge him, his Assistant Deans, and his network of informers and enforcers amongst the skips and porters. It was a lark.

MORE POIGNANT than the collaborative 'rebelliousness' of the 1964–8 generations in Trinity was their capacity to ignore the ever-pressing injustices of the world outside College walls, at home and abroad. Apartheid was in full flow in South Africa, the Vietnam War was gathering force under their noses, and the issue of civil rights was rolling inexorably from Memphis to Magherafelt. (As there weren't many Catholic nationalists in Trinity at the time, and almost all Nor'ners there were Unionist, it's hardly surprising that this last escaped much attention.) Indeed, as Trinity remained an essentially colonial institution, with an overwhelmingly Commonwealth student population, their self-indulgence is less surprising than the revolution they did finally initiate in 1968. For even then, Trinity was typically post-Empire Protestant. But by then, a new consciousness had begun to permeate the place.

It's true that there was a colourful international mix in the 1960s. This survived into the early 1970s. Freshers could revel in the acquaintance of strange others, and learn about them, and from them. Taigs and Trinidadians, Kerrymen and Kiwis, Nigerians and North Americans, all exchanged openly. This did indeed engender awareness, tolerance and fun. Without beatniks,

Beatles and bravado, Trinity might not have made the transition from 1964 to 1968. It certainly wouldn't have done so without the impact in that period of Kadar Asmal and Hardial Bains amongst a new generation of politically aware undergrads.

Asmal, an Asian South-African exile, took up a teaching post in the Law Department in 1964, and immediately set about founding the Irish Anti-Apartheid Movement. In the 1970s, he would become my beloved tutor and mentor. I can only imagine the difficulties he must have faced in those early years. As late as 1974, racism and bigotry still figured within Trinity's student body, especially amongst Northern Irish Loyalists. In 1964, such views must have been as prevalent as sexism. Fortunately, Trinity also had a solid tradition of free thought and left-liberalism. This was best exemplified by Owen Sheehy-Skeffington, who served as one of TCD's Oireachtas senators for most of the 1950s and 1960s. But there were many others. So Kadar did not want for help-meets on campus. It is a tribute to his charm, humour, resilience and persua-siveness that it took him only one generation of students to build moral support and a small army of activists for justice in South Africa. By 1968, they were rolling onto the streets; by 1970 they were rocking them.

Yet the outbreak of student political activism and institutional reform in Trinity in 1968 was not provoked by yet another outrage in South Africa, but by the state visit to Ireland of the king of the Belgians, colonial master of Africa's Congo basin.

Shortly after Asmal had founded the IAAM, Hardial Bains, a Trinity biolo-gist, founded the Communist Party of Ireland (Marxist-Leninist). In its early form, this Maoist group was known as the Trinity Internationalists, a term that stuck. Unlike the IAAM, this strange sect was more interested in attacking potential allies than winning friends. So by 1968, the Internationalists still numbered only a handful of Stalinists, content in their imagined role as *the* Bolshevik revolutionary vanguard in Ireland. It seems now an extraordinary thing that this Inquisitorial gang not only propelled the Trinity body politic out of decades of Rightism and complacency, but kept a hand on the progres-sive tiller until 1976.

Like it or not, it was they who, in 1966, set the agenda for the democratiza-tion of College, which prevailed in the ensuing decade. Their 1966 'Academic

Freedom' programme became the norm in and after 1968, namely: no restrictions on student social, political and academic activity, staff–student equality in campus administration, and full student representation in critical decision-making. In effect: 'Student Power', a great catchphrase of the time. As with the Levellers in Cromwellian England, the Internationalists took the moral high ground in Trinity's political life. This was intertwined with an anti-Imperialist dogma, which eventually came a cropper on the sectarian streets of Belfast. It is ironic that the Internationalists had more effect locally than they ever did nationally, let alone internationally.

In the mid-Sixties there was a pronounced progressive tendency in the student body. Not since the Forties Prometheans had there been such a strong Leftist surge. The Republican Club was on a roll, and had seized the Hist ballot box with its prize-winning rhetoric. Republican Socialist, Eoin Ó Murchú was elected an officer, and he, with Cian Ó hEagartaigh and other radicals, formed a sixth column for women's rights therein. The Labour Club boasted about Conor Cruise O'Brien, Justin Keating, David Thornley and a new wave of socialism.

But all this remained somehow academic until King Baudouin of Belgium came in 1968 to view the Book of Kells. His Majesty would have been better advised to visit Harrods in London. The Internationalists protested. It took only a garda scuffle and a torn-down banner to ignite the flame. The Internationalists became martyrs to 'police brutality'. By the end of Baudouin's visit, a revolution had begun. As with the fall of any *ancien régime*, there's a prelude when the writing is on the wall. Only after some precipitating event are reforms offered, too late and too little, to satisfy the urge for complete change. In themselves, these placatory gestures encourage the thrust for transformation. So it was in Trinity in that year, and for some years afterwards.

Provost McConnell presiding over the Board, (whom I would later satirize as the dormouse at the Mad Hatter's Tea Party), played the role of Louis XVI. His Mirabeaus were already in negotiation about the right of students to distribute Marxist literature on campus, and for the recognition of student rights, as such. Then, in unmanageable succession, came the demonstrations against Enoch Powell, King Baudouin, U Thant, Dr Christian Barnard and Brian Lenihan. 'Events, dear boy!' So an inquiry was set up by the Board, which had far-reaching consequences for College life. Actually, though the others got a rough ride, Powell never came. He was warned off by the SRC, the Scholars and the Provost for fear of 'violent student disorder'. McConnell never truly recovered from this flight from the treasured principle of free speech in a university. He did, nonetheless, deliver full women's rights in the same year.

All this was happening as student protest ran riot throughout Europe and the US. Not since 1848 had such a shower of privileged bowsies appeared to be at the forefront of a righteous struggle for justice in the world. The year 1968 started with images of American troops, beseiged in Vietnam, responding with the massacre at My Lai; for evil measure, their South Vietnamese partners blowing a Viet Cong prisoner's brains out. The year continued with the assassination of Martin Luther King, and the explosion across America of the Black Civil Rights and Anti-Vietnam War movements. In Warsaw and Prague students demanded freedom from Moscow, while in Paris, typically, they demanded revolution, and almost got it. Irish students simply rose to the occasion.

By the year's end UCD was paralysed with occupations and demonstrations, while in Trinity the Left had come into its own. The cosy, charming, even fashionable worlds of the Elizabethan Society, Boat Club and Philosophical Society suddenly appeared silly and irrelevant. The Students Representative Council donned both Red and Green, and the Blues were dispelled. Though it took another few years to drive them from power, the days of a conservative Protestant and Anglo student ascendancy in Trinity were over.

I guess that in those last, headline-grabbing years of the 1960s, between the Baudouin kerfuffle and the Springbok fracas, thousands of socially concerned, Catholic secondary-school students resolved to go to Trinity: kids who had collected for Biafra, competed in school debates about famine, war and exploitation, and listened carefully to Bob Dylan. Even *scoláirí na Gaeilge* (Irish language students) must have seen the anti-colonialist thrust of it all, and filled out their Trinity applications *as Bearla* (in English) enthusiastically. Though in their case, the attraction of the outstanding Máirtín Ó Cadhain in the Department of Modern Irish must have been pretty irresistible anyway.

In that context, it must be said that Trinity's faculty and syllabus had long been ahead of that which may be imagined. Although the institution – its structures, rules and ethos – was stuck in the past, and many of its students also, the University Council had kept abreast of modern educational needs. In the 1960s the College Board would be obliged to make major reforms of the institution as well.

By 1968, in spite of the Catholic hierarchy's ban upon them entering Trinity, a steady stream of Southern Irish Catholics had registered. After 1970, when the bishops lifted the ban, this stream became a river, and, from 1974, a flood. In those years there was still a healthy component of British and overseas students. But it wasn't much longer before a new, less challenging homogeneity prevailed. Nowadays, northside and southside Dublin domesticity and transport links play a greater role in determining the undergraduate composition of Dublin's universities than any other factors. As regards undergraduate diversity, TCD and UCD might as well have merged in 1970. In this respect, there was another irresistible force building around Trinity's walls in that period.

From 1960, governmental investment and involvement in post-primary education increased markedly. In 1967, free secondary education was introduced, resulting in large increases in pupil numbers. In 1970 a third-level student grants scheme took that a stage further. Also, in 1968 the Higher Education Authority (HEA) was set up as an umbrella body for all Irish universities. Throughout this decade, Trinity came under increasing pressure from the government to integrate into a state education system. TCD had been in receipt of government funding since 1923. By the late 1960s, it could not function effectively without it. Minister for Education Brian Lenihan Sr knew this. For years, Trinity had huffed and puffed about its independence. Eventually the government threatened to blow it down with a proposal in 1967 for merger with UCD. This threat brought Trinity to its senses. Ireland needed lots of new university places for a burgeoning population of school-leavers; Trinity would now have to play its part, fully.

In 1969, I was one of the last students in almost 400 years to matriculate into Trinity under its own entrance examination. By the time I left College in 1976, Trinity operated under the HEA, and was also signed up to the Central Admissions Office, with its new points system. Any show of Trinity's independence after that was nominal. In addition, by the time I registered for General Studies (aka General Doss), the overriding political issue in Irish society was kicking in with a vengeance. Southern Catholics were no more able than Southern Protestants to deal successfully with the situation unfolding in Northern Ireland.

Our impotence would later, wrongly, be characterized as cynical indifference.

The Northern Ireland Civil Rights and People's Democracy movements of 1968/69 had an immediate impact upon Trinity's student body. It is to the credit of the majority of Southern Protestants, who formed a plurality of the undergraduate population at the time, that they sided with justice not bigotry. Many of their Northern counterparts did the same. So, before Catholics began to pour into Trinity, the undergraduate consensus in TCD was for equality of rights and political freedom in Northern Ireland.

Sadly, during my time in College, the situation 'over the Border' slipped beyond such good reasoning. The vicious Protestant backlash against the civil righters, and the partisan intervention of British forces, led to a bloody, dirty and numbing war of intimidation, destruction and terror by all combatants. In this cataclysm, sides were also taken by Trinity students, often bitterly. By the mid-Seventies, any possibility of an equitable resolution to the Troubles had evaporated, and along with it, any unity of the students' movement born a decade before. The hope and optimism of the Sixties 'revolution' in Trinity had soured, and the fruit was internecine feuding, impotence and an internalization of progressive politics.

Yet in spite of this slide into darkness, in 1970, the mainly Protestant College Historical Society had elected a Jesuit-educated Northern Catholic as its Auditor, over an equally talented Protestant Brahmin whose father was effectively the Unionist senator for TCD in the Oireachtas. How impressive both Judge Deeny and Senator Ross Jr remain today! It was a pleasure in my Junior Freshman year to witness them in action against one another, using only words as a weapon.

Donnell Deeny and Shane Ross are not the only significant characters whom I recall in Trinity at the end of the 1960s. As a schoolboy political activist, in my first term in College, I also focused on the Student Representative Council. The president of the SRC at the time was the late lamented Paul Tansey. Paul had a nose for sham, folly and injustice, which he would excoriate with an irreverent sense of humour and fearless intellectual candour. He also had a fine sense of what needed to be done to solve a problem, or advance a cause.

The SRC in the late 1960s remained a toothless body, by no means at the head of the burgeoning student activism of the time. Alan Mathews had done well as SRC president in 1968 to secure democratic student representation in the College reforms of that year. But, in spite of paid sabbatical, Board representation, and a plethora of new staff–student committees, the result was diffusion. The Central Societies Committee and Central Athletics Committee still laid equal claim to the SRC to represent student interests, and student representatives on the new joint managerial committees were elected as if in rotten boroughs. This was Student Power as sham. The real Provost, Secretary Giltrap, must have rubbed his hands. No doubt informed by his canny predecessor, Joe Revington, Tansey established a programme to rectify this, and a dynasty to achieve it. In the next five years, the SRC steadily took the leadership of the student movement in Trinity, and obtained the necessary structures and powers to act upon that responsibility.

In 1970, in pursuit of the demand for better library facilities and opening hours, hundreds of students followed Paul Tansey into the New (Koralek) Library for an overnight 'sit-in'. I can think of no better 'Sixties' image than us all, at 3 am, stoned and cross-legged, watching Polanski's *Cul-de-Sac*, projected onto a library wall by the DU Film Society, on 16mm. In black and white, of course! By 1970, students had stopped requesting and started demanding. This sit-in was the first of many such actions and victories to come. Finally, in Trinity, the 1950s had passed and the 1970s had begun.

It is a weird yet valid measure of the success of this progress toward a powerful, all-encompassing student body, that the Internationalists devoted all their energies in 1975 to winning its presidency. After almost ten years agitating in College, the Internationalist David Vipond was elected as the first president of Trinity's Student Union. Vipond, a high-school scholar, was a decent chap in spite of his rhetoric. But the times had overtaken his revolutionary mission. His tenure as an anti-Imperialist student leader was followed by a Thermidorian reaction; and the Left was put back in its peripheral place. The late-Seventies Student Union presidents, Alex White and Joe Duffy, may be regarded as a last Sixties Leftist fling before authoritarianism, subservience, complacency and indifference set in for the long term. This time, it was to be a Catholic middle-class malaise.

Today, I often meet College lecturers who miss the concerned student activism of the 1960s–70s era. They bemoan the unquestioning consumption of today's undergraduates, their compliance, their conformism. The faculty we once fiercely berated, now regards us fondly as a reflection of something Universities should be: cauldrons of challenging thought and action, of human engagement. In retrospect, much of our effort may seem to have been a self-indulgent failure. Our generation of alumni are growing old in a world that appears just as bad, if not worse. Poverty, ignorance, injustice, war and famine have not diminished. But it is my hope that the example of Trinity in that period will not be forgotten, and will eventually inspire.

Perhaps, one day, in the absence of peasants, students will be revolting again …

John Stephenson (1969–76: G.S.) was director of Dublin's Project Arts Centre in the late 1970s, he secured both their current premises and favoured Arts Council and City Council cliency. In 1980, he directed the biggest ever festival of the Irish arts abroad, **A Sense of Ireland**, in London. In 1996, he was project manager for Dublin's first St Patrick's Day Festival. After decades as an arts/media producer and commentator, he retired from active duty and is now working on a novel.

Front Square TCD, as seen through the main entrance.
Photo by Photographic Centre, TCD.